Communicating by Telephone

INTERNATIONAL SERIES IN EXPERIMENTAL SOCIAL PSYCHOLOGY

Series Editor: MICHAEL ARGYLE, *University of Oxford*

Communicating by Telephone

by

D. R. RUTTER
Institute of Social and Applied Psychology
University of Kent at Canterbury

PERGAMON PRESS

OXFORD · NEW YORK · BEIJING · FRANKFURT
SÃO PAULO · SYDNEY · TOKYO · TORONTO

U.K.	Pergamon Press, Headington Hill Hall, Oxford OX3 0BW, England
U.S.A.	Pergamon Press, Maxwell House, Fairview Park, Elmsford, New York 10523, U.S.A.
PEOPLE'S REPUBLIC OF CHINA	Pergamon Press, Room 4037, Qianmen Hotel, Beijing, People's Republic of China
FEDERAL REPUBLIC OF GERMANY	Pergamon Press, Hammerweg 6, D-6242 Kronberg, Federal Republic of Germany
BRAZIL	Pergamon Editora, Rua Eça de Queiros, 346, CEP 04011, Paraiso, Sao Paulo, Brazil
AUSTRALIA	Pergamon Press Australia, P.O. Box 544, Potts Point, N.S.W. 2011, Australia
JAPAN	Pergamon Press, 8th Floor, Matsuoka Central Building, 1-7-1 Nishishinjuku, Shinjuku-ku, Tokyo 160, Japan
CANADA	Pergamon Press Canada, Suite No. 271, 253 College Street, Toronto, Ontario, Canada M5T 1R5

Preface

The purpose of this book is twofold: to examine the contribution which social psychology has made to telecommunications; and to consider how telecommunications have in turn contributed to social psychology. The emphasis throughout will be on experimental research and theory, and there will be five chapters. The first will chart the history and development of the telephone, from its invention in 1876 to the present day. Particular attention will be paid to its uses and effectiveness, especially in interviewing and surveys, crisis intervention and counselling, and conferences and teaching. Chapter 2 will introduce the theoretical background to the main arguments of the book, and will concentrate on nonverbal communication, especially looking and eye-contact, seeing, and cuelessness. Chapter 3 will examine outcome research, particularly transmission of information and problem-solving, persuasion, and person perception, and Chapter 4 will explore process, which includes the content and style of interactions. The book will end with a discussion of recent research on teaching and learning by telephone.

Many people, of course, have helped me to write the book, and I am delighted to have the opportunity to thank them. The Economic and Social Research Council, the Medical Research Council, and the Mental Health Foundation have continued to support my research financially; Rupert Brown, Noel Clark, Michael Dewey, Kevin Durkin, Delice Gambrill, Patricia Grounds, Ann Harding, Nigel Kemp, Ian Morley, Donald Pennington, Lyn Quine, Beatrice Shire, Geoffrey Stephenson, Janet Thomas, Hilarie Tucker, and Julius Wishner have been my principal colleagues, both in the research itself and as the book was drafted; Marco de Alberdi, Peter Bull, Brian Champness, Howard Giles, and Derek Rogers have, at various times, made helpful comments on the cluelessness model; and, throughout, Michael Argyle has been an incisive, constructive, and supportive editor. I am grateful to them all.

Acknowledgements

Figures 1.1 and 1.3 are reproduced with the permission of the Controller of Her Majesty's Stationery Office.

Figures 1.2 and 1.4 are reproduced with the permission of British Telecom.

Figure 2.1 is reproduced from Paterson, M. L. (1982) A sequential functional model of nonverbal exchange, *Psychological Review*, The American Psychological Association. Reprinted by permission of the publisher and author.

Figure 2.2 is reproduced from Kendon, A. (1967) Some functions of gaze direction in social interaction, *Acta Psychologica*, with permission from the North-Holland Publishing Company, Amsterdam.

Figure 2.3 is reproduced from Argyle, M. & Dean, J. (1965) Eye-contact, distance and affiliation, *Sociometry*, with permission from the authors and the publisher, The American Psychological Association.

Tables 4.3 and 4.7 are reproduced from Kemp, N. J. & Rutter, D. R. (1986) Social interaction in blind people: an experimental analysis, *Human Relations*, with permission from the authors and the publisher, Plenum Publishing Corporation, New York.

Figure 4.3 is reproduced from Short, J., Williams, E. & Christie, B. (1976) *The Social Psychology of Telecommunications*, Wiley. Reprinted by permission of John Wiley & Sons Ltd.

Table 4.5 is reproduced from Rutter, D. R. & Stephenson, G. M. (1977) The role of visual communication in synchronising conversation, *European Journal of Social Psychology*, Wiley. Reprinted by permission of John Wiley & Sons Ltd.

Tables 5.4 and 5.5 are reproduced from McConnell, D. & Sharples, N. (1983) Distance teaching by CYCLOPS: an educational evaluation of the Open University's telewriting system, *British Journal of Educational Technology*. Reprinted by permission of the Council of Educational Technology.

Figures 5.3 and 5.4 are reproduced from Rutter, D. E. & Robinson, B. (1981) An experimental analysis of teaching by telephone. In G. M. Stephenson and J. H. Davis (eds.), *Progress in Applied Social Psychology*, Wiley. Reprinted by permission of John Wiley & Sons Ltd.

Figures 5.5, 5.6, 5.7, 5.8, 5.9, 5.10, 5.11 and Table 5. are reproduced from Rutter, D. R. (1984) *Looking and Seeing: the role of visual communication in social interaction*, Wiley. Reprinted by permission of John Wiley & Sons Ltd.

Figure 5.12 is reproduced from McConnell, D. (1982) CYCLOPS tablewriting tutorials. *Teaching at a Distance*, Open University ©, by permission of the Open University Press.

Contents

1

History and Survey of the Telephone

HISTORY

"One day, every town in America will have a telephone."
(Mayor of a small American town, c. 1880)

"My department is in possession of full knowledge of
the details of the invention [the telephone], and the
possible use of the telephone is limited."
(Engineer-in-Chief, British Post Office, 1877)

On 14 February 1876 Alexander Graham Bell filed an application with the U.S. Patent Office. The device for which he claimed was an electromagnetic voice transmitter, a receiver, and a wire to connect them, and the name he gave it was the "electric-speaking telephone". Despite a rival application a few hours later from another inventor, Elisha Gray, Bell alone was successful, and his patent was granted on 7 March. The telephone had been born.*

Events moved quickly. In June the same year the invention was exhibited at the American Centennial Celebrations in Philadelphia, and in October came the first successful "long-distance" demonstration, from Boston to Cambridgeport, a distance of two miles. The following year Bell offered to sell his patent to Western Union, who were already involved in telegraphy, but the offer was rejected and instead the company turned to Gray and Edison. Bell's response was to form a company of his own, the Bell Telephone Company, and by January 1878 he had opened the first commercial switchboard, in New Haven, Connecticut, with eight lines and twenty-one customers. By 1879 he had sued Western Union successfully for infringement of his original patent, and by 1893 he had established a virtual monopoly worldwide. Bell the entrepreneur was no less a figure than Bell the inventor.

The 1880s and 90s were a time of expansion and consolidation. By March 1880 there were 138 exchanges in the U.S.A., with some 30,000

---

*Useful introductions to the history of the telephone and recent developments in technology are to be found in *Van Nostrand's Scientific Encyclopaedia*; *Enclyclopaedia Britannica*; No. 3, Volume 22, 1976, of the journal, *Electronics and Power*; and *Handbook of Data Communications*, published by the National Computing Centre, Manchester, 1982.

subscribers, and by 1887 there were almost 750 exchanges, with 150,000 subscribers and as many miles of cable. The first automatic exchanges were installed in the late 1890s. Long-distance calls were commonplace by the turn of the century, and the first transcontinental call, from New York to San Francisco, was made in 1915. In 1956 came the first transatlantic cable, with the capacity for sixty calls at a time, and in 1962 the first experimental telecommunications satellite was launched, Telstar. Regular commercial service was made possible by the first geostationary satellite, launched in 1963, and the service came into operation in 1965, with Early Bird.

Today, in the mid-1980s, it is estimated that the nationwide network in the U.S.A. has the capacity to make 14 million billion connections. Fifty million long-distance calls are handled each day, including twenty million between states. Well over 90% of American households have the telephone, and there are more than 1.2 billion miles of circuitry, much of it now able to handle not just the voice but visual information, telegraphic messages, and computer data too. The U.S.A. connects with around 250 other countries, some seventy-five by subscriber direct dialling, and two-thirds of overseas links are by satellite. For several years now the annual growth rate in the number of international calls has been 25% or 30%.

In Britain, meanwhile, the pace of development has been a little slower. The first telephone exchange was opened in 1879, in the City of London, with seven or eight subscribers. By the end of the year there were two more, with 200 subscribers altogether, and by 1887 the number of subscribers had reached 26,000. In May 1889 the National Telephone Company was formed to amalgamate the many existing private companies, and by the end of 1911 the whole British network had been taken over by the Post Office — with the exception of Portsmouth, which joined in 1914, and Hull, which remains independent to this day. The first automatic exchange was opened in 1912, more than a decade behind the U.S.A.

Today there are almost 30 million telephones in Britain, and 78% of households are connected (1984), almost double the figure for ten years ago — still well behind the U.S.A. but ahead of much of Europe (Fig. 1.1). Every day some 60 million calls are made, and there are direct dialling links to 161 countries (1985) and over 90% of the world's estimated 600 million telephones. The rate of growth and development continues to be rapid (Fig. 1.2). In 1981 the telecommunications and postal divisions of the Post Office were separated, and telecommunications and data transmission became the responsibility of a new public corporation, British Telecom. In its first financial year the corporation made a profit of over £450 million on a turnover of over £5700 million, and today its sales are over £6 billion a year and its workforce numbers almost a quarter of a million. Late in 1984 it became a denationalised public limited company. At the same time, the government took the first step in breaking British

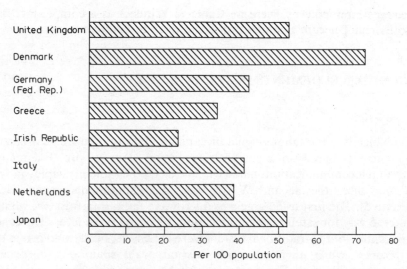

FIG. 1.1. Telephone ownership: international comparison for 1983.
Source: *Social Trends*, 1986 edition, London: H.M.S.O.
Note: Equivalent figure for the U.S.A. is over 90%.

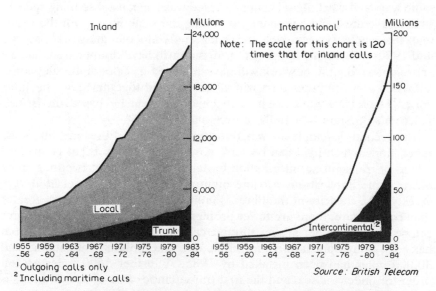

FIG. 1.2. Number of telephone calls originating from the U.K.: 1955–1984.
Source: *Social Trends*, 1985 edition, London: H.M.S.O.

Telecom's monopoly by licensing Cable & Wireless as a competitor. By 1986 British Telecom's annual profit had risen to £2000m.

RECENT DEVELOPMENTS IN TECHNOLOGY

Transmission

The voice is a continuous signal of varying intensity, and Bell's original telephone was based on analogue transmission along a wire. For many years all telecommunications made use of exactly the same principle, and it was only after the Second World War that experiments began with alternatives. The first to emerge was microwave radio transmission, which paved the way for satellite communications a decade or so later. The long copper cables of the traditional system were expensive, bulky, and prone to interference, while microwave transmission could span long distances without any cable at all. For most purposes, however, cable continued to be essential, and the other main goal for research was to find ways of improving transmission along it. It was here that two extremely important developments were to take place, and together they have brought about a fundamental change in telecommunications throughout the world.

The first was digital coding. Although the voice is an analogue signal, if it is sampled very frequently it can be represented digitally, as a series of "on–off" pulses. In fact, almost any information can be represented in the same way, and what digital coding offered was a means of sending speech, writing, pictures, and computer data along the same lines, with the result that the whole system could be integrated into one network. By the mid-1990s in Britain analogue transmission will have disappeared, and an entirely new, digital, network will have replaced it. Telegraph, telephone, television and computer data will all be handled together, and the Integrated Digital Network, as it is to be called, will be based on British Telecom's "System X" family of exchanges.

The second development was fibre optics. Optical fibres are tiny glass tubes along which light can be sent, powered by lasers. Light is an ideal means of transmitting information in digital form, since it is either on or off, and the implications for telecommunications were appreciated very quickly. The capacity of the fibres is immense, some twenty times greater than copper wire, there are fewer problems of interference, and the fibres can be bound together in slim, durable cables. From 1984 British Telecom has been using optical fibres for all its new and replacement cabling, and 30,000 miles had been installed by 1985. A further 3600 miles are on order for under the sea, and the first transatlantic cable of optical fibres is due to open in 1988. Together, digital coding and fibre optics are expected to be the basis of telecommunications well into the next century, and they represent perhaps the most important development since the telephone was invented.

Instruments and Services

While the technology of transmission has developed apace, there have also been significant improvements in the range of instruments and services available for everyday use at home and at work. Push-button telephones are replacing dial machines — though in Britain, at least, the time to make a connection will remain the same until the digital network is in operation — and there are many available refinements. In Britain, for example, there are machines which store and "remember" numbers, dial and redial automatically, and play prerecorded messages; there are machines which have visual displays to show the number being dialled, and others which display predetermined numbers on a touch-sensitive VDU, which the subscriber simply touches to "dial"; and there are machines, worn as wrist watches or pendants, which act as alarms and call prearranged locations when a button is pressed. Increasing numbers of telephones are being fitted to cars, and in 1984 the first train telephone was installed in Britain, to be followed the same year by the first aeroplane telephone. The Integrated Digital Network, moreover, will mean that shopping and banking will soon be possible at the press of a button, with not so much as a word spoken. Similar systems have been available in the U.S.A. for several years.

The other main development has been the videotelephone. The traditional telephone, of course, means that speaker and listener have no visual contact. The purpose of the videotelephone was to restore the missing information, at least in part. The best known of the prototypes was the Picturephone of AT & T, a desk-top unit consisting of a loudspeaking telephone, a camera with zoom lens, a 5 inch × $5\frac{1}{2}$ inch monochrome monitor, and a built-in microphone. The normal camera position gave a head-and-shoulders image of the speaker, but close-ups were possible too, and even material on the desk could be transmitted, by means of a mirror, though the resolution was insufficient for typescript. Each machine was equipped with a "privacy button" so that the speaker could switch off the camera but, even so, neither the Picturephone nor its British equivalent, the Post Office Viewphone, were well received. The ostensible reason was cost.

Group Networks

Audio systems

Although the telephone has traditionally been a medium for two people, there are now a number of systems which will accommodate small groups.

Probably the most widely used is the "conference call". Participants use their own receivers and the public lines, and they are "bridged" together by the operator. The lines are open, so that everyone can hear and speak to everyone else, and up to eight or nine people can normally take part. The main advantage of the conference call is its flexibility and ease of use, but it is time-consuming and costly to set up, and the acoustic quality is sometimes unsatisfactory. Instead, many organisations now install their own "dedicated" networks on private lines with their own operators.

The second system is the loudspeaking telephone, and the best known prototypes were the British Post Office LST 4 and Bell Telephones' Speakerphone. In both the models the handset is connected to a speaker/amplifier unit, so that participants speak into a built-in microphone, while the incoming signal is amplified and reproduced through the loudspeaker. In principle, the systems were intended to accommodate as many as a dozen people around one unit but, because the microphone is unidirectional and requires the speaker to sit no more than 18 inches away, it is seldom possible to cater for more than three or four. Furthermore, only one person can speak at a time, and the automatic voice-switching mechanism which determines which of the two ends is "on" often removes opening and closing syllables — voice clipping, as it is known. Unfortunately, the switch can also be triggered by signals other than voices.

In general, the loudspeaking telephone has not been well received, but improved versions are now becoming available. British Telecom, for example, has replaced the LST 4 with DORIC — and more recently still with HARMONY and LST 8 — and all three allow speakers to sit up to 10 feet away. There is much less voice-clipping than before, because of a faster switching mechanism, and the transmitter is more sensitive, the volume is greater, and the entire machine is smaller and more manageable. Like their predecessors, the new units can all be bridged in to conference calls.

The third and last of the group audio systems is the Remote Meeting Table, whose principal user has been the British Civil Service. One of the problems with both the conference call and the loudspeaking telephone is that individual speakers are hard to identify unless they announce themselves each time they contribute. It was this in part which the Remote Meeting Table was designed to overcome. Two tables of up to six people are linked by a telephone line, and every participant has a microphone. People at the first table are each represented by a loudspeaker at the other end and, each time they speak, their voice is reproduced through their "own" loudspeaker, their name appears in letters over the top, and a light comes on. Participants and loudspeakers are placed alternately round the table, and the physical positions of the "absent" contributors are thus reproduced.

Video systems

Although audio networks are often sufficient, people sometimes ask for vision as well. One solution, of course, is to bridge together a number of videotelephones in a conference call but, because the videotelephone has proved unpopular, alternatives have had to be invented. The result, in Britain, has been British Telecom's Confravision. Special studios have been set up in a number of cities, and each can be linked with any of the others, though normally only one at a time. Each has two cameras, one for the group and one for documents, and there are two monitors, one showing the "home" group and one showing the other group. The system was piloted in the 1970s, and it is now in full operation. Moreover, a digital video-conferencing service, which links ordinary offices by means of the new integrated digital network, opened in February 1984. Similar networks have been developed elsewhere, particularly by Bell Telephones in North America.

Computer-mediated systems

The very first computer-mediated network is said to have been installed in 1970, at the Office of Emergency Preparedness of the Executive Office of the President of the U.S.A. Many developments have followed, but the essentials are similar. Every participant has a computer terminal, into which material can be typed, and all the terminals are linked to a central computer by public or dedicated lines. Every contribution is labelled and stored, and is then available for all the participants to retrieve, unless the sender chooses otherwise. Participants need not be "on-line" at the same time — though if they are not the network amounts to little more than a postal service — and most of the current systems allow members a certain amount of "private" space which is not accessible to others. Many systems have now been established, especially in the U.S.A., and they are particularly common among groups of scientists and branches of government. Useful reviews are to be found in books by Hiltz and Turoff (1978), Johansen, Vallee and Spangler (1979), and Christie (1981).

One other important development, this time from Britain, has been CYCLOPS, a computer-based machine devised at the Open University for tutorial teaching by telephone (Read, 1978; McConnell, 1982). The purpose of CYCLOPS is to allow visual information, particularly graphics, to be transmitted at the same time as speech, and it is most commonly used to link two "study centres" together, each with perhaps three or four people grouped together round a monitor and loudspeaking telephone. Prerecorded graphics can be presented from a cassette player, and material can be added "live" by means of a lightsensitive pen which is applied direct to the screen or through a special "scribble pad". All the information appears on both monitors, and both groups of participants can transmit.

USES AND EFFECTIVENESS

Domestic and Business

From the moment it was invented, the telephone was seized upon as a system for industrial organisations, and its introduction into the home followed well behind. As long ago as the mid-1970s, however, over 90% of American households had been connected, and there were clear patterns in the way the telephone was used (Mayer, 1977). Almost 50% of calls, for example, were to locations within a 2-mile radius; around 20% of calls from any one house went to the same receiving number and the next four numbers accounted for a further 30% or 40%; 50% of calls lasted less than a minute, but there was a disproportionately large number over 20 minutes; and the heaviest users were families with teenage children who had recently moved to a new area in the same city. Family and friends, in other words, were the people Americans telephoned most, and teenagers — who were responsible, it was said, for most of the calls over 20 minutes — were probably the heaviest users of all (Keller, 1977). Further detailed analyses are to be found in Pool (1977).

In Britain, the pattern appears to be much the same as in the U.S.A., though calls are generally more expensive and the system is less well developed. Many households, however, still do not have the telephone (Fig. 1.3) — despite the relative cheapness of calling against writing (Fig. 1.4) — and the number of *public* call-boxes is under 80,000. In 1983 the average family of two adults and two children spent approximately 1.2% of its gross income on the telephone and communications, exactly double the percentage of 15 years earlier (Family Expenditure Survey 1983: London, H.M.S.O.).

As to systematic research on the uses and effectiveness of the telephone, almost all the work has been conducted in business organisations rather than the home, and there have been two main types. The first consists of attempts to assess the impact of the telephone on everyday life, while the second is concerned with psychological impact. The most common approach to everyday impact has been to examine *economic* issues. Cherry (1971), for example, noted that if one counts the number of telephones in a country and then examines gross national product, the two figures will correlate positively and strongly. The relationship holds even in relatively underdeveloped countries and in regions within countries. Apart from creating wealth, the telephone can also help to save energy and conserve the environment by substituting for travel, and it is here that the major benefits are often said to be found. What is sometimes forgotten, however,

Percentage of households with:	Professional, employers, and managers		Intermediate non-manual		Junior non-manual		Skilled manual and own account non-professional		Semi-skilled manual and personal service		Unskilled manual		All heads of household[1]		
	1979	1983	1979	1983	1979	1983	1979	1983	1979	1983	1979	1983	1979	1983	1984
Refrigerator[2]	96	97	95	96	93	96	92	95	88	91	82	90	92	94	94
Deep-freezer[2]	61	77	47	61	36	49	41	61	28	43	18	36	40	57	61
Washing machine	85	89	72	79	71	72	80	86	67	73	57	68	74	80	79
Tumble drier	30	42	20	30	14	22	19	29	12	21	8	14	18	28	29
Dishwasher	12	15	3	6	1	2	1	2	1	1	—	—	3	5	5
Telephone	90	95	82	88	74	81	65	76	49	63	39	53	67	77	78
Central heating	78	83	66	75	58	66	50	61	41	50	36	49	55	64	66
Television Colour	79	91	66	83	66	80	71	84	55	71	44	65	66	81	83
Black and white only	18	7	28	14	30	18	27	14	42	26	50	31	31	17	14
Video recorder	–	24	–	18	–	12	–	20	–	12	–	12	–	17	24
Home computer	–	–	–	–	–	–	–	–	–	–	–	–	–	–	9

[1]Includes members of the armed forces, full-time students, people in inadequately described occupations, and all who have never worked.
[2]Fridge-freezers are included in both Refridgerator and Deep-freezers.

Source: General Household Survey.

FIG. 1.3. Availability of the telephone and other durable goods by socio-economic group of head of household.

Source: Social Trends, 1986 edition, London: H.M.S.O.

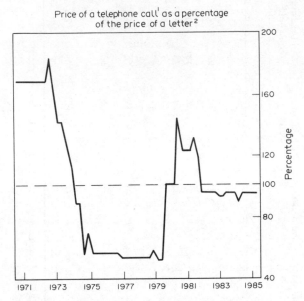

Price of a telephone call[1] as a percentage
of the price of a letter[2]

[1] Cheap rate, direct dialled call, over 56 km, of 3 minutes
duration, including VAT

[2] First class letter weighing up to 60 g (2oz up to March 1975)

FIG. 1.4. Price of a telephone call as a percentage of the price of a letter: United Kingdom.
Source: *Social Trends*, 1986 edition, London: H.M.S.O.

in the economic arguments, is the paradox that the telephone *generates* travel perhaps even more than it substitutes for it, for the more frequently people make contact by telephone the more they appear to want face-to-face meetings to follow (Short, Williams and Christie, 1976). Moreover, the reverse is the case as well: the opening of the Severn Bridge produced jammed telephone switchboards between England and Wales; and cheap flights to America were followed by an enormous increase in transatlantic telephone calls.

The other main approach to the everyday impact of the telephone has been to explore the *social* impact, and the most recent concern has been decentralisation. The new integrated digital networks will mean that, at least for the purely "work" aspects of an organisation, face-to-face contact may no longer be necessary, for people can work from computer terminals in scattered offices or at home (Christie, 1981). As early as the mid-1970s the Hardman Report on decentralising the British Civil Service was acknowledging the potential role of telecommunications, and there has even been speculation that new types of "rural urban" structure might begin to develop (Goldmark, 1972a, 1972b). With decentralisation, however, come psychological distance and central control. The effect that they would have is unpredictable and incalculable.

From explorations of the economic and social effects of telecommunications have come attempts to produce explanatory models, and one which has received particular attention in Britain is the Telecommunications Impact Model of Reid (1971). The aim of the model is to establish how far an organisation's face-to-face communications could be transferred to the telephone. The first measure it examines is the *amount* of communication in the organisation. Next the *types* of meeting which occur are counted, and an estimate is made of what proportion could be handled effectively by telephone. After that, economic calculations are made as to which *mode* or system of telecommunications would be appropriate — though measures like users' attitudes and the accessibility of the equipment are included in the equation too — and finally the possible implications for *relocating* the organisation are explored.

Perhaps because the amount, mode, and location parts of the model are subject to transitory changes in costs, which are difficult to accommodate, much of the research has concentrated on the "type" dimension, and has tried to build taxonomies of meetings. Reid himself was Director of the Communications Studies Group at University College, London — funded largely by the British Post Office — and one of the group's early projects (Pye *et al.*, 1973) was DACOM, Description and Classification of Meetings. Managers were asked to classify meetings on a number of dimensions, including "functions" and "activities", and pilot analyses were conducted to look for patterns in their responses. Meetings for "problem-solving and gathering background information" were the most common, it emerged, with "persuasion" some way behind, and "social chat" further away still. In an extensive follow-up by Connell (1974), based on a controlled survey of Post Office business customers, "problem solving" and "information seeking" were confirmed as the leaders.

Models like Reid's are based on simple economic assumptions — that telecommunications can be regarded as a substitute for travel, and that what matters most is the "effectiveness" of the communication, where "effectiveness" denotes task efficiency. What they fail to consider in any detail is the psychological impact of telecommunications, and it is here that the second main line of research developed. Most of the work is concerned with people's attitudes to the telephone, and much of the material is to be found in unpublished reports from commercial companies and experimental community projects. Three organisations in particular will be used as illustrations: Bell Telephones; the American Rural Society Project; and British Telecom.

Perhaps the most common approach to measuring users' reactions has been to ask respondents to think back to recent meetings they have attended and to say how suitable each of a variety of media would have been. The method is one which Bell Telephones in particular have favoured, and a considerable amount of their research made use of it in the 1970s. Klemmer (1974), for example, reviewed a survey by Snyder (1970) of more than 3000 of Bell Telephones' own staff. The question they were asked was which of a range of media would make acceptable substitutes for face-to-face, and 85% of the respondents insisted that they needed both sound and vision. Fifty per cent, however, were prepared to make do with slides and blackboards for the graphic component and to sacrifice facial information, but 15% would entertain no alternative at all to closed-circuit television. Only 2% would accept sound alone.

Another approach by Bell Telephones has been to give people the hypothetical choice between travel and telecommunications. Kollen and Garwood (1974), for example, questioned 30,000 Canadians as they were travelling across the country by road, rail and air, and asked them which of a number of telecommunications systems they regarded as acceptable substitutes. Of the third who replied, only 20% said they would be willing to telephone instead. The journeys, it should be added, were all between major cities, and of course rather different results might well have emerged for local travel.

The second organisation, the American New Rural Society Project, developed from the ideas of Goldmark (1972a, 1972b), whose work I mentioned earlier in the section. Goldmark's vision was that tele-communications would lead to new types of urban structure, and one of the objectives of the project was to try to predict the likely effects upon the members of the new society. A particular concern was to determine the conditions under which people believed it was essential — not just bene-ficial — to be able to see the other person. The one occasion above all, it emerged, was meeting new people (Christie, 1973).

The third and last of the organisations is British Telecom. One of the methods of conducting research which British Telecom has favoured is to fund research teams in academic institutions, and perhaps the most promi-nent has been the Communications Studies Group at University College, London, to which I have referred already. One of the questions which they too were concerned to answer was how people would react to the new forms of telecommunications, but what distinguished their approach from the others was that respondents were first asked to test the equipment. Christie and Holloway (1975), for example, set up a variety of systems and asked managers from industry and government to take part in simulated meetings over one or other of them. Closed-circuit television, audio networks with normal, automatic or voice switching, and micro-phone–speaker links with open lines were all included, and afterwards the subjects were asked to complete a series of questions about their experi-ences. A variety of meetings were hypothesised in the questionnaire, and the factors which were varied were acquaintance (the meeting would be with strangers or with acquaintances), task (negotiating or exchanging information), and travel (short or long distance between those attending). The main question was whether the respondents would choose to travel or to use the system they had just tried, and all three variables had significant effects: new people meant travelling to meet face-to-face; negotiation meant the same; and the only distances which justified telephoning and not travelling were long ones. The critical division, it transpired, was between telecommunications overall and face-to-face — not least, perhaps, because that was the pattern of responding the phrasing of the questions encouraged — and differences between the various types of telecommunications medium did not emerge.

In a follow-up to Christie and Holloway, Thomas and Williams (1975) went on to explore the division between face-to-face and tele-communications in more detail. Once again, subjects met over one or another of a variety of media, but this time they were asked how satisfactory they would find their particular medium for each of a number of hypothetical occasions. A series of very extensive studies was combined — 193 users of British Telecom's Confravision, 190 users of Bell Telephones' equivalent in Eastern Canada, 140 Civil Service users of British Telecom's Remote Meeting Table, and 186 users of the University of Quebec's audio conferencing system of loudspeaking telephones — and the outcome was just as before. Acquaintance and task were found to be significant sources of variance, but type of telecommunications medium was not. Whether respondents would actually have *chosen* their medium was not, unfortunately, included as a question, but research by Champness (1973) suggests that a similar pattern would have emerged. The more satisfactory the respondents found the medium to be — Confravision was the favourite in that particular study — the less likely their desire to travel to meet face-to-face.

One final issue which sometimes concerns respondents is privacy and security, and here too British Telecom and the Communications Studies Group have reported a number of findings. Champness (1972a) found in a laboratory study that closed-circuit television was rated significantly less private than either audio or face-to-face, and similar scales suggested that video and audio networks might both be regarded as less private than face-to-face (Champness, 1972b). British Telecom's Confravision (Champness, 1973) and Bell Canada's conference television system (Williams and Holloway, 1974) were both found to arouse suspicion about security among their users, and the effect was especially marked for the latter. The main explanations of the difference were that British Telecom stresses privacy in its promotional literature on Confravision and that, unlike the Bell system, Confravision does not have a technician sitting in to monitor the proceedings.

Interviewing and Surveys

Uses

From the point of view of social psychology, one of the limitations of the literature on domestic and business uses of the telephone is that much of it has been about people's attitudes, and very little is about the *processes* of communicating by telephone and the *outcomes* of those processes. For most social psychologists, process and outcome are the central theoretical concerns of their discipline, and much of the remainder of the book will be devoted to them. Interestingly enough, however, they have also been considered in the literature on interviewing by telephone, and a variety of questions have arisen.

Perhaps the first question is simply what types of interviewing can be conducted by telephone. The answer is almost any. Much the most common uses include public opinion polling, consumer advertising and market research, and television audience research — where the telephone has all but supplanted both face-to-face and postal methods — but there are many other examples too including, in recent years, a surprising number from health and psychology: health beliefs (Cummings, 1979); the mental state of psychiatric patients (Simon *et al.*, 1974; Schnelle, 1979); "daily marital behaviour" (Christensen and King, 1982); depression in the general population (Aneschensel *et al.*, 1982); parent–child problems in the home (Brown *et al.*, 1983); and the provision of care for mentally handicapped people in residential homes (Weissman-Frisch *et al.*, 1983). The best known of all, however, is probably the California Disability Survey (Shanks *et al.*, 1981; Freeman *et al.*, 1982) a large-scale project covering the whole of California. Its purpose was to discover the incidence of disability and disabling conditions in the general population, and then to estimate what services people needed and how far the assistance of government was being used. The projecct included more than 50,000 people in more than 30,000 households, and it was based entirely on computer-assisted interviewing, as we shall see later in the section.

Sampling

The second question to ask is how satisfactory a sample does the telephone method allow. In fact, there are two issues — how representative of the population is a telephone sample, and what is the typical response rate — and it is the former which has received the greater attention. The problem, of course, is that since not everyone has the telephone not everyone has an opportunity to be chosen. A considerable amount of research has therefore been devoted to the biases which one can expect, and useful reviews are to be found in the standard texts on the subject (e.g.

Blankenship, 1977; Lucas and Adams, 1977; Dillman *et al.*, 1976; Groves and Kahn, 1979; Frey, 1983).

Early interview studies generally made use of telephone directories, sampling at random from listed numbers, but a variety of biases soon became clear. Middle-class, middle-aged urban residents were over-represented, while highly mobile people, blacks, and those over retirement age were all under-represented (e.g. Perry, 1968; Kegeles *et al.*, 1969; Ibsen, 1974; McGuire and Leroy, 1977; Lucas and Adams, 1977; Herzog *et al.*, 1983). Also excluded were people with non-listed, ex-directory numbers, who often were of high socio-demographic status and lived in small geographical clusters (e.g. Glasser and Metzger, 1972; Blankenship, 1977).

The solution was to abandon the telephone directory and to adopt random digit dialling, in which random strings of numbers — or random once the area code had been dialled — were made up, so that listed and non-listed numbers all had an equal probability of inclusion. In general, the method has been well received, and the consensus in the literature is that it offers a very close approximation to alternative approaches, such as postal questionnaires to randomly selected addresses (e.g. Groves, 1978; Cummings, 1979; Wolfle, 1979; Jordon *et al.*, 1980; Freeman *et al.*, 1982). Biases which may still be present can sometimes be overcome by supplementary postal questionnaires or even face-to-face meetings, but then, of course, the chief advantage of the telephone is lost — its cheapness (Herman, 1977; McGuire and Leroy, 1977).

Once contact has been made with a particular household, the question then is who in the household to sample. The traditional approach is to use either the Kish (1949) or Troldahl-Carter (1964) methods, both of which provide the interviewer with random selection procedures to apply once initial facts such as the number of people over criterion age and the number in each sex have been established. Facts of that kind, however, are not always easy to find out, and they may even lead to refusals (e.g. Czaja *et al.*, 1982; Hagan and Collier, 1983). Alternative approaches have therefore been tried from time to time, and one of the most attractive is to ask to speak to whoever has the next or most recent birthday. The method is said to be very effective (e.g. O'Rourke and Blair, 1983; Salmon and Nichols, 1983).

Representativeness, I suggested, is the first of two questions to ask about sampling. The second is response rate, and this time there is less agreement in the literature. Wiseman and McDonald (1979), for example, reviewed the reports of thirty-two major consumer research firms and manufacturers in the U.S.A. and found that high non-response rates were very common, though they were often due to factors which could have been controlled. Brown *et al.* (1983), in their survey of parent–child problems in the home, likewise reported a large number of refusals and failures to complete the interview, while Groves (1979) argued that the way to increase response rates and compliance was to improve one's technique of questioning so that respondents would be reassured about the importance, legitimacy, and confidentiality of the interview. Other writers, however, have found no difference between the telephone and face-to-face response rates (e.g. Weaver *et al*., 1975; Quinn *et al*., 1980). What matters most, perhaps, is not the medium of communication at all but the nature of the questions being asked.

A more useful approach than simply recording refusal rates is to try to account for them when they do occur, and here a variety of studies have been conducted. Weaver *et al*. (1975), for example, reported an overall refusal rate of 10.9%, and a large proportion of those who refused or were unobtainable were black. Old people especially were likely not to respond. O'Neill (1979) found the "resistors" were disproportionately blue-collar workers, especially skilled craftsmen, with lower education and income than the general population, and he confirmed that many were over 65. Calls to urban areas, Kerin and Peterson (1963) reported, were less likely to lead to completions than were non-urban calls, and refusals were more common during the day than at other times, while non-responses — people were out — were greatest in the evening. Letting the telephone ring four times, reported Smead and Wilcox (1980), was sufficient to reach more than 96% of people who *were* at home — more rings would be necessary in Britain, because the time between them is shorter and fewer homes have multiple receivers — while the best time of all to ring, according to Vigderhous (1981), was weekday evenings in the Spring and Autumn.

As to how to improve response rates, two main approaches have been tested. The first is the telephone equivalent of the "foot-in-the-door" technique used face-to-face (de Jong, 1979). A degree of success was reported by Groves and Magilavy (1981). Two brief questions were asked on the first occasion, and subjects who agreed to answer those were more likely to agree to be interviewed at length than those who were pitched straight in. The improvement was not considerable, however, and the authors concluded that the technique would seldom be worth the extra cost. The second approach is simply to offer money, and Gunn and Rhodes (1981) reported that $25 was sufficient to raise their completion rate for a 25-minute interview from less than 60% to around 70%. Their subjects were medical practitioners.

Response validity

The third issue concerns validity, that is, whether subjects give "true" responses which are the same as they would give over another medium. To an extent, of course, if one's sample is not properly representative of the population, the pattern of responses one obtains will *necessarily* lack validity — but the more commonly asked question has been how the telephone might affect the responses a *particular* subject gives. At the beginning of the section I suggested that psychological processes and outcomes had been important concerns in the literature on telephone interviewing, just as in theoretical social psychology, and one of the main examples has been interviewer effects. Interviewer effects occur when a given interviewer obtains answers to questions which differ systematically from answers from the same respondents to the same questions but by a different interviewer. Rosenthal (1966) explored a whole range of effects in psychological experiments, and a number of writers have subsequently examined their role in telephone interviewing.

As to the extent of interviewer effects, there is little agreement in the literature. Tucker (1983), for example, examined eleven national polls conducted for CBS News and the *New York Times* in 1980, and found that any effects were small and inconsistent. Singer and Frankel (1982), however, reported that varying the interviewer had much greater effects than varying how much information respondents were given about the purpose and proposed content of the interview — though disclosing the purpose did lead to an increase in refusals to answer the more sensitive questions. Dillman *et al*. (1976), nevertheless, could find no evidence of interviewer effects in their research — though only the sex of the interviewer was considered — but race appears to be important in racial interviews (Cotter *et al*., 1982), and even the rhythm of the interviewer's speech may sometimes be significant (Natale, 1978), long pauses leading to a negative impression and hence a reluctance to respond.

Aside from interviewer effects, the main concern of the literature on validity has been to compare telephone responses with face-to-face responses, for that is the most basic issue, especially for practical purposes — even though the validity of face-to-face responses themselves may be extremely difficult to test. Many studies have been conducted. Kegeles *et al*. (1969), for example, among the early writers, argued that the telephone was able to produce perfectly acceptable responses, and their conclusion was confirmed by Lucas and Adams (1977) in their standard text. Both factual and sensitive questions, it seemed, produced much the same answers as face-to-face. Among later writers, however, there have sometimes been doubts. Herman (1977), for example, in a survey of trade union voting, found that respondents were more likely to refuse to declare their vote than face-to-face, and were less likely to report unlawful campaign practices — though responses on most other issues were unaffected. Likewise, Jordan *et al*. (1980) found differences on sensitive items, this time in a survey of household income and attitudes, but, overall, estimated Wolfle (1979), under 2% of responses to single items were likely to differ from the true population value in large, properly conducted surveys.

Other writers, in general, have argued in favour of the telephone. Rogers

(1976), for example, in a survey of knowledge, attitudes, and personal affairs, found that telephone and face-to-face responses were similar, a conclusion reiterated by Quinn *et al*. (1980). Christensen and King (1982), in their study of everyday married life, reported that the correlation they found between marital behaviour and marital satisfaction was similar to the values recorded in previous studies, and Brown *et al*. (1983) likewise found in favour of the telephone in their survey of parent–child problems in the home. What is more, similar conclusions have come even from studies of mental health. Thus, Schnelle (1979), for example, reported that the telephone provided valid baseline data against which to evaluate patients' psychotherapy, and Aneschensel *et al*. (1982), in their study of depression in the general population, found that the telephone revealed just the same incidence as face-to-face. Even the most intimate details, it seems, therefore, *can* be measured, and adequate responses *will* generally be obtained.

Computer-assisted telephone interviewing (CATI)

The over-riding concern of practitioners has been not sampling and validity but cost-effectiveness, and it is principally the cheapness and convenience of the telephone which have been its greatest attraction. Cost-effectiveness, indeed, is what brings us to the fourth and final issue, the role of computers in telephone interviewing and surveys. Telephone interviewing originally meant that an interviewer read from a paper questionnaire, recorded the respondent's answers on the pages, and analysed the data later. With the advent of microcomputers, however, a whole range of refinements has become possible, and together they make up the area of computer-assisted telephone interviewing, or CATI, as it is now generally known.

CATI began in the early 1970s and by 1983 it was sufficiently developed as a research technique to warrant an entire issue of the journal, *Sociological Methods and Research*. The issue was edited by Freeman and Shanks, and it also included papers by Fink, Palit and Sharp, Nicholls, Groves, and Sudman, many of whose names we have encountered already. By 1984 there were more than a dozen CATI survey systems in the U.S.A. (Groves and Mathiowetz, 1984), including the first major project, the California Disability Survey (Shanks and colleagues), to which I referred earlier, and the National Health Interview Survey conducted by Groves and his colleagues of the Survey Research Center. They all had three things in common: an interactive computer to control the content and order of the questions; a telephone interviewer who read the questions from a VDU; and on-line response recording through the interviewer's keyboard (Shanks, 1983).

As to the effectiveness of CATI, response-rates and validity are said to be similar to those for conventional telephone interviews — as indeed they should be since there is no reason why the respondent should be aware of the computer — and there are many advantages. In particular, individual questions can be selected randomly or systematically, contingency questions can be administered, data collected earlier in the interview or in previous interviews can be recalled, and responses and interviewer comments can be recorded verbatim (Shure and Mekker, 1978; Groves, 1983; Palit and Sharp, 1983; Groves and Mathiowetz, 1984). However, costs can be very high, especially when extensive training programmes have to be used and when networks to microcomputers are linked to larger "host" machines. Nevertheless, the gains are generally considered to outweigh the disadvantages very comfortably, and CATI looks set for a promising future.

Crisis Intervention and Counselling

Hotline services

Crisis intervention and counselling by telephone began in Britain, in 1953, with the formation of the Samaritans. The Samaritans offer a 24-hour service, staffed by volunteers, and their aim is simply to offer a listening ear to anyone who makes contact, for whatever reason. They are known especially for their work with the suicidal. In 1984 there were some 180 branches throughout the United Kingdom, with 20,000 volunteers, and there were almost 330,000 first-time callers, an increase of 10,000 over 1983.

Since 1953 enormous numbers of similar organisations have grown up throughout the world. Together they have become known as telephone "hotline" services (De Cell, 1972), but, in fact, it is useful to distinguish two rather different types of organisation: emergency crisis intervention services; and long-term counselling services. The Samaritans belong principally to the former category, and so too, in this country, do organisations such as the College Niteline service, and Gayline. In the U.S.A., similarly, there are many general services organised both by local communities and educational institutions (e.g. Briggs, 1972; Delworth et al., 1972; Berman et al., 1973; Hurley and George, 1974; Horn et al., 1982) — the first said to be the Los Angeles Suicide Prevention Center founded in 1958 — but there are specialist services too. Adolescents, for example, have their own networks (e.g. Garell, 1969; Garell and Bissiri, 1969; Musgrave, 1971; Hurley and George, 1974); and there are also organisations for giving careers advice (e.g. Snipes and McDaniels, 1982; Roach et al., 1983, for helping with drug problems (e.g. Yasser, 1970; Delworth et al., 1972; Schmitz and Mickelson, 1972; Hurley and George, 1974), and even for dealing with child abuse (e.g. Tapp et al., 1974). Many of the services rely on voluntary helpers, and some will act as referral agencies while others are strictly non-directive. Many are open all day and all night, and some — the counselling service of the University of Texas at Austin, for example — even offer information and advice in the form of tape-recordings. Over 150 tapes on common problems of physical and mental health are available at Austin, each lasting 8–10 minutes, and callers simply describe their problem to the duty operator who then plays an appropriate recording. Over 100 calls a day are received, and face-to-face counselling is made available as well whenever it is thought advisable (Hill and Harmon, 1976; Iscoe *et al.*, 1979).

Given the range of crisis services now available, one of the most important questions is how extensively they are used, and for what. There is a considerable amount of published data. Berman *et al.* (1973), for example, reported that more than half the calls received by the George Washington University hotline were for psychological problems, a finding reiterated by Horn *et al.* (1982) for a hospital walk-in and telephone enquiry service operated by social workers. "Chronic" callers, those who make repeated contact, are generally found to be a minority (e.g. Speer, 1971). It has also been reported that the types of call show regular seasonal variations (e.g. King *et al.*, 1974) and even change systematically from hour to hour, with men more likely than women to call between midnight and 2 a.m., for example (Morgan and King, 1977). Unfortunately, because the services are often very busy, calls sometimes take a long time to be answered (e.g. McGee *et al.*, 1972), but encouraging callers to be brief (e.g. Morrison *et al.*, 1976) is something which most of the organisations explicitly reject.

Crisis intervention, I suggested, is the first type of hotline service, and the second is longer-term counselling. Once again there is a considerable literature. Sometimes the telephone is used as a supplement or adjunct to routine face-to-face psychotherapy, to provide an emotional "safety valve" (Chiles, 1974), a "therapeutic umbrella" (Grumet, 1979), or simply a means of keeping in touch (Rosenblum, 1969; Miller, 1973). In other circumstances the telephone may *substitute* for face-to-face (Rosenbaum, 1977; Ranan and Blodgett, 1983), especially for clients who welcome the anonymity and less threatening nature of the medium (Lester, 1974; Grumet, 1979; Wark, 1982). But, as well as general psychotherapy, a number of specialist forms of counselling have been set up by telephone. Catanzaro and Green (1970), for example, followed up alcoholic patients by telephone, and Shiffman (1982) developed a special "Stay-Quit Line" for people who had given up smoking and were afraid of relapsing.

Other specialist services have made use of *group* counselling by telephone. Lindstrom *et al.* (1976), for example, were able to conclude that the telephone was just as effective as face-to-face for running weight-watchers' classes, while Evans and colleagues (Evans and Jaureguy, 1981; Jaureguy and Evans, 1983) reported that the telephone made a useful medium for blind people. Veterans who had been blinded in battle were counselled in small groups over conference calls, and a variety of comparisons were made with a control group who received nothing. Depression and loneliness revealed no difference, but the counselled group reported greater involvement with other people. The main benefits of the telephone for groups, it is argued, just as for individuals, are anonymity, reduced travel, and cheapness.

Staff selection and training

Once a hotline service has been set up, whether for crisis intervention or for long-term counselling, there are then two main questions to ask: how to select and train the volunteers; and how to evaluate what they do. Both the questions depend upon first defining the aims and objectives of the particular service but, since aims and objectives are often hard to articulate, and in any case may lead to criteria which cannot be sensibly quantified, most organisations have proceeded intuitively.

As to selection, a variety of empirical studies have been published but, interestingly enough, almost all of them consist of retrospective analyses, often comparing volunteers who succeeded in being selected with those who did not. Schoenfeld *et al*. (1976), for example, found that rejection was associated with a variety of sociodemographic and personality variables: separation, divorce and widowhood; low educational achievements and intelligence; high levels of drinking, depression, and suicidal thoughts and attempts; and a history of psychological or psychiatric treatment. Candidates who achieved the most positive ratings as recruits were often college graduates, and more than half were frequent or moderate drinkers, against a quarter for those with the poorest ratings. There were differences too in the candidates' scores on the MMPI. The MMPI was also able to predict conscientious attendance and "interviewer effectiveness", according to Evans (1976, 1977), and King *et al*. (1980) managed to discriminate experienced counsellors from controls by means of the California Psychological Inventory. Measures of listening and empathy have often been said to be especially useful for selection (e.g. Coonfield *et al*., 1976; Gray, Nida and Coonfield, 1976), and one paper even reported a criterion which was based on candidates' physiological responses to tape-recorded histories and slides of child abuse (Stone and Taylor, 1981).

Other studies have concentrated on volunteers' attitudes. Turner (1973), for example, organised a recruitment drive for a campus hotline in Washington, and compared students who volunteered with those who were ambivalent and those who refused. Men were evenly distributed across the three groups, while women fell disproportionately into the ambivalent group. The main motivation for men was to help other people, while women hoped to learn and achieve. Volunteers as a group were more self-controlled, tolerant, and dedicated to social improvement than the remainder. In a similar study in New Zealand, based this time not on a campus network but the organisation, Youthline, Drummond (1980) could find relatively little which volunteers had in common. Most had further education and were motivated at least in part to contribute to the organisation, but around two-thirds belonged to no other fellowship organisation or church group, and there were no particular occupations which stood out. In one other study, based once more in the U.S.A., Elkins and Cohen (1982) studied volunteers' dogmatism. While knowledge and skills increased with training, and both were related inversely to dogmatism, dogmatism itself remained unchanged.

The paper by Elkins and Cohen takes us from selection to training, and here too there have been a variety of published reports, though few of them, unfortunately, are based on established theoretical and empirical principles. One of the leading groups has been Evans and his colleagues at the University of Western Ontario, and their particular interest is microteaching, which consists of intensive laboratory sessions based on role-play simulations and audiovisual techniques of teaching. Students who had undergone microteaching were found to be more empathic with callers subsequently than those who had had sensitivity training or no training at all, and they were also less directive and received more favourable ratings overall (Evans et al., 1978). The training sessions were carefully structured, with an emphasis on counselling techniques, particularly facilitation, paraphrasing, reflection of feeling, and attending. The group also found that microteaching was more effective than programmed learning (Uhlemann et al., 1980).

Other writers have used a diversity of approaches, and each has been influenced by a particular view of what hotline services are about. Brockopp (1970), for example, argued that forming relationships with clients was less important than offering therapy, and he developed a programme accordingly (Brockopp and Yasser, 1970). Dixon and Burns (1974), however, viewed hotline counselling as a process of crisis resolution, for which social learning theory provided a valuable theoretical framework, with an emphasis on participant learning, simulation, and modelling, akin to the methods of Evans and his colleagues. Another approach has been to regard volunteer services as "quasi-professional" organisations, even though they are generally staffed by volunteers (Viney, 1983), and yet another has been to concentrate on the long-term consequences of hotline work for the volunteers themselves. Prolonged service, it is now recognised, may lead to "burnout", and at least one of the major organisations — the Austin, Texas counselling service — offers special workshops to deal with the problem (Baron and Cohen, 1982). Detailed attention is paid to the development and recognition of burnout, and advice is given on how individuals and organisations can help to cope with it.

Effectiveness of services

Evaluating counselling and psychotherapy of whatever sort is extremely difficult and, when much of the purpose of a telephone system is to allow for anonymity, the difficulty is greater still. The first stage ought to be to define the organisation's aims and objectives, so that some attempt can be made to measure how sensible the aims and objectives are and how close the organisation comes to reaching them (e.g. Lester, 1970, 1971, 1972). In fact, however, so formal an approach has seldom if ever been taken, for statements of aims and objectives have generally not been made. Instead, evaluations have gone straight to the more practical issues, and three main types of study have been conducted: analyses of feedback from callers; examinations of staff behaviour or the process of counselling; and estimates of the impact of hotlines on suicide rates. All three approaches have produced valuable results but, for a detailed and thorough critique of the methodological issues, see the excellent review by Auerbach and Kilmann (1977). As those authors suggest:

"Evaluation in this context, however, poses numerous problems. With growth has come diversity. The great majority of programs operate with nonprofessionals as their primary staff resource and these service providers differ in how, the degree to which, and the effectiveness with which they are trained. In addition, most agencies are no longer directly oriented around suicide prevention. Some focus on referral, others on information giving, and others on direct clinical services for a range of problems in either the phone-in or face-to-face setting. With no theoretical model to dictate selection of crucial independent and dependent variables and hypotheses to be tested, the process of evaluation is necessarily oriented around a particular program's priorities or researchers' preferences as to choice of variables. Thus, many studies are arbitrarily selective in terms of variables examined and measurement procedures employed, and it is difficult to generalize findings across studies."

(Auerbach and Kilmann, 1977, p. 1191)

Of the three types of evaluation research, the least developed is the first, on callers' feedback. What is more, most of it has concentrated on college hotlines, though there are one or two exceptions. Hornblow and Sloane (1980), for example, recontacted callers to a community service 48 hours after they had rung off, and found that two-thirds gave the maximum possible rating to the counsellor to whom they had spoken — against only 10% for counsellors rating themselves. For roughly the same proportion the counsellor had correctly identified one of the caller's two strongest feelings at the time, and for half the cases the counsellor and caller agreed on the rank-ordering of the various problems for severity. Two-thirds of callers who had agreed to take some specific course of action had complied by the time the follow-up contact was made. In later studies, Snipes and McDaniels (1982) found similarly that around two-thirds of callers were satisfied with the help they had received, from a careers information service, and Shiffman (1982) reported similar success with the smokers' "Stay-Quit Line".

Of the college research, the most extensive has been by Slaikeu and his colleagues, at Austin, Texas, but there is also some interesting work from King at Auburn. McGowen and King (1980) approached 100 students who had heard of the university's service but had never used it, and found that respondents had positive expectations both about the help they would receive if they did decide to make contact and the impact it would have on their lives. Of those who *had* used the service, 67% of men reported that it had helped, and 80% of women — though the sample was only 66 from a distribution of 3000 questionnaires. The people who reported the greatest impact on their everyday lives were female callers to male counsellors.

As for Slaikeu's research itself, perhaps its main achievement has been to begin to find out not just how satisfied or compliant the caller may be, but what it is about the call which produces the effect. Since the counsellor's behaviour is likely to be the most important aspect of the process, Slaikeu's work takes us from the first group of studies, on callers' feedback, to the second, on counsellor performance. For several of the leading commentators (for example, Lester and Brockopp, 1973; McGee, 1974; France, 1975), counsellor performance is the most important criterion of effectiveness.

One of Slaikeu's more recent studies was published by Slaikeu and Willis (1978). Contact was renewed with callers 5 days after their initial call, and respondents reported a significant decrease in the severity of their problem, with the call itself perceived as the most important factor and the simple passage of time the second. Content analysis of the calls revealed that the most helpful things the counsellor could do were to give clear and accurate information, to be supportive and reassuring, and to try to provide a new perspective on the caller's problem. The caller's preference for active advice was something which Libow and Doty (1976) had also reported in a similar study — though many organisations explicitly discourage it, their aims and objectives being instead to listen and to allow callers to talk through their problems without intervention.

The main emphasis of Slaikeu's work has been on compliance, in particular whether callers will keep appointments for face-to-face counselling made during their initial telephone crisis calls, and whether compliance correlates with the counsellor's behaviour. In the very first study, twenty pairs of calls were examined, one "show" and one "no show" for each of twenty counsellors (Slaikeu *et al.*, 1973). Two main measures emerged as significant predictors, the rated "concreteness" of the counsellor in dealing with the caller, and the caller's own motivation. However, since no independent evidence was presented that breaking or cancelling the subsequent appointment indicated failure — the assumption the team had made implicitly — a second study was conducted (Slaikeu *et al.*, 1975). Once again, caller's motivation had a significant effect, though not this time the counsellor's "concreteness". The most important finding, however, was to emerge from the questionnaire which callers were given as a follow-up. Far from staying away because the service had failed them many had been motivated by the contact to take specific action to solve their problem or to find help at another agency. A further important point about the study was the very high response rate to the questionnaire, 95% for the "shows", 70% for the "no shows", and 93% for those who cancelled. The explanation was that respondents were contacted by telephone.

Subsequent work by Slaikeu and his colleagues has moved on to objective measures of counsellors' performance (Blumenthal, Tulkin and Slaikeu, 1976; Slaikeu, 1979) — something which is very welcome though still uncommon (Auerbach and Kilmann, 1977) — but the remaining work on counsellors' behaviour has kept firmly to subjective ratings. What is more, satisfaction and compliance have been all but ignored, as indeed have any other measures of outcome, and detailed ratings of behaviour have been conducted apparently for their own sake — though presumably still with the *implicit* goal of trying to understand outcome. Several of the studies have used "dummy" calls — bogus calls by anonymous staff pretending to be clients, so that counsellors do not realise they are being monitored (e.g. Bleach and Claiborn, 1974; Carothers and Inslee, 1974; O'Donnell and George, 1977) — but others have been open (e.g. D'Augelli *et al.*, 1978; Delfin, 1978; Kalafat *et al.*, 1979). The most common ratings have been based on the warmth, empathy, and genuiness scales of Truax and Carkhuff (1967), and the most common finding, perhaps, is that counsellors with the highest scores are often considered the most effective (Auerbach and Kilmann, 1977). The balance of evidence suggests that volunteers are rated as positively as professionals (O'Donnell and George, 1977), and that there is little in the argument that counsellors and callers should have similar value systems if the relationship is to succeed (Kalafat *et al.*, 1979). Novices may sometimes be better than experienced counsellors at encouraging callers to talk (D'Augelli *et al.*, 1978), but training does, on the whole, tend to improve performance overall (O'Donnell and George, 1977; Kalafat *et al.*, 1979).

The third and final type of evaluation research has attempted to estimate the impact of hotline services on suicide rates. Some of the best research has been conducted in Britain, on the Samaritans organisation, which was the first major service to be set up in the world, as we have seen, and which even today has the suicidal as its principal target group. To demonstrate any form of cause–effect relationship where the dependent measure is

suicide or prevented suicide is, of course, extremely difficult both methodologically and ethically, but one particular approach has been used a number
of times — comparison of suicide rates between towns which have a
Samaritans branch and matched towns which do not.

The original reason for such a design was that, as the Samaritans began
to develop throughout Britain, so the national suicide rate fell, while
outside the U.K. there were as yet no Samaritans branches and no decline
in suicide (Fox, 1975). By 1975 there were 165 branches in the U.K. and
Eire, with an estimated one million calls each year (Yorke, 1977), and by
1978 the British suicide rate had fallen from 12 per 100,000 in 1963 to 8
per 100,000. The national changeover to North Sea gas may, of course,
have been one significant factor (Kreitman, 1976), together with the
general improvement in professional medical and psychiatric services
(Barraclough, 1972), but there remained the possibility that the Samaritans had made at least some contribution.

The first major study was by Bagley (1968), and it has become something of a classic. Suicide rates are published not for towns but for county
boroughs, and what Bagley did was to compare the first county boroughs to
have a Samaritans branch with fifteen matched controls where there was
no branch. Matching was based on two sets of variables, the first a number
of what Bagley called "ecological" measures, the second a set of "predictor" variables, which he believed ought to be associated with suicide. The
main ecological measures were social class distribution and recent changes
in the population structure, while the "predictor" variables were the
proportion of the population aged 65 or over, the number of women per
thousand men, and a further index of social class. The upshot of the
matching was that Bradford, Swansea, and Ipswich, for example, which
had Samaritans branches, were compared respectively with Leeds, New-
port and Lincoln, which did not. The mean suicide rates were then
examined for the period between the opening of the branch and 1964, and
for an equal period leading up to the opening, and the difference between
the two was calculated for each pair of towns. For Samaritan towns there
was a decrease after the opening of 6%, while for control towns there was
an increase of 20% using the "ecological" measures and an increase of 7%
using the "predictor" measures. Both comparisons were statistically reliable, and the Samaritans, it was concluded, were a success.

Bagley's findings were widely accepted (Fox, 1975; Bridge *et al.*, 1977).
According to Jennings, Barraclough and Moss (1978), however, more
recent statistics have raised a number of questions, for, since 1970, the
decline in the suicide rate has slowed down, despite a continuing growth in
the number of Samaritans branches. It may, of course, be that a "ceiling"
has been reached, or even that the suicide rate would have *increased*
without the Samaritans — the number of new Samaritans clients continues
to rise each year — but, whatever the reason, Jennings *et al.* believed that

Bagley's findings should be tested again, incorporating more towns, a wider time span, and more rigorous matching. They therefore repeated the study, using the original fifteen Samaritan towns and a number of others as well, but this time with newly selected controls and with data up to 1973. No significant differences between Samaritan and control towns were found.

Jennings *et al.*'s study has itself attracted a degree of criticism (Bagley, 1977; Lawton, 1977). Moreover, it remains unclear whether applying the later methods to Bagley's original data would have removed the significant effects he reported: that is, whether the difference in findings is attributable to differences in methodology or to the fact that they were based on data from different times. Whatever the real explanation, however, there is an even more important problem of interpretation: if there *is* a decline in the suicide rate when a Samaritan branch is set up, both the decline and the setting-up may be attributable to some third factor. That is, the correlation may be illusory, for something about the town — presumably the social conditions or changes in those conditions — may have led to both the Samaritans and the decline in suicide (Auerbach and Kilmann, 1977). The only satisfactory approach, methodologically, would be a *a priori* random assignment of new branches — but that, of course, is not possible.

Although it is established that the Samaritans *do* attract the suicidal, and so that the organisation reaches at least part of its principal target (Barraclough and Shea, 1970), two further questions have been asked in the recent literature: are the parasuicidal equally attracted; and might an increase in publicity make a difference? The first of the questions was raised by Greer and Anderson (1979), who examined a series of 325 patients admitted to King's College Hospital, London after making deliberate but "unsuccessful" attempts on their lives — the definition of parasuicide. Twenty-eight per cent had not heard of the Samaritans or knew very little about them; 13% had made contact at some time in their lives; but only 1.4% had done so immediately before the present crisis. In contrast, for people who "succeed" in killing themselves, the suicide rate is ten times higher among Samaritans clients than the rest of the population and reaches its peak during the month immediately after the contact (Barraclough and Shea, 1970). According to Greer and Anderson the most common reasons the patients gave for not making contact were that they "didn't think of it" (20% of patients), that they "wanted temporary oblivion" (20% of patients), and that the "Samaritans wouldn't help" anyway (16% of patients). Teenagers especially were unfamiliar with the organisation, and the authors concluded that publicity should be directed at that group in particular, and should concentrate on why people *fail* to make contact, in the hope of changing their beliefs.

The second question, whether publicity would make a difference, was raised by Holding (1975). From February to April 1972, BBC Television presented a weekly documentary series about the Samaritans, called "The Befrienders". The emphasis was on the Samaritans as a suicide-prevention organisation, and Holding simply counted the number of calls one particular branch, Edinburgh, received during the 11 weeks of transmission. Though the rates of suicide and parasuicide were unchanged, the number of calls rose by 140%, suggesting that publicity had indeed increased the community's awareness. The majority of callers, it is said of the Samaritans, are *not* suicidal (Holding, 1975), and awareness of the service and the frequency with which it is used may well be the most valuable criteria of effectiveness. Simply knowing that someone is there is probably what matters most.

Conferences and Teaching

Conferences

Conferences by telephone began in the 1970s. Although local conference call networks had been available for some time, it was only then that large-scale systems were developed, capable of linking even continents together. One of the reasons for growth was the advent of computer networks, as we have seen, but the other development which led eventually to telephone conferences was the communications satellite. Communications satellites had first been launched in the late 1950s, but it was 20 years before their potential for large-scale international organisations began to be exploited. One such organisation is UNESCO, which each year holds a world General Conference. In 1976 the venue was Nairobi and as an experiment the satellite, "Symphonie", was used to connect Nairobi with headquarters in Paris. Links by telephone, video, telex, and facsimile machines for transmitting photocopies were all made available. Many benefits were reported — not least that the Paris staff could supply last-minute information very quickly and were able to be involved in the proceedings in a way which hitherto had been impossible — and the entire experiment was said to be a great success (Sommerlad, Seeger and Brown, 1978).

Teaching

Unlike conferences by telephone, teaching by telephone began early, in Iowa in the 1930s. Today it is very widespread, particularly in the U.S.A. and Europe, and an enormous variety of students and courses are now taught by telephone methods. Most commonly, at least in the U.S.A., the telephone lines are used for audio lectures, perhaps as part of a package which includes correspondence and television material, but they may also be used for tutorials. In the early days courses were taught by telephone for experimental purposes or as a means of introducing expert lecturers to students who were long distances away. Now, however, they have become an established part of core teaching in their own right, most often in further education and where students are unable to travel to the central institution. English as a foreign language, for example, is now widely taught by telephone; there are many courses for in-service teacher training and for post-qualifying professionals in continuing education; and there are even classes in music and fine art, made possible by the new developments in telephone technology.

The organisations which are generally said to have the most sophisticated systems at present are, in the U.S.A., the University of Wisconsin–Extension and, in Europe, the British Open University. Wisconsin is the size of England, but with a scattered population of five million who have to endure long, harsh winters. The University of Wisconsin–Extension was founded expressly to provide off-campus education. for the whole state, and its staff now exceeds that of most conventional British universities. Central to the system is the Educational Telephone Network (ETN) which was established in 1965, initially to provide continuing education for doctors. The ETN consists of over 200 study centres, all linked together by dedicated lines, and each centre has microphones and loudspeakers so that participants can speak to and from anywhere in the system, as if they were connected to a giant party line. By 1970 the invention of a device called the Electrowriter had made possible the transmission of graphics, and a second network was set up, the Statewide Engineering Education Network (SEEN).

As well as ETN and SEEN there are three other systems at Wisconsin, the first of which, DIAL-ACCESS, was introduced in 1974. DIAL-ACCESS is a library of cassette tapes, and subscribers simply dial the number of whichever recording they wish to hear. Like ETN the system was devised originally for doctors, to provide an authoritative reference library, particularly for emergencies, but it now extends to a wide variety of disciplines with over 4000 tapes and more than 100,000 callers a year. The second system, Administrative Teleconference Network (ATN) was set up in 1977, mainly as a private conference call network between the university's campuses. The third of the services, MEET-ME, was established in 1978, again as a conference call network, but this time for linking domestic telephones, as many as twenty at a time. DIAL-ACCESS, ATN, and MEET-ME together absorb 21% of Wisconsin's telephone teaching budget: SEEN accounts for 16%, and ETN takes 42%. As to the effectiveness of the various systems, a detailed discussion will be held over until Chapter 5, but useful descriptions of what is available at Wisconsin and how it is used are to be found in a variety of reports by Parker (Parker, 1974, 1976; Parker and Baird, 1978; Parker, Baird and Gilbertson, 1978;

Parker and Zornosa, 1980) and, especially, a paper by Reid and Champness (1983).

In Britain there has been much less call for telephone teaching, for obvious geographical reasons, but the one institution which makes extensive use of it is the Open University. The Open University is a "university of the air", founded in the late 1960s for people who wished to study for degrees but had not followed traditional routes into higher education. There is no campus, only a central administration, and most of the teaching is done by television, radio, printed course material, and correspondence with tutors and counsellors who are co-ordinated through the thirteen regional offices. Apart from occasional summer schools, the only face-to-face contact which students have with staff or with one another is through tutorials, which typically meet perhaps five or six times a year.

Although student numbers have always been high — around 74,000 in 1983 — in the early days of the university there were relatively few courses, so that face-to-face tutorials were the most economic way to organise small-group teaching. By the mid-1970s, however, the number of courses had risen dramatically, so much so that any one region might find itself with very few students on a given course, and perhaps no tutor at all. The telephone thus became an increasingly attractive proposition, no longer something special for disadvantaged students who were geographically isolated or housebound through disability, but something to be exploited more generally.

To date the Open University has not been able to establish a full dedicated network like Wisconsin's ETN, but three systems are in common use: the conference call; the loudspeaking telephone; and CYCLOPS. The conference call is the most widely used, allowing for up to eight or nine students to be linked to the tutor through their own domestic telephones. Loudspeaking telephones have been less popular because they have to be installed in study centres and are often unsatisfactory technically — though recent improvements in design are expected to help considerably.

CYCLOPS, the newest of the systems, was introduced only in the late 1970s, and offers perhaps the greatest promise of all. Designed by the Open University itself, it resembles Wisconsin's Electrowriter, allowing graphics to be transmitted at the same time as speech. As we have seen, it is typically used to link two study centres together, each with three or four people grouped round a monitor and loudspeaking telephone. Prerecorded graphics can be presented from a cassette player, and material can be added or removed by hand, through a light-sensitive pen applied direct to the screen or a special "scribble pad". All the information appears on both monitors, and both groups of participants can transmit — so that a drawing, for example, can be made on the screen at one centre and embellished or even erased at the other. At present, CYCLOPS is available only in the East Midlands Region of the Open University, where it has all but replaced ordinary conference calls, and preliminary trials are nearing completion. The results of those trials, together with other evaluations of the Open University's telephone teaching, will be included in Chapter 5. More detailed descriptions of the various systems are to be found in reviews by Turok (1975, 1977), Read (1978), Robinson (1981), McConnell (1982), McConnell and Sharples (1983), and Harris and Tarrant (1983).

REFERENCES

ANESHENSEL, C.S., FRERICHS, R.R., CLARK, V.A. and YOKOPENIC, P.A. (1982) Measuring depression in the community: a comparison of telephone and personal interviews. *Public Opinion Quarterly*, **46**, 110–21.
AUERBACH, S.M. and KILMANN, P.R. (1977) Crisis intervention: a review of outcome research. *Psychological Bulletin*, **84**, 1189–1217.
BAGLEY, C. (1968) The evaluation of a suicide prevention scheme by an ecological method. *Social Science and Medicine*, **2**, 1–14.
BAGLEY, C. (1977) Suicide prevention by the Samaritans. *Lancet*, **1977ii**, 348–9.
BARON, A. and COHEN, R.B. (1982) Helping telephone counsellers cope with burnout: a consciousness-raising workshop. *Personnel and Guidance Journal*, **60**, 508–10.
BARRACLOUGH, B.M. (1972) A medical approach to suicide prevention. *Social Science and Medicine*, **6**, 661–71.
BARRACLOUGH, B.M. and SHEA, M. (1970) Suicide and Samaritan clients. *Lancet*, **1970ii**, 868–70.
BERMAN, P.J., DAVIS, A.W. and PHILLIPS, E.L. (1973) George Washington University volunteer hotline: a descriptive study. *Psychological Reports*, **33**, 364–6.
BLANKENSHIP, A.B. (1977) Listed versus unlisted numbers in telephone-survey samples. *Journal of Advertising Research*, **17**, 39–42.
BLEACH, G. and CLAIRBORN, W.L. (1974) Initial evaluation of hot-line telephone crisis centres. *Community Mental Health Journal*, **10**, 387–94.
BLUMENTHAL, D., TULKIN, S.R. and SLAIKEU, K.A. (1976) Analysis of temporal variables in telephone calls to a suicide and crisis service: a comparison of clients who show for appointments and those who do not show. *Psychotherapy: Theory, Research and Practice*, **13**, 177–82.
BRIDGE, T.P., POTKIN, S.G., ZUNG, W.W.K. and SOLDO, B.J. (1977) Suicide prevention centers: ecological study of effectivensss. *Journal of Nervous and Mental Disease*, **164**, 18–24.
BRIGGS, B.C. (1972) Instant help by telephone. *American Journal of Nursing*, **72**, 731–2.
BROCKOPP, G.W. (1970) The telephone call: conversation or therapy. *Crisis Intervention*, **2**, 73–5.
BROCKOPP, G.W. and YASSER, A. (1970) Training the volunteer telephone therapist. *Crisis Intervention*, **2**, 65–72.
BROWN, J.H., CUNNINGHAM, G. and BIRKIMER, J.D. (1983) A telephone home survey to identify parent-child problems and maintaining conditions. *Child and Family Behaviour Therapy*, **5**, 85–92.
CAROTHERS, J.E. and INSLEE, L.J. (1974) Level of empathic understanding offered by volunteer telephone services. *Journal of Counselling Psyscology*, **21**, 274–6.
CATANZARO, R.J. and GREEN, W.G. (1970) WATS telephone therapy: new follow-up technique for alcoholics. *American Journal of Psychiatry*, **126**, 1024–7.
CHAMPNESS, B.G. (1972a) Attitudes towards person–person media. *Communications Studies Group* paper No. E/72011/CH.
CHAMPNESS, B.G. (1972b) Feeling towards media in group situations. *Communications Studies Group* paper No. E/72160/CH.
CHAMPNESS, B.G. (1973) The assessment of user reactions to confravision: II. Analysis and conclusions. *Communications Studies Group* paper No. E/73250/CH.

CHERRY, C. (1971) *World Communication: Threat or Promise*? London: Wiley.

CHILES, J.A. (1974) A practical therapeutic use of the telephone. *American Journal of Psychiatry*, **131**, 1030–1.

CHRISTENSEN, A. and KING, C.E. (1982) Telephone survey of daily marital behaviour. *Behavioural Assessment*, **4**, 327–8.

CHRISTIE, B. (1973) Appendix M. *In* P.C. Goldmark *et al.*, *The 1972/73 New Rural Society Project*. Unpublished report: Fairfield University, Connecticut.

CHRISTIE, B. (1981) *Face to File Communication: a psychological approach to information systems*. Chichester: Wiley

CHRISTIE, B. and HOLLOWAY, S. (1975) Factors affecting the use of telecommunications by management. *Journal of Occupational Psychology*, **48**, 3–9.

CONNELL, S. (1974) The 1973 Office Communications survey. *Communications Studies Group* paper No. P/74067/CN.

COONFIELD, T.J., NIDA, R.A. and GRAY, B. (1976) Research report: the assessment of telephone crisis workers. *Crisis Intervention*, **7**, 2–9.

COTTER, P.R., COHEN, J. and COULTER, P.B. (1982) Race-of-interviewer effects in telephone interviews. *Public Opinion Quarterly*, **46**, 278–84.

CUMMINGS, K.M. (1979) Random digit dialling: a sampling technique for telephone surveys. *Public Opinion Quarterly*, **43**, 233–44.

CZAJA, R., BLAIR, J. and SEBESTIK, J.P. (1982) Respondent selection in a telephone survey: a comparison of three techniques. *Journal of Marketing Research*, **19**, 381–5.

D'AUGELLI, A.R. *et al.* (1978) The verbal helping behaviour of experienced and novice telephone counsellers. *Journal of Community Psychology*, **6**, 222–8.

DECELL, L.A. (1972) International hotline survey: a preliminary report. *Proceedings of the Annual Convention of the American Psychological Association*, **7**, 807–8.

DEJONG, W. (1979) An examination of self-perception mediation of the foot-in-the-door effect. *Journal of Personality and Social Psychology*, **37**, 2221–39.

DELFIN, P.E. (1978) Components of effective telephone intervention: a critical incidents analysis. *Crisis Intervention*, **9**, 50–68.

DELWORTH, V., RUDOW, E.H. and TAUB, J. (1972) *Crisis Centre/Hotline: a guidebook to beginning and operating*. Springfield, Illinois: Charles C. Thomas.

DILLMAN, D.A., GALLEGOS, J.G. and FREY, J.H. (1976) Reducing refusal rates for telephone interviews. *Public Opinion Quarterly*, **40**, 66–78.

DIXON, M.C. and BURNS, J.L. (1974) Crisis theory, active learning and the training of telephone crisis volunteers. *Journal of Community Psychology*, **2**, 120–5.

DRUMMOND, W.J. (1980) Profiles of youthliners and issues relating to a telephone counselling service in a New Zealand city. *Adolescence*, **15**, 159–70.

ELKINS, R.L. and COHEN, C.R. (1982) A comparison of the effects of pre-job training and job experience on non-professional telephone crisis counsellers. *Suicide and Life-Threatening Behaviour*, **12**, 84–9.

EVANS, D.R. (1976) The use of the MMPI to predict conscientious hot-line workers. *Journal of Clinical Psychology*, **32**, 684–6.

EVANS, D.R. (1977) Use of the MMPI to predict effective hotline workers. *Journal of Clinical Psychology*, **33**, 1113–14.

EVANS, D.R., UHLEMANN, M.R. and HEARN, M.T. (1978) Microcounselling and sensitivity training with hotline workers. *Journal of Community Psychology*, **6**, 139–46.

EVANS, R.L. and JAUREGUY, B.M. (1981) Telephone counselling with visually impaired adults. *International Journal of Rehabilitation Research*, **4**, 550–2.

FOX, R. (1975) The suicide drop — why? *Royal Society of Health Journal*, **95**, 9–14.

FRANCE, O.K. (1975) Effects of caller value orientation and of worker training and experience on the functioning of lay volunteer crisis telephone workers. *American Journal of Community Psychology*, **3**, 197–220.

FREEMAN, H.E., KIECOLT, K.J., NICHOLLS, W.L. and SHANKS, J.M. (1982) Telephone sampling bias in surveying disability. *Public Opinion Quarterly*, **46**, 392–407.

FREY, J.H. (1983) *Survey Research by Telephone*. Beverly Hills, Calif.: Sage.

GARELL, D.C. (1969) A hotline telephone service for young people in crisis. *Children*, **16**, 177–80.

GARELL, D.C. and BISSIRI, G.R. (1969) Children's Hospital: Los Angeles sets up its own adolescent hotline. *California's Health*, **27**, 8–10.

GLASSER, G.J. and METZGER, G.D. (1972) Random-digit dialing as a method of telephone sampling. *Journal of Marketing Research*, **9**, 59–64.

GOLDMARK, P.C. (1972a) Tomorrow we will communicate to our jobs. *The Futurist*, April, 55–8.

GOLDMARK, P.C. (1972b) Communication and community. *Scientific American*, **227**, 142-50.

GRAY B., NIDA, R.A. and COONFIELD, T.J. (1976) Empathic listening test: an instrument for the selection and training of telephone crisis workers. *Journal of Community Psychology*, **4**, 199–205.

GREER, S. and ANDERSON, M. (1979) Samaritan contact among 325 parasuicide patients. *British Journal of Psychiatry*, **135**, 263–8.

GROVES, R.M. (1978) An empirical comparison of two telephone sample designs. *Journal of Marketing Research*, **15**, 622–31.

GROVES, R.M. (1979) Actors and questions in telephone and personal interview surveys. *Public Opinion Quarterly*, **43**, 190–205.

GROVES, R.M. (1983) Implications of CATI: costs, errors and organization of telephone survey research. *Sociological Methods and Research*, **12**, 199–215.

GROVES, R.M. and KAHN, R.L. (1979) *Surveys by Telephone: a national comparison with personal interviews*. New York: Academic Press.

GROVES, R.M. and MAGILAVY, L.J. (1981) Increasing response rates to telephone surveys: a door in the face for foot-in-the-door? *Public Opinion Quarterly*, **45**, 346–58.

GROVES, R.M. and MATHIOWETZ, N.A. (1984) Computer assisted telephone interviewing: effects on interviewers and respondents. *Public Opinion Quarterly*, **48**, 356–69.

GRUMET, G.W. (1979) Telephone therapy: a review and case report. *American Journal of Orthopsychiatry*, **49**, 574–84.

GUNN, W.J. and RHODES, I.N. (1981) Physician response rates to a telephone survey: effects of monetary incentive level. *Public Opinion Quarterly*, **45**, 109–15.

HAGAN, D.E. and COLLIER, C.M. (1983) Must respondent selection procedures for telephone surveys be invasive? *Public Opinion Quarterly*, **47**, 547–56.

HARRIS, N.D.C. and TARRANT, R.D. (1983) Teleconferencing and distance learning. *British Journal of Educational Technology*, **14**, 103–8.

HERMAN, J.B. (1977) Mixed-mode data collection: telephone and personal interviewing. *Journal of Applied Psychology*, **62**, 399–404.

HERZOG, A.R., RODGERS, W.L. and KULKA, R.A. (1983) Interviewing older adults: a comparison of telephone and face-to-face modalities. *Public Opinion Quarterly*, **47**, 405–18.

HILL, F.E. and HARMON, M. (1976) The use of telephone tapes in a telephone counselling programme. *Crisis Intervention*, **7**, 88–96.

HILTZ, S.R. and TUROFF, M. (1978) *The Network Nation: human communication via computer*. Reading, Mass.: Addison-Wesley.

HOLDING, T.A. (1974) The B.B.C. "Befrienders" series and its effects. *British Journal of Psychiatry*, **124**, 470–2.

HORN, B., MANVELE, G.M. and OLVANY, B.F. (1982) *Social Work in Health Care*, **7**, 47–56.

HORNBLOW, A.R. and SLOANE, H.R. (1980) Evaluating the effectiveness of a telephone counselling service. *British Journal of Psychiatry*, **137**, 377–8.

HURLEY, J.T. and GEORGE, R.L. (1974) Telephone counselling: charlatan or helper. *College Student Journal*, **8**, 36–41.

IBSEN, C.A. (1974) Telephone interviews in social research: some methodological considerations. *Quality and Quantity*, **8**, 181–92.

ISCOE, I., HILL, F.E., HARMON, M. and COFFMAN, D.A. (1979) Telephone counselling via cassette tapes. *Journal of Counselling Psychology*, **26**, 166–8.

JAUREGUY, B.M. and EVANS, R.L. (1983) Short term group counselling of visually impaired people by telephone. *Journal of Visual Impairment and Blindness*, **77**, 150–2.

JENNINGS, C., BARRACLOUGH, B.M. and MOSS, J.R. (1978) Have the Samaritans lowered the suicide rate? A controlled study. *Psychological Medicine*, **8**, 413–22.

JOHANSEN, R., VALLEE, J. and SPANGLER, K. (1979) *Electronic Meetings: Technical Alternatives and Social Choices*. New York: Addison-Wesley.

JORDAN, L.A., MARCUS, A.C. and REEDER, L.G. (1980) Response styles in telephone and household interviewing: a field experiment. *Public Opinion Quarterly*, **44**, 210-22.

KALAFAT, J., BOROTO, D.R. and FRANCE, K. (1979) Relationships among experience level and value orientation and the performance of para-professional telephone counsellers. *American Journal of Community Psychology*, **7**, 167–80.

KEGELES, S.S., FINK, C.F. and KIRSCHT, J.P. (1969) Interviewing a national sample by long-distance telephone. *Public Opinion Quarterly*, **33**, 412–19.

KELLER, S. (1977) The telephone in new (and old) communities. *In* I. de S. Pool (ed.), *The Social Impact of the Telephone*, pp. 281–98. Cambridge, Mass. MIT Press.

KERIN, R.A. and PETERSON, R.A. (1983) Scheduling telephone interviews: lessons from 250,000 dialings. *Journal of Advertising Research*, **23**, 41–7.

KING, G.D., MORGAN, J.P. and SMITH, B. (1974) The telephone counselling center as a community mental health assessment tool. *American Journal of Community Psychology*, **2**, 53–60.

KING, G.D., McGOWEN, R., DOONAN, R. and SCHWEIBERT, D. (1980) The selection of paraprofessional telephone counsellers using the California Psychological Inventory. *American Journal of Community Psychology*, **8**, 495–501.

KLEMMER, E.T. (1974) Some current questions regarding subscriber services. Paper to *Seventh International Symposium on Human Factors in Telecommunications*. Montreal, Canada.

KOLLEN, J.H. and GARWOOD, J. (1974) The replacement of travel by telecommunications. Paper to *Eighteenth International Congress of Applied Psychology*. Montreal, Canada.

KREITMAN, N. (1976) The coal gas story: United Kingdom suicide rates, 1960–71. *British Journal of Preventive and Social Medicine*, **30**, 86–93.

LAWTON, A. (1977) Suicide prevention by the Samaritans. *Lancet*, **1977ii**, 706.

LESTER, D. (1970) Steps toward the evaluation of a suicide prevention center: parts 1 to 4. *Crisis Intervention*, **2**, Supplements 1–4.

LESTER, D. (1971) Geographical location of callers to a suicide prevention center: note on the evaluation of suicide prevention programs. *Psychological Reports*, **28**, 421–2.

LESTER, D. (1972) The evaluation of telephone counselling services. *Crisis Intervention*, **4**, 53–60.

LESTER, D. (1974) The unique qualities of telephone therapy. *Psychotherapy: Theory, Research and Practice*, **11**, 219–21.

LESTER, D. and BROCKOPP, G.W. (1973) *Crisis Intervention and Counselling by Telephone*. Springfield, Illinois: Charles C. Thomas.

LIBOW, J.A. and DOTY, D.W. (1976) An evaluation of empathic listening in telephone counselling. *Journal of Counselling Psychology*, **23**, 532–7.

LINDSTROM, L.L., BALCH, P. and REESE, S. (1976) In person versus telephone treatment for obesity. *Journal of Behaviour Therapy and Experimental Psychiatry*, **7**, 367–9.

LUCAS, W.A. and ADAMS, W.C. (1977) *An Assessment of Telephone Survey Methods*. Santa Monica, CA: Rand.

McCONNELL, D. (1982) CYCLOPS telewriting tutorials. *Teaching at a Distance*, **22**, 20–5.

McCONNELL, D. and SHARPLES, M. (1983) Distance teaching by CYCLOPS: an educational evaluation of the Open University's telewriting system. *British Journal of Educational Technology*, **14**, 109–26.

McGEE, R.K. (1974) *Crisis Intervention in the Community*. Baltimore, Maryland: University Park Press.

McGEE, R.K., RICHARD, W.C. and BERCUN, C. (1972) A survey of telephone answering services in suicide prevention and crisis intervention agencies. *Life-Threatening Behaviour*, **2**, 42–7.

McGOWEN, R. and KING, G.D. (1980) Expectations about effectiveness of telephone crisis intervention. *Psychological Reports*, **46**, 640–2.

McGUIRE, B. and LEROY, D.J. (1977) Comparison of mail and telephone methods of studying media contractors. *Journal of Broadcasting*, **21**, 391–400.

MAYER, M. (1977) The telephone and the uses of time. *In* I. de S. Pool (ed.), *The Social Impact of the Telephone*, pp 225–45. Cambridge, Mass.: MIT Press.

MILLER, W.B. (1973) The telephone in outpatient psychotherapy. *American Journal of Psychotherapy*, **27**, 15–26.

MORGAN, J.P. and KING, G.D. (1977) Calls to a telephone counselling centre. *Journal of Community Psychology*, **5**, 112–15.

MORRISON, J.K., FASANO, B.L. and BECKER, R.E. (1976) Systematic reduction of a community mental health team's telephone time with patients. *Psychology*, **13**, 3–6.

MUSGRAVE, L.C. (1971) Hot line takes the heat off. *American Journal of Nursing*, **71**, 756–9.

NATALE, M. (1978) Perceived empathy, warmth and genuineness as affected by interviewer timing of speech in a telephone interview. *Psychotherapy: Theory, Research and Practice*, **15**, 145–52.

O'DONNELL, J.M. and GEORGE, K. (1977) The use of volunteers in a community mental health centre emergency and reception service: a comparative study of professional and lay telephone counselling. *Community Mental Health Journal*, **13**, 3–12.

O'NEILL, M.J. (1979) Estimating the non-response bias due to refusals in telephone surveys. *Public Opinion Quarterly*, **43**, 218–32.

O'ROURKE, D. and BLAIR, J. (1983) Improving random respondent selection in telephone surveys. *Journal of Marketing Research*, **20**, 428–32.

PALIT, C. and SHARP, H. (1983) Microcomputer-assisted telephone interviewing. *Sociological Methods and Research*, **12**, 169–89.

PARKER, L.A. (1974) Educational telephone network and subsidiary communications authorization: educational media for continuing education in Wisconsin. *Educational Technology*, **14**, 34–36.

PARKER, L.A. (1976) Teleconferencing as an educational medium: a ten-year perspective from the University of Wisconsin-Extension. *In* L.A. Parker and B. Riccomini (eds.), *The Status of the Telephone in Education*. Madison: University of Wisconsin-Extension.

PARKER, L.A. and BAIRD, M.A. (1978) Teaching by telephone. *Journal of Communication*, **28**, 137–9.

PARKER, L.A., BAIRD, M.A. and GILBERTSON, D.A. (1978) Introduction to teleconferencing. *In* D.A. Gilbertson and B. Riccomini (eds.), *Technical Design for Audio Teleconferencing*. Madison: University of Wisconsin-Extension.

PARKER, L.A. and ZORNOSA, A. (1980) *Five Year Plan*. Madison: University of Wisconsin-Extension.

PERRY, J.B. (1968) A note on the use of telephone directories as a sample source. *Public Opinion Quarterly*, **32**, 691–5.

POOL, I. de S. (1977) (ed.) *The Social Impact of the Telephone*. Cambridge, Mass.: MIT Press.

PYE, R., CHAMPNESS, B.C., COLLINS, H. and CONNELL, S. (1973) The description and classification of meetings. *Communications Studies Group* paper No. P/73160/PY.

QUINN, R.P., GUTEK, B.A. and WALSH, J.T. (1980) Telephone interviewing: a reappraisal and a field experiment. *Basic and Applied Social Psychology*, **1**, 127–53.

RANAN, W. and BLODGETT, A. (1983) Using telephone therapy for "unreachable" clients. *Social Casework*, **64**, 39–44.

READ, G.A. (1978) *CYCLOPS — an audio-visual system*. Milton Keynes: Open University Press.

REID, A.A.L. (1971) The telecommunications impact model. *Communications Studies Group* paper No. P/71161/RD.

REID, F.J.M. and CHAMPNESS, B.G. (1983) Wisconsin Educational Telephone Network: how to run educational teleconferencing successfully. *British Journal of Educational Technology*, **14**, 85–101.

ROACH, D., REARDON, R., ALEXANDER, J. and CLOUDMAN, D. (1983) Career counselling by telephone. *Journal of College Student Personnel*, **24**, 71–6.

ROBINSON, B. (1981) Telephone tutoring in the Open University: a review. *Teaching at a Distance*, **20**, 57–65.

ROGERS, T.F. (1976) Interviews by telephone and in person: quality of responses and field performance. *Public Opinion Quarterly*, **40**, 51–65.

ROSENBAUM, M. (1977) Premature interruption of psychotherapy: continuation of contact by telephone and correspondence. *American Journal of Psychiatry*, **134**, 200–2.

ROSENBLUM, L. (1969) Telephone therapy. *Psychotherapy: Theory, Research and Practice*, **6**, 241–2.

ROSENTHAL, R. (1966) *Experimenter Effects in Behavioural Research*. New York: Appleton-Century-Crofts.

SALMON, C.T. and NICHOLS, J.S. (1983) The next-birthday method of respondent selection. *Public Opinion Quarterly*, **47**, 270–6.

SCHMITZ, M.B. and MICKELSON, D.J. (1972) Hot-line drug counselling and Rogerian methods. *Personnel and Guidance Journal*, **50**, 357–62.

SCHNELLE, J.F., GENDRICH, J., MCNEES, M.P., HANNA, J. and THOMAS, N.M. (1979) Evaluation of outpatient client progress: time-series telephone interview data. *Journal of Community Psychology*, **7**, 111–17.

SCHOENFELD, L.S., PRESTON, J. and ADAMS, R.L. (1976) Selection of volunteers for telephone crisis intervention centres. *Psychological Reports*, **39**, 725–6.

SHANKS, J.M. (1983) The current status of computer-assisted telephone interviewing: recent progress and future prospects. *Sociological Methods and Research*, **12**, 119–42.

SHANKS, J.M., NICHOLLS, W.L. and FREEMAN, H.E. (1981) The California Disability Survey: design and execution of a computer-assisted telephone study. *Sociological Methods and Research*, **10**, 123–40.

SHIFFMAN, S. (1982) A relapse-prevention hotline. *Bulletin of the Society of Psychologists in Substance Abuse*, **1**, 50–4.

SHORT, J., WILLIAMS, E. and CHRISTIE, B. (1976) *The Social Psychology of Telecommunications*. Chichester: Wiley.

SHURE, G.H. and MEKKER, R.J. (1978) A minicomputer system for multi-person computer-assisted telephone interviewing. *Behaviour Research Methods and Instrumentation*, **10**, 196–202.

SIMON, R.J., FLEISS, J.L., FISHER, B. and GURLAND, B.J. (1974) Two methods of psychiatric interviewing: telephone and face-to-face. *Journal of Psychology*, **88**, 141–6.

SINGER, E. and FRANKEL, M.R. (1982) Informed consent procedures in telephone interviews. *American Sociological Review*, **47**, 416–26.

SLAIKEU, K.A. (1979) Temporal variables in telephone crisis intervention: their relationship to selected process and outcome variables. *Journal of Consulting and Clinical Psychology*, **47**, 193–5.

SLAIKEU, K., LESTER, D. and TULKIN, S.R. (1973) Show versus no show: a comparison of referral calls to a suicide prevention and crisis service. *Journal of Consulting and Clinical Psychology*, **40**, 481–6.

SLAIKEU, K.A., TULKIN, S.R. and SPEER, D.C. (1975) Process and outcome in the evaluation of telephone counselling referrals. *Journal of Consulting and Clinical Psychology*, **43**, 700–7.

SLAIKEU, K.A. and WILLIS, M.A. (1978) Caller feedback on counsellor performance in telephone crisis intervention: a follow-up study. *Crisis Intervention*, **9**, 42–9.

SMEAD, R.J. and WILCOX, J.B. (1980) Ring policy in telephone surveys. *Public Opinion Quarterly*, **44**, 115–16.

SNIPES, J.K. and MCDANIELS, C. (1982) Delivering career information on a toll-free hotline. *Personnel and Guidance Journal*, **60**, 505–8.

SNYDER, F.W. (1970) Travel patterns: implications for new communication facilities. Unpublished report: Bell Telephone Laboratories.

SOMMERLAD, E.L., SEEGER, W. and BROWN, M. (1978) A UNESCO experiment. *Journal of Communication*, **28**, 149–56.

SPEER, D.C. (1971) Rate of caller re-use of a telephone crisis service. *Crisis Intervention*, **3**, 83–6.

STONE, L.E. and TAYLOR, B.K. (1981) Physiological responses to child abuse stimuli as criteria for selection of hotline counsellers. *Journal of General Psychology*, **104**, 103–10.

TAPP, J.T., RYKEN, V. and KALTWASSER, C. (1974) Counselling the abusing parent by telephone. *Crisis Intervention*, **5**, 27–37.

THOMAS, H. and WILLIAMS, E. (1975) The University of Quebec audio conference system: an analysis of users' attitudes. *Communications Studies Group* paper No. P/75190/TH.

TRUAX, C.B. and CARKHUFF, R.R. (1967) *Toward Effective Counseling and Psychotherapy: training and practice*. Chicago: Aldine.

TUCKER, C. (1983) Interviewer effects in telephone surveys. *Public Opinion Quarterly*, **47**, 84–94.

TURNER, J.R. (1973) Personal and situational determinants of volunteer recruitment for a campus "hotline" programme. *Journal of the American College Health Association*, **21**, 353–7.

TUROK, B. (1975) Telephone conferencing for teaching and administration at the Open University. *British Journal of Educational Technology*, **6**, 63–70.

TUROK, B. (1977) Telephony — a passing lunacy or a genuine innovation? *Teaching at a Distance*, **8**, 25–33.

UHLEMANN, M.R., HEARN, M.T. and EVANS, D.R. (1980) Programmed learning in the microtraining paradigm with hotline workers. *American Journal of Community Psychology*, **8**, 603–12.

VIGDERHOUS, G. (1981) Scheduling telephone interviews: a study of seasonal patterns. *Public Opinion Quarterly*, **45**, 250–9.

VINEY, L. (1983) Experiences of volunteer telephone counsellers: a comparison of a professionally oriented and a non-professionally oriented approach to their training. *Journal of Community Psychology*, **11**, 259–68.

WARK, V. (1982) A look at the work of the telephone counselling centre. *Personnel and Guidance Journal*, **61**, 110–12.

WEAVER, C.N., HOLMES, S.L. and GLENN, W.D. (1975) Some characteristics of inaccessible respondents in a telephone survey. *Journal of Applied Psychology*, **60**, 260–2.

WEISSMAN-FRISCH, N., CROWELL, F.A., BELLAMY, G.T. and BOSTWICK, D. (1983) A telephone interview technique for assessing living environments and life styles of retarded adults in community residential facilities. *Behavioural Assessment*, **5**, 219–30.

WILLIAMS, E. and HOLLOWAY, S. (1974) The evaluation of teleconferencing: report of a questionnaire study of users' attitudes to the Bell Canada conference television system. *Communications Studies Group* paper No. P/74247/WL.

WISEMAN, F. and MCDONALD, P. (1979) Noncontact and refusal rates in consumer telephone surveys. *Journal of Marketing Research*, **16**, 478–84.

WOLFLE, L.M. (1979) Characteristics of persons with and without home telephones. *Journal of Marketing Research*, **16**, 421–5.

YASSER, A.M. (1970) Treating the bad trip by telephone. *Crisis Intervention*, **2**, 25–6.

YORKE, M. (1977) *The Samaritan* (Special Issue).

2

Theoretical Background

Introduction

Communication face-to-face is rich in social cues: we can see one another; we know the distance between us; and we may even be able to touch. Over the telephone, in contrast, there is little except the voice, yet vocal cues have been all but ignored in the literature on the telephone, despite their important role in communication. Instead, the focus has been the cues which are lost, especially those from vision.

If communicating by telephone is to be understood properly, however, cues which are present and those which are absent must *both* be considered. The organisation of the chapter will therefore be as follows. First, the main approaches to communication, or the "schools" which have developed in the literature, will be outlined. Next, research on the voice will be reviewed, and that will be followed by looking and eye-contact. Finally, I shall introduce the literature on seeing and cuelessness, which will provide the theoretical framework for the remainder of the book. The chapter is intended both as a background to research on the telephone and as a review of current models of nonverbal communication.

Approaches to Communication

Systematic research on nonverbal communication began in the 1950s, and by the late 1960s a number of traditions or schools had established themselves. The first was structuralism, and the leading members were social anthropologists, notably Birdwhistell, Scheflen, Condon, and Ogston. Nonverbal behaviour, it was argued, and indeed any social behaviour, is underpinned by a system of rules, which are organised hierarchically, like Chomsky's syntactic rules for language. Single elements of behaviour, such as smiles and gestures, are of little interest in their own right, for meaning stems not from individual behaviours but from the way they are integrated together. All behaviours are considered potentially communicative, but the rules underneath, and not the surface structure, are what matters most. The rules are deterministic rather than probabilistic, and the main concern of the approach is to study incidents of communication holistically and naturalistically. Greeting rituals and turn-taking are particular favourites.

The second school, which some might say is actually part of the first, consists of the symbolic interactionists and ethnomethodologists, including Goffman, Garfinkel, Harré, and others. This time, social behaviour is regarded as a performance, presented by an actor for an audience. The performance consists of "social acts", which are elements of behaviour or whole sequences, with agreed, shared meanings in the particular culture. A single headnod might be a social act, as might a complete greeting ritual, and the deciding factor is whether a shared meaning can be demonstrated. Again, the goal of the approach is to extract the rules which define an appropriate, competent repertoire for the given encounter, and a variety of methods are used: participant observation; the recording of participants' "accounts" to tap how they define situations and choose which roles to adopt; analysis of etiquette manuals; and even simple experiments, often designed to detect and identify rules by breaking them.

From the first two schools already there emerge a number of issues or themes which recur throughout the literature on communication. First, *should* we adopt a structural approach, with its emphasis on inferred rules, or might functionalist, behavioural analyses be more valuable both for theory and for practice? Second, *is* it the case that integrated patterns of behaviour should be of more interest, of more theoretical concern, than individual elements of behaviour? Third, how are we to define communication, and how are we to know when meaning has been conveyed? And, fourth, what are we to say of language? Do we believe in one integrated system of communication, or do we believe that language and nonverbal behaviour should be separated — not just for empirical convenience because they are hard to study together, but because they *are* separate systems?

On almost every one of those issues the third school differs fundamentally from the first two. The name of the school is ethology, and the leading members, all European, are Eibl-Eibesfeldt, Blurton-Jones, Grant, and P.K. Smith. Ethology began with Lorenz and Tinbergen and others, as a discipline concerned with animal behaviour, but before long it embraced humans too. Its main purpose is to identify the functions of behaviour, by detailed observation in the natural habitat. Minute descriptive categories of individual elements of behaviour are set up — Grant has over twenty categories of lip and mouth positions, for example, and a similar number of eye and brow configurations, each just discriminable from the next by trained observers — and the observations are used to try to answer four questions: what made the subject do that (immediate causal control); how did the subject come to be someone who would do that (ontogeny); what value does the behaviour have for the subject as an individual (survival value); and why does the subject's species behave in that way (evolution)? The approach is thus biological and functionalist, with an emphasis on the minutiae of behaviour and little concern with language. Meaning, if it is of interest at all, is measured by the effect of the behaviour on the next member of the species, and so amounts to social influence.

The fourth and last of the schools is perhaps best named experimental social psychology, and the leading names this time are Argyle in this country, and Ekman, Mehrabian, Ellsworth, and Patterson in the U.S.A. It is probably in this particular school that the clearest and strongest implications for the telephone are to be found. Like ethologists, experimental social psychologists are concerned with function, but this time functions are inferred from experiments, in which cause–effect relationships are measured between independent and dependent variables, and the reliability of the effects is evaluated statistically. Measurement is often concerned with single elements of behaviour, with little interest in integration between behaviours and with language.

Most of the research by experimental social psychologists has examined either encoding by the sender or decoding by the receiver, and very little has examined both. Communication is most commonly defined according to Wiener *et al.* (1972), who drew an important distinction between "communication" and "behaviour". Communication could be said to exist, they argued, only when there is:

> "(a) a socially shared signal system, that is, a code, (b) an encoder who makes something public via that code, and (c) a decoder who responds systematically to that code".
>
> (Wiener *et al.*, 1972, p. 186)

By "code" was meant:

> "a shared set of behaviours which have shared referents, as in Morse code".
>
> (Wiener *et al.*, 1972, p. 186)

If the three conditions did not obtain, then, even though a decoder might take a particular behaviour as a sign of something — a furrowed brow denoting anger, for example, or pacing suggesting anxiety — communication in this strict sense could not be said to have occurred. The distinction is similar, though not identical, to that made by Ekman and Friesen (1969) between "communicative" and "indicative" behaviours, and since the three conditions are only seldom established by experimentalists, or indeed any of the other schools (Harper, Wiens and Matarazzo, 1978; Bull, 1983), great care must be taken both in describing and in interpreting findings.

For many years, from the mid-1960s, much the most influential theoretical approach among experimentalists was Argyle's. In 1965 Argyle and

Dean published the Intimacy model of social behaviour. Social behaviour, it was argued, is underpinned by both approach and avoidance forces. When two people meet, each may be prepared to tolerate a certain level of intimacy, but there will probably be a conflict of motives until an equilibrium develops. Intimacy was said to be signalled by "eye-contact, physical proximity, intimacy of topic, smiling, etc." (Argyle and Dean, 1965, p. 293), and if the tacitly accepted equilibrium were broken on any one dimension, another would change in compensation. If a subject moved closer, for example, there might be a reduction in eye-contact, or if the topic became more intimate, perhaps smiling would decrease. Quite who would make the compensation — the person who first broke the equilibrium, the partner, or somehow the dyad — was never entirely clear and has remained an issue of controversy but, in any event, the model led to many predictions of the form "if A goes up B will go down", and a vast literature was stimulated by it. It was a truly functionalist model, it was concerned both with single elements of behaviour and with their inter-relationships; it addressed indicative and communicative aspects of behaviour alike and was about both encoding and decoding; and it even had things to say about language.

For fifteen years after Argyle and Dean's paper, there was little theoretical development in the experimental literature, but then came the work of a new American writer, Patterson. For some time Patterson had been interested in gaze and arousal, particularly the way in which the arousal of being looked at leads us to try to make an attribution about the significance of the look. From gaze, Patterson moved on to nonverbal exchange more generally, and he produced what he called a "sequential functional model of nonverbal involvement". For Argyle and Dean, the principal function of nonverbal behaviour had been to signal intimacy, and the signals we use were the intimacy behaviours. For Patterson, however, there were many more functions: providing information, regulating the interaction, expressing intimacy, exercising social control, and facilitating service or task goals, such as giving a medical examination or teaching a student. The behaviours we use to carry out the functions are the nonverbal involvement behaviours, and each individual behaviour can be used for any or all of the functions (Patterson, 1982; Edinger and Patterson, 1983; Patterson, 1983).

An encounter will proceed as follows (Fig. 2.1). To the start of the proceedings each of the participants will bring a variety of *antecedents*, including their personalities, their experiences, and their ways of perceiving the situation and their relationships with the other people. Indirectly, the antecedents will influence both the *nonverbal involvement behaviours* the subject will use and the *functions* he or she perceives in the encounter, but between the antecedents and those two variables are a series of *mediators*. One is the subjects' characteristic styles of behaviour, another is the extent to which their levels of arousal are likely to change as the encounter develops, and another is the way they perceive and evaluate the proceedings. The result of the ensuing exchange, if the other person behaves unexpectedly and the encounter becomes unstable, will be further changes in arousal and in the way the subjects perceive and evaluate the proceedings. Thereafter, feedback to earlier stages in the model will occur, and the proceedings will continue cyclically until the encounter terminates.

One of the achievements of both Argyle and Dean and Patterson was to draw attention to the importance of vision and visual signals in social interaction. For Argyle and Dean reciprocated gaze into the eyes of the other was a signal of intimacy, and for Patterson gaze is one of the

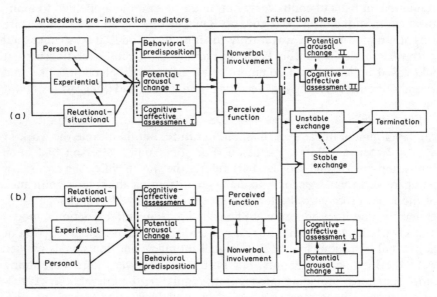

FIG. 2.1. Patterson's sequential fuctional model of nonverbal involvement (Patterson, 1982).

involvement behaviours. What is more, many of the other signals in both the models rely upon vision for their reception. Since the purpose of this chapter is to introduce the theoretical background for our discussion of communicating by telephone, and since it is the visual channel above all which the telephone denies us, the literature on visual communication will provide the focus for the remainder of the chapter. So far as possible, the discussion will be restricted just to the main theoretical and empirical developments. More detailed accounts are to be found in Argyle and Cook (1976), Short, Williams and Christie (1976), Harper, Wiens and Matarazzo (1978), and Rutter (1984).

Voice Quality

Expression of emotions and attitudes

The term "voice quality" is normally taken to refer to pitch, volume, and timbre. Among early writers, the main concern was to discover whether emotions and attitudes could be detected from those measures. Davitz and Davitz (1959), for example, asked speakers to recite the letters of the alphabet in such a way as to express particular emotions, and it was found that judges performed with above-chance success — especially for anger, anxiety, sadness and happiness. There were marked individual differences between both decoders and encoders, however, and Davitz (1964) went on to suggest that, for successful decoding, the most important attributes included "intelligence" and "auditory ability".

The major problem in research on voice quality is to disentangle the variables of interest from content. Davitz's method was to hold the content constant, and many subsequent writers have used the same technique (Harper *et al.*, 1978). There is, however, an alternative, and that is to filter out content electronically, usually by removing the higher frequencies, and then to splice together random segments from what remains. Scherer, in particular, has used the techniques to considerable effect (Scherer, 1979, 1982), and he too has concluded in favour of a variety of emotion-voice links, notably that volume leads to impressions of potency when sounds are rated on semantic-differential scales (Scherer *et al.*, 1972). Even when speech is simulated or manipulated by electronic synthesisers, it appears, there can be good agreement between judges as to what emotion is being expressed (Scherer, 1974, 1982).

Moreover, according to the literature on deception, what the listener detects may be quite different from what the speaker *intends* the listener to detect, for tone of voice is hard to control and sometimes "leaks" to the listener the very emotions and attitudes the speaker is trying to conceal (Ekman and Friesen, 1969, 1974; Zuckerman, DePaulo and Rosenthal, 1981; Ekman, 1986).

Among the most interesting of the more recent literature has been a new theoretical approach, from Scherer (1986). Scherer's concern was that, though the evidence appeared to show that listeners were relatively accurate in judging affect from the voice, little progress had been made in defining which particular voice quality was associated with which particular judgement. That is, while decoders were generally found to be accurate, little was known about how emotions were encoded and which were the cues decoders used.

Scherer's solution was to propose a "component patterning model" of affective states, which said that voice quality was associated with the physiological responses which characterised a given emotion, and that there were three main categories: "wide or narrow": "relaxed or tense": and "full or thin". Fear and terror, for example, would produce a narrow, tense, thin voice; elation and joy a wide, medium-tense, medium-full voice; and rage a narrow, very tense, and extremely full voice. Though most of the existing literature has restricted itself to the relaxed-tense category, the findings are generally favourable, and the model is set to provide a welcome framework for future research.

Personality

The second issue has been whether certain types of personality are characterised by certain types of voice. The experimental techniques have been the same as in the previous section (Brown and Bradshaw, 1985), but this time there is perhaps less agreement on findings. Among the best-known writers to use the constant-content method was Addington (1968), whose study examined the effects upon listeners of standard content spoken with varying degrees of breathiness, nasal tone, and so on. Listeners rated speakers on forty bipolar scales, and there was good agreement on which characteristics should be ascribed to each speaker and which to each voice quality. Breathiness in male voices, for example, was said by listeners to denote youth and artistic ability, while nasal tones in women produced the descriptions, "crude", "unattractive", "foolish", "lethargic", "unemotional", and "self-effacing". Aronovitch (1976), using correlational techniques in natural settings, was able to confirm that identical voice qualities were used very differently for attributions about men as against women. There was nothing to suggest, of course, in either Addington (1968) or Aronovitch (1976) that the ratings were valid — only that they were reliable — but, in an experiment by Friedman *et al*. (1969) an interesting example of validity *was* demonstrated. "Type A" people, who are said to be especially prone to coronary disease, were readily distinguishable from control subjects — or, at least, many of them were — and among the critical measures was "explosive speech intonations".

The most extensive study to have used filtering and random splicing is one by Scherer (1979, 1982) which has become known as the jury study and has provided data on many issues. Subjects in the U.S.A. and Germany took part in a mock jury experiment, and their speech was recorded and masked. Speakers, their peers, and American and German voice experts all then rated the speakers' personality characteristics. Overall, agreement was poor, but there were strong associations between peers and experts, especially for American speakers. Again, of course, the data say nothing about validity, but they point to at least a degree of inter-rater reliability, if only at the level of personality stereotypes.

As to experiments with synthesisers, among the best known is one by

Brown *et al*. (1975). Real speech samples were taken, and were manipulated to produce a range of fundamental frequencies and speech rates. Among ratings commonly found to be affected in the previous literature, the authors argued, were "competence" and "benevolence", and the same was true here. Increasing fundamental frequency led to a decrease in both; increasing its variability from moment to moment led to an increase in benevolence; and decreasing the variability led to a decrease in both. The most marked finding, however, came from speech rate (confirming research by Scherer), for increasing speech rate led to an increase in perceived competence, while the results for benevolence revealed an inverted-U curve. A major problem, however, was that the manipulations were so strong that the passages were not always regarded as natural. Apple *et al*. (1979), indeed, argued that some of Brown's increases in fundamental frequency were sufficient to make what was a man's voice sound like a woman's. With smaller changes, they found, quite different results emerged, and, as Scherer acknowledges in his review (Scherer, 1979), the whole area appears to be especially sensitive to methodological variation.

Psychopathology

The third issue has been whether psychiatric patients can be detected from voice quality, and useful reviews have appeared in edited volumes by Darby (1981, 1985). The most common approach has been based on the spectograph. The spectograph is a machine which reproduces frequency and amplitude in visual form on a paper chart or its more modern computer equivalent. One of the earliest reports was by Ostwald (1965), and he simply gave examples from a variety of subjects, including one or two schizophrenic patients. Hargreaves *et al*. (1965), however, went further, and were able to show that, for twenty-five of a sample of thirty-two acutely depressed patients, day-to-day changes in the voice corresponded to fluctuations in mood. The "typical" depressed voice, insofar as there was one, showed a lack of volume in comparison with the "normal" voice, and a lack of high overtones, giving a "dull, lifeless quality with diminished inflection". Sometimes, however, the voice would rise in frequency, "in a kind of pathetic whimper" — though other subjects in the group were quite different. The authors were also able to show that spectographic measures predicted clinical ratings of mood (Starkweather, 1967). Formal comparisons with normal controls, it should be noted, were not included in the group's work, and the methods of selecting subjects — including the criteria with respect to medication — were reported only briefly. For a further discussion, see Ostwald (1981).

Other studies have concentrated on schizophrenic patients. Spoerri (1966), for example, interviewed each of 350 patients for 10-40 minutes, and recordings of the proceedings were then analysed for pitch, intensity and duration. Though many of the patients apparently produced unusual results, no one pattern predominated, and conclusions were difficult to draw (see also Müller-Suur, 1981). Saxman and Burk (1968), however, were more successful. They compared depressed schizophrenic in-patients with a normal control group from the general population, and each subject read a short passage aloud and gave a brief impromptu talk. There was no difference between the schizophrenic and control groups in fundamental frequency, but schizophrenic patients showed greater variability than the controls from moment to moment, though only in the reading task — where they were also slower than the controls. The findings overall, the authors suggested, were probably an indication of psychopathology in general, rather than schizophrenia in particular, a view echoed by Alpert (1981) and Darby (1985). The evidence also suggests that vocal abnormalities in psychiatric patients may be situation-specific and not a stable characteristic (Rice *et al.*, 1969; Darby, 1981, 1985) — exactly the same as we shall find later for looking and eye-contact.

Speech Disturbance

Speech disturbances are normally divided into two categories (Mahl, 1956). First there are "ers" and "ums" (or, in American English, "ahs"), which are known as filled pauses and which appear to be an index of linguistic planning and may sometimes be used to hold the floor during what would otherwise be periods of silent ambiguity. Then there are all the other measures, which together are known as "non-ah" disturbances and include sentence correction, sentence incompletion, stutters, indecipherable intruding sounds, slips of the tongue, omissions, and repetitions. Filled pauses are scarcely disturbances at all, since they serve linguistic functions closely associated with content (e.g. Beattie, 1983), and our main concern is therefore with "non-ah" disturbances.

The principal issue in the literature has been whether speech disturbance may be associated with anxiety, and the earliest research consisted mainly of clinical studies. Mahl (1956), for example, examined two patients and found that, as GSR activity increased, during "conflicted" passages in therapy, so speech disturbances increased. Panek and Martin (1959) confirmed the finding, and Boomer (1963), in a single-case study, reported that speech disturbance correlated with "non-purposive body movements". In each of the three papers, if should be noted, speech disturbances were expressed as a ratio with the number of words by the speaker, giving a "speech disturbance ratio".

In more recent work, the most common approach has been to manipulate anxiety experimentally, and there are a variety of useful reviews, including Mahl and Schulze (1964), Cook (1969), Siegman (1978), and

Scherer (1979). Trait anxiety has not produced consistent results — indeed some, including Cook (1969), argue that it is unrelated to speech distur- bance — but there is good agreement that speech disturbance *is* affected by situational or transient anxiety. Krause and Pilisuk (1961), for example, asked subjects to report their experiences under conditions which did or did not arouse anxiety, and anxiety led to a clear increase in speech disturbance. Kasl and Mahl (1965) interviewed subjects on a variety of anxiety-arousing topics, and again there was strong evidence that anxiety led to speech disturbance, and that increases in speech disturbance corres- ponded with increases in palmar sweating. Jurich and Jurich (1974) found similar effects, and so too did Siegman and Pope and their colleagues in a series of studies reviewed in Siegman and Pope (1972). There is also evidence from Mehrabian (1971) that, when subjects are *presumably* anxious — when they are asked to deceive, for example — again their speech disturbance rises. Anxiety and associated states, in summary, appear to have clear effects on speech disturbance, and the findings are among the most persuasive in all the literature on the voice.

Temporal Characteristics of Speech

The principal time-based measures of speech are speech rate, silences, number and length of utterances, and interruptions. The measures are intended to be purely formal — that is, content-free — and they are closely associated with the patterning of interaction, especially turn-taking. Those particular functions, however, are the subject of later chapters in the book, and here I shall consider only the remaining literature. Once again, there are useful reviews — particularly Mahl and Schulze (1964), Rochester (1973), Harper *et al.* (1978), Feldstein and Welkowitz (1978), Siegman (1978), and Scherer (1979) — and the main areas of interest, it will be found, have been the same as for voice quality, namely, the expression of emotions and attitudes, personality, and psychopathology.

Expression of emotions and attitudes

The main concern, as with speech disturbance, has been anxiety, and the principal measures have been verbal productivity (time spent speaking and number of words spoken) and speech rate (number of words per unit of time). The early literature was reviewed by Murray (1971), who concluded that, though clear effects for speech rate had not been demonstrated, if only because there had been relatively few studies, trait anxiety appeared to produce an increase in verbal productivity and a decrease in silence, while situational anxiety led to the opposite. Trait and situational anxiety could be combined, he suggested — though his logic was not entirely clear

— with the result that anxiety and verbal productivity were related by an inverted-U.

Subsequent research has produced variable results. Siegman and Pope (1972) examined psychiatric patients and reported that, in comparison with "low-anxiety days", "high-anxiety days" were associated with increased speech rate and decreased silence. Manipulating situational anxiety in psychiatrically normal subjects, they found, raised "verbal quantity" but had no effect on silence, supporting the findings of Pope *et al.* (1970) that anxiety raised verbal output but did not affect speech rate. Yet other findings, however, suggest that anxiety may lead to *more frequent, longer* pauses (Siegman, 1978), and it was Siegman himself who tried to produce a reconciliation. Anxiety, he argued, was a drive, and its effect upon pausing was U-shaped. Trait anxiety, he suggested, should produce a decrease in the frequency and/or duration of long pauses. Highly anxious speakers would compensate for their generally higher speech rate by using more frequent and longer pauses so that they could plan what to say and say it fluently.

Despite its attractions, Siegman's model receives only limited support from the evidence (Scherer, 1979), and, as Scherer himself points out, one of the main reasons for the inconclusive state of the literature may be its disregard for social psychological variables. We have seen already that social context may influence the voice and speech — over and above anxiety and other motivational and cognitive factors — and it is here that attention should now be focused. Self-presentation and the perceived demands of the audience are likely to be especially important.

Apart from anxiety, the only other variables of interest have been affiliation and leadership. Mehrabian (1972), for example, conducted a series of experiments in the waiting-room, and found that both verbal productivity and speech rate were associated positively with speakers' reported liking for their interactant — a programmed confederate. Perceived persuasiveness too was found to be correlated with speech rate, apparently against Addington (1971), who had found no relationship between speech rate and credibility. Moreover, people who spoke the most in group discussions, according to Stang (1973), were seen as having the greatest leadership qualities, but "medium" speakers were the most liked — a pattern of findings supported by, amongst others, Sorrentino and Boutillier (1975). In all these studies, however, where the designs are correlational, the results must be treated with considerable caution since content is uncontrolled and can therefore not be disentangled from the measures of interest.

Personality

Rather less has been published on personality than the expression of emotions and attitudes, and the earliest research was concerned with the stability of speech measures within individuals (reviewed by Saslow and Matarazzo, 1959). Individuals do behave consistently, it appears, but external factors can produce variations (e.g. Matarazzo and Wiens, 1972; Siegman, 1978). One particular factor is the behaviour of the other person, and it is well established that, for example, the length of one person's utterances will be positively correlated with the other's. Two real-life examples have been reported from conversations between NASA. Mission Control and astronauts circling the earth (Matarazzo *et al.*, 1964) and President Kennedy's replies to reporters' questions at press conferences (Ray and Webb, 1966).

As to what may be responsible for stable individual differences, the most frequently studied personality trait has been extroversion. Siegman and Pope (1965), for example, found that extroversion was associated with shorter latencies, fewer brief filled pauses, and fewer silent pauses, and Ramsay (1966, 1968) reported that silences between sound bursts were on average shorter for extroverts than introverts. A variety of American studies have indicated a positive association between verbal productivity and extroversion or related traits (e.g. Cope, 1969; Weinstein and Hanson, 1975), and British studies have reported the same (e.g. Carment *et al.*, 1965; Patterson and Holmes, 1966; Rutter, Morley and Graham, 1972; Campbell and Rushton, 1978). As in the case of anxiety, Siegman (1978) suggests that the effects are due largely to cognitive and motivational factors associated with the trait — especially "cognitive activity" and "impulsivity" — but Scherer (1979) argues once more for greater attention to situational factors and their interaction with personality.

Psychopathology

The literature on psychopathology is extensive, and a review is to be found in Rutter (in press). The very first studies were conducted by Chapple and his colleagues in the 1940s, using the Interaction Chronograph (Chapple, 1939), a push-button event-recorder operated by a technician seated out of sight of the speakers. Chapple and Lindemann (1942) conducted standardised interviews with forty psychiatric patients and fifty normal controls, and reported that latencies and simultaneous speech especially discriminated between psychotic, neurotic, and normal subjects. Chapple *et al.* (1960), however, were unable to separate schizophrenic from non-schizophrenic subjects, and there was marked variability from patient to patient and noticeable moment-to-moment fluctuation. Variation within groups was also the principal finding of Matarazzo and Saslow (1961).

Despite the original assumptions that standardising the interview would eliminate effects of content from research with the Interaction Chronograph, it soon became clear that they still remained. It was also difficult to control for operator bias. The eventual outcome was a new line of research by Feldstein and his colleagues, reviewed by Jaffe and Feldstein (1970), Feldstein (1972), Feldstein and Welkowitz (1978), and Scherer (1982). The standardised interview was replaced by conversation (where the hope was that effects of content would be non-systematic because content was free to develop at random), and the Interaction Chronograph was replaced by an automated computer-based system known as Automatic Vocal Transaction Analysis: AVTA (Cassotta et al., 1964).

Most of the group's work was concerned with normal speakers, but two recent papers have examined psychiatric patients. In the first, by Glaister et al. (1980), five schizophrenic patients were monitored, and their speech-silence sequences were tracked. For four of the five a degree of response-matching was found with the partner but, while partners alternated between periods of speech and silence of almost equal length, patients were much less stable. When patients spent longer in silence than speech — they were observed on several occasions — their clinical ratings were found to have deteriorated correspondingly. In the other paper, by Feldstein et al. (1982), autistic subjects aged 14–20 were observed in interaction once with one of their parents and once with an experimenter. The parent also met the experimenter separately and, while parent and experimenter achieved good "temporal synchrony" — lack of pausing or disruption at turn-taking — patients with parents and patients with experimenter did not.

In one final group of studies, I examined psychiatric patients myself. The first experiment, by Rutter and Stephenson (1972), monitored twenty acute schizophrenic patients and twenty acutely depressed patients, each matched individually with an acute chest patient. Each of the patients was given a standardised clinical interview, by an interviewer who was trained to behave consistently, and speech was scored from tape-recordings by means of a simple push-button event-recorder similar to the Interaction Chronograph. The principal measures were verbal productivity (proportion of time spent speaking, number and average length of utterances, number of words), interruptions (number and duration), proportion of time spent in mutual silence, speech rate, filled pause ratio, and speech disturbance ratio. The schizophrenic patients, it emerged, were very similar to their controls, but the depressed group spent longer in silence on average than their controls, and proportionately less time listening to the interviewer.

In the subsequent studies, I changed to free conversation as Feldstein had done. In the first of two experiments reported in Rutter (1977a), I examined four groups of acute patients: schizophrenic, depressed, people with neurotic and personality disorders, and chest patient controls. Each subject held two conversations, one with a patient from the same diagnostic category, and one with a nurse. Only one significant main effect of diagnostic category was revealed — though a number of the detailed comparisons between groups were also statistically reliable — and the similarities were much more striking than the differences, as was also to emerge for looking and eye-contact. In the other experiment reported in the 1977a paper, chronic and acute schizophrenic patients were compared, and no single difference was detected. Almost half the chronic patients approached initially, however, were found to be mute, and their elimination from the study meant that the eventual sample was highly selected.

The final study, by Rutter (1977b), was concerned with the issue of competence and performance. If schizophrenic patients do sometimes show different speech patterns from other subjects, is it that they have failed to learn the "rules" of speaking and so lack competence, or is it that the acute phase of the illness prevents their behaving according to those rules and impairs merely their performance? The most useful approach, I reasoned, would be to compare acute patients with those who were in remission, and to include a control group once again, consisting of chest patients. I also chose to manipulate topic — so that each patient and partner (a nurse) conversed once about an impersonal subject and once about an arousing topic — and it was topic alone which produced significant main effects. There were no effects of diagnostic category and no interactions between diagnosis and topic. The question to which the experiment had been addressed, therefore, remained unanswered, but once again there was evidence that content and "non-content" measures of speech could simply not be separated. It is precisely those links — between content, style, and outcome — which will provide the theoretical focus for much of the remainder of the book.

LOOKING AND EYE-CONTACT

The Pattern of Gaze

Speech and the timing of looks

From time to time during social encounters, people look at one another in the region of the eyes, and sometimes their eyes meet to make eye-contact. The first question for the literature to resolve was whether any regularity or pattern might be detectable, and a tentative answer appeared in a classic paper, by Kendon (1967). In an "exploratory" study, based in his Oxford laboratory, Kendon found that each member of a pair would typically look at the other about 50% of the time — though the range was considerable — and the figure for mutual looking, or eye-contact as it is generally known, approached 25%. Glances were generally fewer and shorter during speech than listening, and bursts of eye-contact seldom lasted more than a second. The findings were similar to those already published by Nielsen (1962), whose work is less well known for some reason, and it was also to emerge that there are stable individual differences (Kendon and Cook, 1969). That is, some of us look a lot, and some

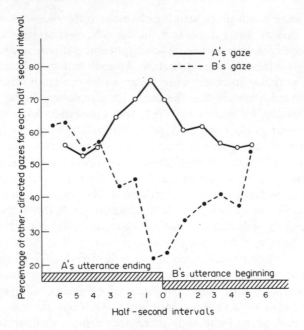

FIG. 2.2. Kendon (1967): The timing of looks in relation to speech.

of us look a little, but each of us behaves consistently from encounter to encounter.

The other feature of Kendon's paper was a detailed analysis of precisely when in the flow of conversation each look occurred. The most important findings concerned the beginnings and endings of so-called long utterances, those which lasted 5 seconds or more. What emerged was that, as the speaker came to the end of an utterance, he would generally look up at the listener, who would then look away and continue to do so until he was well underway himself (Fig. 2.2). The figure was more than 70% in both cases. If the speaker failed to look up at the end of the utterance, there was generally a delay before the new speaker took over, if indeed he took over at all. Gaze, it appeared, was closely synchronised with speech, so much so, Kendon speculated, that it probably served as one of the signals for regulating turn-taking. Subsequent writers, as we shall see later, have been less sanguine.

Individual differences

As soon as it was established that individuals behaved consistently from encounter to encounter, attention turned to the possible sources of variation. One of the most extensively investigated has been sex, and women have almost always been found to look more than men and to engage in more eye-contact (Ellsworth and Ludwig, 1972; Argyle and Cook, 1976;

Harper, Wiens and Matarazzo, 1978; Rutter, 1984). As to why, two main interpretations have been suggested, the first based on motivation, the second information. The motivational account argues that women have a greater need than men for affiliation, while the informational account says that they are more dependent on social cues and feedback. There may also, of course, be situational factors which interact (Exline, 1971).

The second variable of interest has been personality, but this time the findings are less clear. Need for affiliation, dominance, and extroversion have been the main traits to receive attention, and both "correlational" and "between-groups" designs have been used. Correlational studies take a random selection of subjects and correlate individuals' scores on the particular measure of personality with their levels of gaze, while between-groups designs typically select extreme groups on the personality measure and compare their mean levels of looking. In general, correlational studies have not produced significant effects but between-groups studies have. Little attempt at theoretical integration has been made, however, but such accounts as do exist are very similar to those for sex differences, in that they are based on either motivation or information (Rutter, 1984).

The third and final variable is psychopathology, which of the three has the longest history in the literature on gaze. Research methods have ranged from clinical case studies to controlled experiments, and psychotic children, schizophrenic adults, and depressed adults have all been investigated extensively. The most common finding has been that all three groups look very little during social interaction, indeed sometimes not at all (Rutter, 1973, 1984). More recent evidence, however, some of it from my own research on schizophrenic and depressed patients, has suggested that a significant proportion of the variance may be attributable to the setting in which the behaviour is observed. Almost all the early literature was based on clinical interviews, typically about the patient's disorder, and the result was gaze aversion. When the setting and topic were changed, however, to less structured conversations with other patients or nurses about unemotive, everyday interests like television, patients looked quite normally. The gaze aversion of the early literature, in other words, was situation-specific (Rutter, 1973, 1976, 1977), and what produced it was probably something very simple, like embarrassment (Rutter and O'Brien, 1980). People who are socially withdrawn are embarrassed about discussing their case histories and their disorders, and like perfectly normal people who are embarrassed they look away; when the setting changes to remove their embarrassment, they behave normally.

Emotion and the Expressive Functions of Gaze

The Intimacy model of Argyle and Dean (1965)

Towards the end of his paper, Kendon (1967) turned from the structure of gaze to its possible functions, and he suggested that there were three:

expression; regulation; and monitoring. The expressive function, which has attracted much the most interest among research workers, was concerned with how we convey our emotions and attitudes to one another. Two main types of study have developed: encoding studies, which examine the effects of emotion and attitudes on the sender's gaze; and decoding studies, which focus instead on the receiver and examine whether variations in the sender's gaze have measurable effects upon the receiver's perceptions and behaviour. Very few attempts have been made to integrate the two approaches, either theoretically or empirically, but there is one major exception, the intimacy research of Argyle and Dean.

The Intimacy model makes a large number of predictions about dyadic behaviour, as we have seen, but the most important for the literature have concerned the relationship between distance and gaze. It was that particular relationship, indeed, upon which the empirical part of the 1965 paper dwelt, and one of the experiments presented there has become particularly well known. Student subjects were recruited for "an experiment on conversations", and each held three 3-minute discussions with a confederate who posed as another genuine subject. The task was to make up stories about TAT cards. The speakers sat at 90° across a table, and the distance between them, which was manipulated by moving the subject after each conversation, was 2 feet, 6 feet, or 10 feet, measured eye to eye. The confederate stared continuously — with the result, it should be noted, that

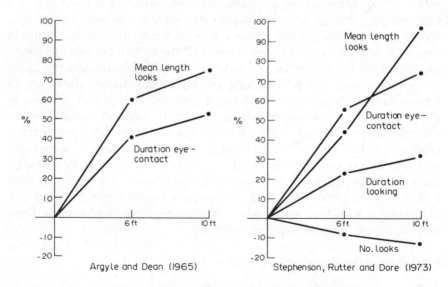

FIG. 2.3. Relationships between gaze and distance.
Note: Findings for 6 ft and 10 ft presented as deviations (%) from the findings for 2 ft.

the subject's looking unavoidably led to eye-contact — and it was therefore necessary to monitor only the subject's behaviour. The observations were made live from behind a one-way screen, and the prediction of the model was supported: the greater the distance between the subject and confederate, the more the subject looked and so the greater the eye-contact, both mean length and overall duration (Fig. 2.3).

The paper quickly became a classic — though it was later to provoke a lively debate about methods of observation (Rutter, 1984) — and the relationship between distance and gaze has proved exceptionally robust. Quite why there is a relationship, however, remains uncertain. The original interpretation was based on emotion and motivation, of course, but other accounts have turned to the concept of information (Chapman 1975: Russo, 1975; Pennington and Rutter, 1981; Swain, Stephenson and Dewey, 1982). The motivational interpretation, which was the basis of the Intimacy model, argues that people engage in more eye-contact at greater distances because they are trying to restore the motivational balance which the increase in distance has violated. The informational interpretation argues instead that an increase in distance leads to a greater dependence on feedback, and gaze is the most useful means of trying to find it.

Encoding studies

One of the virtues of the Intimacy model was that it sought to encompass both encoding and decoding studies. Almost all the remaining literature, unfortunately, has been divided between the two, and it has seldom been easy to see any clear relationship between them. As to encoding studies, first of all, three main groups of variables have been explored: attraction and approval; dominance, status and power; and the emotions of embarrassment, shame and sorrow.

Attraction and approval have produced much the most extensive literature, and there have been three types of study: correlational studies, in which natural variations in liking and approval are examined and correlated with gaze; experimental studies, in which independent variables are manipulated and their effects upon the encoder's gaze are monitored; and role-playing studies, in which subjects are asked to imagine themselves in a variety of settings and relationships, and to behave as they believe they actually would. Dominance, status and power have received much less attention, and all the studies have made use of traditional experimental techniques or role-playing. Embarrassment, shame and sorrow have received less attention still, and only traditional experimental techniques have been used.

For all three groups of variables, the findings are extremely diffuse and complex, and there is no clear pattern to discern. There has been little attempt at integration, either theoretical or empirical, and there are in any case serious methodological weaknesses in much of the research. Many of the studies lacked ecological validity, especially perhaps those based on role-playing, and many of the others were so poorly controlled that apparently encouraging results could not be properly understood because it was impossible to know which particular affective state had caused them, if any. The only conclusion to draw, I think, is that if people experience a positive emotion or make a positive attribution about the encounter, they will probably look more than if their experiences are negative. Theoretically, existing models could say very little, and it was only with the emergence of the attributional approach that any real progress was to be made.

Decoding studies

Decoding studies are less easy than encoding studies to classify, but three main issues have been explored in the literature: whether people are aware of how much they are looked at; whether being looked at is arousing; and whether gaze is used for making attributions about the sender. In general, it emerges, people are not aware of how much they are looked at, though people who do notice gaze appear to form different impressions of the sender from those who do not. However, irrespective of awareness, being looked at does produce detectable effects upon physiological arousal, whether measured peripherally by GSR, for example, or centrally by EEG. Interpretation, however, is not straightforward, since it is impossible to say from the literature whether the critical variable is the emotionally arousing properties of the stimulus or its informational complexity. Just as with both Intimacy and encoding, either type of interpretation is possible.

Research on attributions based on gaze has been much more extensive, and two main types of study have been conducted. In the first, subjects interact with confederates, whose gaze is programmed to vary in systematic ways, and at the end of the encounter they record the impressions they have formed, generally by completing rating scales. In the second, they merely observe, and the stimulus material is typically presented in the form of videotape recordings or films. Very few studies, unfortunately, have combined the two approaches, even though there is little reason to assume that participants and observers will behave in the same way. Nevertheless, the literature does suggest that gaze leads people to make attributions — not least, perhaps, because of demand characteristics — but it is difficult to find any clear pattern since the task and context are particularly important variables. Prolonged gaze, for example, in one setting may produce a quite different attribution from the identical behaviour elsewhere.

*Arousal, attribution, and social influence: the Ellsworth–Patterson
model*

Apart from the literature on encoding and decoding, there is one final
group of studies to examine, those concerned with gaze as a source of social
influence. It is here that at last we begin to detect a significant theoretical
advance on the work of Argyle and Dean. The Intimacy model, I have
suggested already, dominated the literature until the middle or late 1970s,
and it was the work on social influence which first began to offer an
alternative. Interestingly enough, it was also the work on social influence
which first made extensive and systematic use of the field rather than the
laboratory.

The most important of the early studies came from Ellsworth and her
colleagues. The first was published by Ellsworth, Carlsmith and Henson
(1972) and reported a series of experiments designed to test the hypothesis
that staring elicits avoidance. A stare was defined as a gaze or look which
persists regardless of the behaviour of the other person, and it was
considered to be a threat to the receiver. If escape were impossible at first,
tension and arousal would mount, and the response when it finally came
would be exaggerated.

The first experiment reported in the paper was conducted at a road
junction controlled by traffic lights. The experimenter, riding a motor
scooter, pulled up next to the target and stared at the driver until the lights
changed to green. The dependent measure was the time it took the target
to cross the intersection, and experimental subjects were found to cross
more quickly than controls (Fig. 2.4). Subsequent experiments demonstrated that the same happened when drivers were stared at by a pedestrian,
that pedestrians at pedestrian crossings were affected in the same way too,

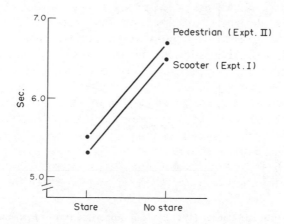

FIG. 2.4. Ellsworth *et al*. (1972): Mean crossing times.

and that the sex of the starer was immaterial. The results could not be explained by saying that staring violates the norms of everyday experience since an equally unusual, albeit asocial, stimulus had no effect — a young woman sitting hammering and picking at the pavement. Instead, Ellsworth offered two other interpretations, and she appeared to favour the second:

> "The first is that staring is generally perceived as a signal of hostile intent, as in primates, and elicits avoidance or, in some circumstances, counterattack. The second is that gazing at a person's face is an extremely salient stimulus with interpersonal implications which cannot be ignored. The stare, in effect, is a demand for a response, and in a situation where there is no appropriate response, tension will be evoked, and the subject will be motivated to escape the situation."
>
> (Ellsworth, Carlsmith and Henson, 1972, p. 311)

A considerable number of experiments followed, some of them on further types of aversive setting — such as the invasion of personal space — but others on more positive forms of interaction, such as trying to attract help (Fig. 2.5). Often, it became clear, staring was not aversive, and Ellsworth began to wonder whether it might simply be a non-specific activator. That is, when I stare at you, you become aroused — perhaps because my behaviour forces you to interact with me — and you cast around for an explanation and a suitable response. If you succeed, your arousal falls; but, if not, you eventually take flight. Gaze has no particular

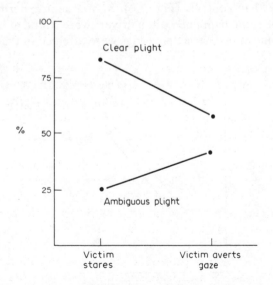

FIG. 2.5. Ellsworth and Langer (1976): Mean proportion (%) of bystanders who helped a "victim in distress".

meaning of its own, and we have to attribute one — by using the context — before we can make a behavioural response. In other words, gaze was a *salient* stimulus, which *aroused* and *involved* the receiver and was difficult to ignore. It had no intrinsic meaning, and the receiver had to resort to contextual information to try to interpret it.

The distinctive feature of Ellsworth's model was, thus, its emphasis on arousal and attribution. Encoding and decoding studies had produced enormous literatures, but what had been missing from them both was any serious attempt at theoretical integration. Now, at last, there was a promising new approach, and what mattered most was to try to develop the model in a little more detail, and to examine how well it could accommodate the existing literature.

At the start of the chapter I introduced the work of Patterson, and it was Patterson's model which provided what was needed. Where Argyle and Dean had spoken of "intimacy behaviours", Patterson used the term "immediacy behaviours". In general, he believed, the evidence supported the Intimacy model, and compensation between behaviours was, indeed, the rule. However, as we have seen already, compensation did not always occur, and reciprocation was sometimes found instead. The reason, suggested Patterson, was that the immediacy behaviours serve not just intimacy but a number of other functions too and, since their roles will sometimes conflict, the results will be inconsistent. Patterson's first major achievement was to account for that inconsistency.

Like Ellsworth, Patterson argued that arousal was the key — and indeed Ellsworth was to write that Patterson's approach was simply one version of the "general theoretical point of view" at which she had herself arrived (Ellsworth, 1978). Sometimes, Patterson suggested, a change in A's intimacy behaviours would arouse B, but sometimes it would not. When arousal did occur, B would make an attribution, and if it was negative he would compensate, but if it was positive he would reciprocate. If there was no arousal, there would be no attribution and no change in behaviour. Though compensation might be the general rule, reciprocation was thus perfectly possible, as indeed were *decreases* in arousal. Like Ellsworth (1978), Patterson conceded that where arousal should be located in the chain from stimulus to attribution to behavioural response was uncertain, and he also acknowledged that what determined whether an attribution would be positive or negative was not yet clear, though individual differences and contextual factors, including the history of the relationship, were likely to be important. The Intimacy model could now be seen as just a "special case" (Ellsworth, 1978) of the theory which Ellsworth and Patterson had proposed, and the introduction of reciprocation was to be welcomed. By the inclusion of compensation and reciprocation within one general theoretical framework, equilibrium theory was encompassed and the literature was both strengthened and integrated.

The work of Ellsworth and Patterson, I believe, is the most successful attempt so far to integrate the literature on decoding — and what is more the approach can readily be extended to encoding. Research on encoding explored discrete empirical areas — attraction and approval; dominance, status and power; embarrassment, shame and sorrow — and there were no obvious links. In fact, however, there was a simple pattern: when we become aroused (for whatever reason) we make an attribution, and if the attribution is positive we look more but if it is negative we look less. Encoding and decoding are thus *both* underpinned by attribution, and it was possible at last to integrate the literature on expression within one single theoretical framework.

Information and the Regulatory and Monitoring Functions of Gaze

The central concept in the literature on expression, as we have seen, is emotion. From time to time, it is true, alternative interpretations of the findings have been offered, making use instead of the concept of information, but it is only when we turn to Kendon's other two functions, regulation and monitoring, that information comes to the fore. Regulation is concerned with how we use visual signals to help open and close encounters and synchronise transitions from speaker to speaker, and monitoring is concerned with how we gather feedback from one another. This time, emotion plays no part, and gaze is regarded simply as a means of exchanging information.

The regulatory function

The most basic function of the look is to seek and offer attention. By looking, we declare that we wish to communicate and that the channel is open. We look and turn our head towards the other person, then we turn our whole body, and only finally do we speak. Averting the eyes serves the opposite function, and often there are implicit norms. According to Goffman (1963), for example, a fundamental "rule" for gaze among strangers is "civil inattention". First look briefly, then look away to signal that the other person is of no special concern, and continue with your business. Should you wish to venture a conversation, however, proceed cautiously and first establish whether the other person will be willing to join in: simply break the rule of civil inattention and look a second time.

More significant in the literature on regulation has been research on transitions from speaker to speaker and, as we saw earlier, the pioneer was Kendon (1967). Kendon reported that long utterances typically began with the speaker looking away and ended with him looking up, and from this he concluded that gaze helps to synchronise turn-taking. There were, however, criticisms: the data referred only to the beginnings and endings of long utterances and could not properly be extrapolated to turn-taking; and, in any case, the findings were often not confirmed by subsequent research. Beattie (1978) and Rutter *et al.* (1978), in the only studies designed expressly to replicate Kendon, both concluded against him.

If the supposed role of gaze in turn-taking is not supported by the evidence, how then do we manage to make smooth transitions from speaker to speaker? Kendon himself had suggested that a variety of signals apart from gaze were used, and indeed there is a wealth of published research, of which the most important is probably the work of the ethno-methodologist, Sacks, and the psychologist, Duncan. Useful reviews of both the approaches are available from a variety of sources, among which Goodwin (1981) and Beattie (1983) are perhaps the most accessible.

What emerged from Sacks and Duncan is that looking plays almost no part in turn-taking. Some of the signals are verbal, some are vocal, and some are nonverbal, but consistently gaze fails to distinguish between floor changes which are accomplished smoothly and those which involve inter-ruption. What then, if looking plays so little part, can we say about those nonverbal signals, like nodding and gestures of the hands, which certainly are important in turn-taking? Are they not transmitted visually, and do they not have to be seen? The answer is that indeed they do, but SEEING and LOOKING are different. Looking is gaze directed at the eyes, and seeing we might define as visual contact with the whole person, precisely the thing we are denied when we talk over the telephone. When we look, all we can do is monitor the other person's eyes, and that tells us very little. Only seeing can give us the information we need and, though visual communication does play an important part in regulating social encoun-ters, as I shall try to demonstrate later, it is seeing and not looking which is the crucial measure. Exactly the same, it will emerge, is true of monitoring.

The monitoring function

At the same time as sending signals to express our emotions and attitudes, and perhaps to help us regulate the flow of conversation, the eyes take in information, enabling us to monitor the other person's behaviour and responses, and so to control and correct our own performance (Argyle and Kendon, 1967). It was this that Kendon called the monitoring function of gaze, and out of his descriptive work have come three main develop-ments. The first consists of attempts to separate the expressive, regulatory, and monitoring functions experimentally; the second explores the conse-quences of overloading the subject with information; and the third examines more closely the particular *sorts* of information we monitor and require.

As we saw earlier, it is sometimes possible to interpret findings which apparently support the expressive function of gaze as actually supporting the monitoring function. What was needed was some means of resolving the ambiguity experimentally, and in fact two main approaches emerged. The first was associated with Argyle and his colleagues (Argyle *et al.*, 1973), and consisted of a somewhat elaborate laboratory arrangement in which two people conversed through a one-way screen, so that the first could see the second but the second could not see the first. If monitoring predominates, it was argued, those who could see should look normally because they were still able to monitor their partner; but if the more important functions of gaze were to send rather than receive signals, they should look very little because they were invisible and looking could serve no purpose.

The results of the experiment were that subjects who could see looked more than those who could not, whether they were speaking or listening, but the latter still looked about 25% of the time. Looking, incidentally, was defined as directing the gaze towards where the partner's eyes would have been, had they been visible. Monitoring, it was concluded, was the predominant function but, as the authors acknowledged, the results were not easy to disentangle: the setting was unusual, to say the least; and some of the looking may simply have resulted from habit since, even if we cannot see the other person or we are invisible ourselves, we may find it hard to "switch off" our gaze. Furthermore, there was no way of knowing whether subjects were trying to *look* or to *see* as they gazed in the direction of the other person. The distinction between looking and seeing may not have been important for Argyle and his colleagues but, as we have begun to observe already, it is crucial to a proper understanding of the literature.

The other experimental approach to disentangling the functions of gaze — one which we have taken ourselves — is to examine the *relationship* between the two people, generally comparing friends with strangers. The first of the papers was by Rutter and Stephenson (1979b), and it is one I mentioned earlier, in the discussion of the Intimacy model. If looking is primarily affective, we argued, friends should look at each other more than should strangers, according to the literature on expressive encoding; but if it is mainly concerned with collecting information, they should look less than strangers, since they are familiar with each other's responses already and should have less need to check them. Since we expected the monitoring function to predominate, we predicted that friends should look less than strangers, and indeed they did. Moreover, friends used considerably shorter but more frequent utterances than strangers, with the result that they spent significantly less time than strangers speaking and significantly more time in silence. Because they knew each other's beliefs and attitudes before the conversation started, friends needed less time to explore them, we argued. In other words, just as they had looked less than strangers because they needed less information, so they spoke less. Subsequent experiments of our own supported the argument (Pennington and Rutter, 1981; Swain, Stephenson and Dewey, 1982), but the literature is by no means consistent (Rubin, 1970; Russo, 1975; Coutts and Schneider, 1976).

The second approach to the monitoring function has been to examine what happens to people when they are overloaded with information. One of the reasons, according to Kendon, that we look away from time to time during social encounters is to shut out information and avoid distraction. Indeed, he argued, that is partly why we look away at the beginning of utterances, for planning demands concentration. Few attempts have been made to examine Kendon's suggestions experimentally, but such evidence as does exist has generally supported what he said. Difficult tasks appear to lead to less looking than easy tasks (Exline and Winters, 1965); uncertainty and stress make us look away (Allen and Guy, 1977); and complex sentences are associated with gaze aversion, as are periods of planning denoted by filled pauses (Cegala, Alexander and Sokuvitz, 1979; Erlichman, 1981; Beattie, 1981).

The third and final approach to monitoring has been to examine the *types* of information which people seek. Do we look simply to find out whether our partner is looking, or is the information we need something else? Duncan, we saw earlier, believed that looking was not important — at least for regulation — and even writers like Kendon and Ellsworth have conceded that gaze is only one of the sources of information which concern us, with facial expression, posture, gesture, and so on, at least as important. What we are confronted with once again, therefore, is the problem which arose in the case of the regulatory function: if looking is defined as gaze directed "in the eye" (Argyle and Dean, 1965), in such a way that the individuals' "eyes would meet" if they looked simultaneously (Kendon, 1967), most of the information we seek is simply not accessible to us until we stop *looking* and move our eyes away, so that we can *see* the whole person. Access to the whole person, not just to the eyes, is what we really require, and that is something which only SEEING, and not LOOKING, can give us.

Looking, eye-contact and chance

In 1968 there appeared a paper by Strongman and Champness. Much of the early research on gaze, inspired perhaps by Argyle and Dean, had concentrated on eye-contact and had all but ignored individual looking. Indeed, the Intimacy model itself was explicitly based on eye-contact, as we have seen already, and looking was regarded as something separate, even unimportant. Imagine, however, said Strongman and Champness, that the two participants in a dyadic conversation were robots, and each was programmed to look and look away at random, independently of its partner. Sometimes, merely by chance, both would happen to be looking, and eye-contact would occur. If A was the duration of the first robot's

TABLE 2.1. *Rutter* et al. *(1977): Actual and predicted eye-contact*

	Actual EC (seconds)		Predicted EC (seconds)		
	Mean	S.D.	Mean	S.D.	r
Stephenson, Rutter and Dore (1973)	116.3	54.5	120.7	56.8	0.99
Rutter et al. (1978) first experiment	216.3	82.2	215.8	81.5	0.99
Rutter et al. (1978) second experiment	279.8	108.6	283.0	108.0	0.97
Lazzerini and Stephenson (1975)	54.0	27.0	50.8	26.0	0.97
Rutter (1976) first study	109.5	55.0	106.5	55.7	0.98
Rutter (1976) second study	167.6	132.4	164.3	132.2	0.99

looking, B the duration of the second, and T the duration of the encounter, the duration of eye-contact would be AB/T. Could it be, they asked, that real people operate in the same way, so that in everyday encounters in which each subject is free to look and look away at will, eye-contact occurs simply because the two individuals happen, by chance, to be looking at the same time? Though the data which Strongman and Champness themselves presented were equivocal, subsequent findings by Argyle and Ingham (1972) were reasonably supportive. For several years, however, the issue was forgotten, and experimenters continued to study whichever of the measures they happened to prefer.

Then, in 1977, we published a paper ourselves (Rutter *et al.*, 1977). The report was very brief, but it re-examined every one of our studies in which pairs of naive subjects had been asked to hold an experimental conversation and their visual behaviour had been recorded. There were six studies altogether, with a wide variety of subjects, relationships, tasks, and purposes. For each set of data, the difference between the actual and expected durations of eye-contact was calculated, together with the correlation between them, and the results were very clear. In every case, the actual and expected values were almost identical, the correlation between the two was at least 0.97, and the proportion of variance explained was thus 95% or more (Table 2.1). In every one of our experiments, the findings were entirely consistent with the prediction, and the duration of eye-contact, we therefore concluded, was apparently nothing more than a chance product of individual looking.

In a later paper (Rutter *et al.*, 1984) we were able to take the argument further, this time concentrating on the implications of our findings. Among our published experiments were three which had been designed originally to explore gaze and distance: Stephenson, Rutter and Dore (1973); Pennington and Rutter, (1981); Swain, Stephenson and Dewey (1982). In all three cases, eye-contact had been shown to increase with distance, just as Argyle and Dean (1965) had reported, but the issue now was whether the effect might in reality be attributable to individual looking. Our analysis this time used linear regression, and the chance prediction was again confirmed: the actual and predicted values were very close; the correlations were 0.96 or more; and well over 90% of the variance was explained. What for Argyle and Dean had been a product of the *dyad* could now, we knew, be readily explained at the *individual* level.

Some time after our 1977 paper was published, there appeared two statistical commentaries on our work, one by Wagner *et al.* (1983), the other by Hargreaves and Fuller (1984). The point which concerned them both was our use of correlation, for, as they were able to demonstrate very clearly, the range of possible values for eye-contact was considerably restricted, given the range of values for looking, and our correlations might therefore be spuriously high. Eye-contact could not, for example, exceed the lower of the two values for looking, and our results might simply be a statistical artifact.

The argument, I acknowledge, is well made and moreover the familiar problems of interpreting correlation and regression mean that cause–effect relationships are difficult to disentangle. The substantive question, however, is whether one can build models of eye-contact which take no account of looking — and whether our correlations are "genuine" or "spurious", either way the answer is the same. If chance is responsible, eye-contact is dependent on looking (or perhaps the reverse); and if the results are an artifact of the constraints, then *still* there is dependency. *Statistically* there may be a debate, but *theoretically* there is not: looking predicts eye-contact, whatever the explanation.

What concerned us most about our findings, as I suggested earlier, was their implications, and there were two: methodological, and theoretical. The methodological implication concerns the use of confederates. In Argyle and Dean (1965), and indeed in many subsequent experiments, one member of the pair was a confederate who was programmed to stare continuously at the genuine subject's eyes. Not only is staring an unusual form of behaviour in everyday life — something which itself makes the methodology questionable — but eye-contact necessarily occurs every time the genuine subject looks, so that the measure of interest is after all controlled by a single member of the pair, and looking and eye-contact cannot possibly be disentangled.

The theoretical implications of the findings are perhaps even more fundamental. First, they undermine the Intimacy model which, as I have remarked a number of times already, was explicitly founded on eye-contact and not individual looking. Certainly it might be possible to recast the model in individual terms, but then, of course, it would be a very different model and it is hard to see that anything substantive would remain.

Acknowledging some of the problems, Argyle has himself suggested revisions (Argyle and Cook, 1976). Many more signals, he concedes, contribute to intimacy than was envisaged originally, and so too do social norms. Moreover, compensation, he suggests, need not be restricted to just one dimension, and an almost infinite number of combinations is possible — with the result, unfortunately, that predictions are even harder to make than before. Above all, though, he concedes, violations of intimacy do sometimes lead to reciprocation and not to compensation at all — as recent research has shown very clearly. It is for that reason more than any other that the Intimacy model has been largely superseded and the attributional approach of Ellsworth and Patterson has come to replace it.

The second theoretical implication of our findings is that they reinforce the view that emotion and motivation have played too large a part in the literature and that greater consideration should be given to information-processing models. But, and this is the third and final point, even though looking may well be more significant than eye-contact, we now know from the literature on regulation and monitoring that the types of information which people seek and exchange are mostly *inaccessible* to looking. What really matters, once again, is not LOOKING but SEEING.

SEEING AND CUELESSNESS

Early Research

By the early 1970s the literature on visual communication was changing, as we have seen. Originally, interest had centred on the structure of gaze — how much did people look and make eye-contact; was there a detectable pattern; did each individual behave consistently from encounter to encounter; and did people differ from one another, and if so what was responsible? But then, structure had been overtaken by function, and the issue now was *why* people looked and made eye-contact. Was it to express their emotions and attitudes; was it to help synchronise the flow of conversation; or was it to monitor the responses of the other person? Emotion was the dominant concept at first, but gradually the literature turned to information-processing. Emotion played no part in regulation and monitoring, and eye-contact, the lynchpin of the emotional approach, was about to be exposed as nothing more than a chance occurrence.

In the mid-1970s came the most important turning-point of all. If information rather than emotion was the crucial concept for looking and eye-contact, the onus was upon experimenters to demonstrate that the information people seek comes from in or around the eyes since that is the only information which looking can give us. In fact, as we now know, looking was not enough and what people really needed to synchronise their encounters and to monitor one another was access to the whole person. Seeing, not looking, was what mattered most.

Although the 1970s were the most active years for the literature on seeing, the beginnings of experimental research can be traced to the 1960s.

Among the most important of the early work was a series of experiments by Moscovici and his colleagues (Moscovici, 1967), and one study in particular, by Moscovici and Plon (1966), raised a number of central issues. Pairs of Parisian *lycée* students were asked to spend twenty minutes discussing the cinema, and there were four experimental conditions: face-to-face, back-to-back, side-by-side facing the front, and face-to-face with a screen in between so that visual communication was precluded. Different channels of communication, the authors argued, require different linguistic codes, and the crucial variables were familiarity and formality. Face-to-face we are able to converse spontaneously but, in an unfamiliar setting such as back-to-back, or a restricted, formal one such as side-by-side, we must take great care to plan and organise what we say, and our language will come to resemble written text, with a high ratio of nouns and connectives to verbs. The screen condition, however, should be no different from face-to-face, because the removal of visual contact is not in itself sufficient to make the setting either unfamiliar or formal. Back-to-back and side-by-side, therefore, should both differ from face-to-face but the screen condition should not.

The predictions were confirmed. In both the back-to-back and side-by-side conditions, the ratio of nouns and connectives to verbs was higher than face-to-face, but in the screen condition it was almost identical to face-to-face. The removal of visual contact appeared to be unimportant in itself, just as the authors had argued, and unfamiliarity and formality were quite sufficient to explain the findings. In Moscovici's words:

> "On the whole, verbal output of the back-to-back and side-by-side participants resembled written language, whereas language emitted in the face-to-face and screen discussions was generally like spoken language. The specificity of the two major kinds of linguistic behaviour, speaking and writing, results from the emitter's familiarity with the setting in which the message is produced and from the psycho-sociological connotations of that setting . . . Purely physical factors that affect the visibility of non-linguistic stimuli are not the only important ones."
>
> (Moscovici, 1967, p. 259)

and

> "the grammatical differences between two channels or languages — written and spoken, for instance — *are not due to the conditions of physical stimulation*, but to the relation these channels create between sender and receiver".
>
> (Moscovici, 1967, pp. 258, 259; Moscovici's emphasis)

As we shall see later, Moscovici's notion of "psychosociological connotations" was extremely important, and it was his theoretical account of the findings which had the most significant implications for the subsequent literature.

Apart from Moscovici, the only other leading figure in the early literature was Argyle, and the most important paper this time was by Argyle, Lalljee and Cook (1968). Where Moscovici's work could be said to have centred on the content of conversations, especially the grammatical structure, Argyle, Lalljee and Cook were concerned with style, and with the way we perceive encounters. There were three experiments altogether, each including a variety of manipulations designed to vary the level of visual contact. In one condition, for example, subjects wore dark glasses so that the eyes were invisible; in a second they wore a mask which obscured the face so that only the body could be seen; in a third they wore a different mask with slits for the eyes so that the face was hidden but the eyes were not; and in a fourth a screen was placed between them so that the whole body was obscured and there was no visual contact at all. Sometimes the two subjects were treated equally, but sometimes more of one was hidden than the other so that the arrangements were asymmetrical. The conversations were typically very short, around 90 seconds, and subjects were often required to undergo more than one condition.

Unfortunately, it was difficult to draw any firm conclusions because the results differed from experiment to experiment in ways which had not been predicted. Moreover, the unusual and contrived conditions and procedures meant that there were sometimes very clear demand characteristics which made generalisation hazardous. Nevertheless, there were two important findings. First, the conditions which led to the greatest discomfort and the greatest difficulty in monitoring the other person and maintaining communication were those which were asymmetrical and not those with the lowest level of visual contact overall. Second, visual contact did have significant effects upon the style of speech — pauses were longest when only the face was visible, and interruptions were most frequent when visual contact was precluded altogether — but none of the other measures of style was affected reliably.

Both papers — Moscovici and Plon (1966) and Argyle, Lalljee and Cook (1968) — had made significant contributions, though it was perhaps not generally recognised at the time. Moscovici has sometimes been dismissed by later writers because the experimental manipulations he chose were unusual, and his results could apparently not be explained by the variable which was generally believed at the time to be the most important, namely visual contact. But that, of course, was precisely the point. The grammatical changes which Moscovici revealed were produced not by the physical conditions directly but by the effects of those conditions upon the relationship between the speakers. Given one set of relationships people spoke spontaneously, but given another their language resembled written text. By implication, if the relationship were manipulated in other ways — quite apart from physically — the result would once again be changes in language. The key was how a particular manipulation influenced subjects' "psychosociological connotations".

Where Moscovici had examined grammar, Argyle, Lalljee and Cook moved to the linguistic style which people adopted and the outcomes they reached — in their particular case perceptions of the encounter — and again there were significant effects. What we have, therefore, when the two contributions are combined, is the beginnings of a suggestion that whether or not people are in visual contact affects three principal aspects of social interaction: content, style, and outcome. For the remainder of this chapter, and indeed for the two which follow, content, style, and outcome will provide the framework within which I shall present the literature. Initially I shall keep the three groups of findings separate, but by the end of the discussion I hope it will be clear that they can and should be integrated theoretically. My own attempt at integration will be offered at the end of Chapter 4.

Seeing: the Development of a Research Programme

In the late 1960s, with my colleagues, Morley and Stephenson, I embarked on what was to become more than a decade of research into visual communication. Content, style, and outcome, I have suggested, are the three principal themes, and my purpose in this section is to outline our earliest experiments in brief, to try to make the *theoretical* issues as clear as possible. More extensive discussion of the findings will be held over until Chapters 3 and 4.

Our very first experiments were concerned with outcome, and they were conducted by Morley and Stephenson (1969, 1970). The focus was negotiation and conflict, and the setting was a simulated plant-level negotiation between a union representative and a management representative. The subjects were students, to whom the roles were assigned at random, and their task was to read a detailed description of the dispute, which was based on a genuine case, and then to spend thirty minutes trying to reach a settlement. Half the pairs negotiated face-to-face and half communicated over a sound-only link in which the subjects sat in separate rooms and spoke to each other over a microphone-headphone intercom. Unknown to the subjects, the background descriptions of the dispute had been deliberately worded to give one side the stronger case, management in Morley and Stephenson (1969) and union in Morley and Stephenson (1970a). When the results of the two experiments were combined, it was found that in the sound-only conditions there were more settlements in favour of the side with the stronger case than the other side, but face-to-face the most common outcome was compromise.

What had happened, Morley and Stephenson argued, was this. The sound-only condition lacked social cues, among them those transmitted visually, and it was therefore especially "formal" — where "formal" was simply another word for "lacking social cues". Negotiations consist of a mixture of interpersonal and interparty concerns, and the effect of formality was to disturb the normal balance in such a way that inter-personal considerations were relegated to some extent and the discussion was dominated by the interparty issues. Formality leads one to behave impersonally (even antagonistically, perhaps), to disregard the subtleties of self-presentation, and to concentrate on putting one's case as thoroughly as possible in the pursuit above all of victory. With increased attention to the issues, the relative merits of the two cases come to the fore and are evaluated objectively, and the stonger case simply carries itself. Face-to-face, where the full range of social cues is available, interpersonal considerations are less easy to disregard, the objective merits of the case are less prominent, and compromise becomes the most likely result.

The implication of Morley and Stephenson's findings was that, if we were to understand *outcome* properly, we needed next to examine the *processes* at work during the discussions. Content especially was likely to give us the insight we needed, but it was only in a paper by Stephenson, Ayling and Rutter (1976) that we first began any serious exploration. Again the focus of the experiment was industrial relations, but this time the sessions were debates, and subjects were not asked to reach an agreement. First they completed a questionnaire about union–management relations, and pairs were then formed so that one member was broadly pro-union and the other pro-management. There then followed a 15-minute discussion, either face-to-face or over a sound-only link, and the task was simply to discuss one or two of the items which had revealed a disagreement. The sessions were tape-recorded, and transcribed and typed verbatim, and then they were analysed by Morley and Stephenson's own coding system, Conference Process Analysis (Morley and Stephenson, 1977).

The findings were very much as the outcome studies had led us to expect, though they were perhaps less clearcut than we might have hoped. First, there was evidence that subjects were especially task-oriented in the sound-only condition, keeping to the task they had been set and digressing very little. Second, there was evidence too that depersonalisation set in, for subjects were less likely to praise their partner than face-to-face, and were more likely to refer to the *party* they "represented" than to themselves and their partners as *individuals*. Unexpectedly, it also emerged that, for task-orientation, medium of communication and union–management status interacted, with union subjects more task-oriented in the sound-only condition than face-to-face, but management subjects tending in the opposite direction. The climate of industrial relations in Britain at the time the experiment was conducted was such that unions were widely believed to be stronger than managements. Most of the experimental sessions therefore concentrated on union affairs and, since union subjects came armed with the stronger case, their behaviour in the sound-only condition was precisely what Morley and Stephenson would have predicted — concentration on interparty issues and disregard for interpersonal considerations.

From the research of Morley and Stephenson and Stephenson, Ayling and Rutter we were able to confirm that whether people could see one another in social encounters did indeed affect the outcome and the content of their interaction. We now turned finally to style, and the first of our papers was published by Rutter and Stephenson (1977). The sessions we analysed were those which Stephenson, Ayling and Rutter (1976) had already examined for their content analysis, and our expectation was that, since vision appeared to be important for regulating turn-taking, sound-only conversations would be marked by poor synchronisation. That is, there would be more silence and interruption than face-to-face, and there would be differences in the structure of what was said as the sound-only subjects compensated for the lack of visual signals by, perhaps, slowing their rate of speech, using longer utterances and grammatically more formal structures, asking more questions, giving more acknowledgement and attention signals, and making more filled pauses and speech errors through planning and anxiety.

In the event, the findings were quite different from what we had predicted, but they did nevertheless support our overall expectation. While silence failed to distinguish between the conditions, interruptions — which generally took the form of overlapping speech — were significantly more numerous and longer *face-to-face* than in the sound-only condition, the opposite of our prediction. Compensation for visual signals, the subject of our second prediction, scarcely occurred at all. There was no difference in speech rate, grammatical structure, or filled pausing, but utterances *were* on average longer in the sound-only condition than face-to-face, and there was more evidence of speech errors. Much the strongest of the effects, however, were those for interruptions, especially their duration, and it was interruptions which led us to our interpretation. Visual communication did play an important part in synchronising conversation, we argued, but it was not quite the one we had anticipated:

> "Face-to-face, interruption can occur freely because the visual chan-
> nel allows the communication of nonverbal signals which maintain
> the interaction and prevent the breakdown which interruption might
> otherwise produce. Without the visual channel, such nonverbal sig-
> nals cannot be communicated, and speech assumes greater importance
> in regulating the interaction. Accordingly, since interruptions may

threaten the continuity of the encounter, they are made less frequently, with the consequence that utterances are longer in the audio
condition simply because they are less often broken by interruption.
The raised incidence of speech disturbance probably stems from
anxiety (Cook, 1969) the result either of the novelty of the situation
or of the increased concern with speech. In summary, the role of
visual communication seems to be to enable participants to converse
spontaneously and interrupt freely without threatening the continuity
of the interaction."

(Rutter and Stephenson, 1977, p. 35)

Despite the apparent confidence of our conclusion, we were well aware
that caution was necessary. Throughout the literature it had been assumed
that the only important difference between sound-only conditions and
face-to-face was the absence of visual contact, and by implication the same
applied to the telephone in everyday life. In fact, however, there is another
difference, of course, namely physical separation. Face-to-face we are in
visual contact and we sit together in the same room, but in the sound-only
condition or over the telephone we lack both visual contact and physical
presence, for we are hidden out of sight in separate rooms. Despite the
assumptions of the literature, physical presence might conceivably be the
more important, or indeed the two might even interact. What was needed,
as we made clear at the time, was some means of disentangling the
variables. We therefore designed one further experiment, and it was from
that, as we shall see, that our attempt at theoretical integration was to
develop — the CUELESSNESS model.

Cuelessness: a Model

The approach we adopted in our attempt to disentangle physical presence and visual contact was to introduce two new experimental conditions.
In the first, subjects sat in separate rooms and talked to each other over a
closed-circuit television link. Each sat in front of a camera which relayed a
head-and-shoulders image to a monitor placed in front of the partner in the
other room. Thus, while subjects were physically separated, a degree of
visual communication was retained, though, of course, it was somewhat
restricted in comparison with face-to-face since looking and eye-contact
could not occur. Sound was conveyed through the monitors. In the second
condition, a curtain was pulled part-way across the room between the
subjects so that, though they were physically together in the same room,
there was no visual contact between them. Face-to-face and sound-only
conditions were included as before, and the four conditions formed a
two-by-two design: physically together/physically separate, and visual con-
tact/no visual contact.

The experiment was reported by Rutter, Stephenson and Dewey (1981), and our argument was as follows. If the critical variable was physical presence, face-to-face and curtain together should differ from CCTV and sound-only together. However, if visual contact was the critical variable, and not physical presence, the main effect should instead be between face-to-face and CCTV together and curtain and sound-only together. Either way, the original differences between face-to-face and sound-only should be confirmed, at the very least. The experiment was designed to examine content and style, though not outcome, and there were three sets of predictions: conversations in which subjects sat in separate rooms would be more task-oriented, more depersonalised, and less spontaneous than those in which they sat together in the same room; conversations in which visual contact was precluded would be more task-oriented, more depersonalised and less spontaneous than those in which visual communication was free to occur; and sound-only conversations would be more task-oriented, more depersonalised, and less spontaneous than face-to-face conversations. Physical presence, I ought to acknowledge, was not expected to play a significant part, and the first prediction was included in the confident expectation that it would be rejected.

Subjects were recruited through a newspaper advertisement. They first completed an opinion questionnaire, and then they were allocated to spend twenty minutes with another subject discussing any or all of the items on which they disagreed in an effort to persuade the other person to their own point of view. The sessions were tape-recorded and transcribed just as before, and content and style were examined by means of the coding systems reported in Stephenson, Ayling and Rutter (1976) and Rutter and Stephenson (1977). Despite our expectation, only the third hypothesis was supported, and neither physical presence nor visual contact produced significant main effects.

For some considerable time we were quite unable to account for our findings, but then eventually we stumbled upon a pattern. The key was the two new conditions, curtain and CCTV, for what emerged was that, whenever there was a significant difference between face-to-face and sound-only, whether in content or style, curtain and CCTV lay somewhere *in between*. There was only one exception in the seven significant results, and we had discovered something quite unexpected — though, in retrospect, it should really have come as no surprise.

In our 1976 and 1977 papers, in common with most previous writers, we had argued as if the nonverbal cues which visual contact makes available had some special significance, and we had paid little attention to anything else. If instead we now consider physical presence and visual contact together, our four conditions can be placed on a continuum according to the aggregate number of social cues they make available. Face-to-face there are cues from both visual contact and physical presence; in the curtain and CCTV conditions there are one set each; and in the sound-only condition there are neither. Thus, as we move from face-to-face to curtain and CCTV and on to sound-only, the conditions gradually lose social cues — or, to use the word which we invented, they become increasingly *cueless*. Face-to-face, to curtain and CCTV, to sound-only was exactly the rank-order we had found in our results for content and style, and it was cuelessness, we argued, which was responsible. What mattered, therefore, was neither visual contact nor physical presence alone, but the aggregate of social cues each condition made available. The smaller the aggregate of cues from whatever source — visual contact, physical presence, or indeed any other — the more task-oriented and depersonalised the content, the less spontaneous the style, and, at least in negotiations, the more likely the side with the stronger case to win a favourable outcome. Cuelessness, we believe, is the crucial variable which had eluded us for so long, and it is the one concept, I shall argue, which allows us to integrate all our previous findings and indeed much of the remaining literature too.

Our problem now was to say how cuelessness operated. How did it produce its effects upon content, style, and outcome, and how were content, style, and outcome related together? As we saw earlier, in the literature on seeing, Morley and Stephenson (1969, 1970a) had suggested that differences in outcome might well be the product of differences in content. Put another way, cuelessness leads subjects to be task-oriented and depersonalised in the content of their discussions, and it is content which in turn produces the different outcomes. What we now suggested was that style too might be mediated by content, so that task-oriented, depersonalised content produces a deliberate, unspontaneous style as well as particular types of outcome. Outcome and style, we argued, were independent of each other, but both were related to cuelessness through the mediation of content.

When we first elaborated our cuelessness model, in Rutter, Stephenson and Dewey (1981), we suggested that cuelessness had a direct effect upon behaviour, but later we were to argue that there was an intermediate variable, namely psychological distance. When social cues are denied us, though we may be very close physically, we feel distant psychologically, and it is that, we now believe, which produces the effects upon content. Cuelessness leads to psychological distance, psychological distance, leads to task-oriented and depersonalised content, and task-oriented, depersonalised content leads in turn to a deliberate, unspontaneous style and particular types of outcome (Fig. 2.6). Psychological distance, I suggest, is exactly the sort of thing which Moscovici meant by "psychosociological connotations", and it is something which is set from the very beginning of the encounter. Subjects make use of whatever social cues are available and form an impression of psychological closeness or psychological distance —

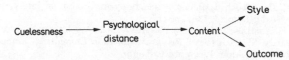

FIG. 2.6. The Cuelessness Model (Rutter, 1984).

the feeling that the other person is "there" or "not there" — and the effects upon content, style, and outcome begin immediately.

Those, we suggested, then, were the processes at work. Later, we were to introduce further refinements, for cuelessness may sometimes lead not to psychological distance but to the very opposite — the closeness which the anonymity of telephone hotlines brings, for example. The result in those cases is an *increase* in personal, intimate content with cuelessness, and a *decrease* in task-oriented problem-solving. What mattered for the present, though, was whether our model would be able to integrate the theoretical and empirical literature, as we hoped, and whether it would be equally applicable to the everyday practical problems of communicating by telephone. In Chapters 3 and 4 we shall find out.

REFERENCES

ADDINGTON, D.W. (1968) The relationship of selected vocal characteristics to personality perception. *Speech Monographs*, **35**, 492–503.

ADDINGTON, D.W. (1971) The effect of vocal variation on ratings of source credibility. *Speech Monographs*, **38**, 242–7.

ALPERT, M. (1981) Speech and disturbances of affect. *In* J. K. Darby (ed.), *Speech Evaluation in Psychiatry*. New York: Grune & Stratton.

APPLE, W., STREETER, L.A. and KRAUSS, R.M. (1979) Effects of pitch and speech rate on personal attributions. *Journal of Personality and Social Psychology*, **37**, 715–27.

ARGYLE, M. and COOK, M. (1976) *Gaze and Mutual Gaze*. London: Cambridge University Press.

ARGYLE, M. and DEAN, J. (1965) Eye-contact, distance and affiliation. *Sociometry*, **28**, 289–304.

ARGYLE, M. and INGHAM, R. (1972) Gaze, mutual gaze and proximity. *Semiotica*, **6**, 32–49.

ARGYLE, M., INGHAM, R., ALKEMA, F. and McCALLIN, M. (1973) The different functions of gaze. *Semiotica*, **7**, 19–32.

ARGYLE, M. and KENDON, A. (1967) The experimental analysis of social performance. In L. Berkowitz (ed.), *Advances in Experimental Social Psychology*, **3**, 55–98. New York: Academic Press.

ARGYLE, M., LALLJEE, M. and COOK, M. (1968) The effects of visibility on interaction in a dyad. *Human Relations*, **21**, 3–17.

ARONOVITCH, C.D. (1976) The voice of personality: stereotyped judgements and their relation to voice quality and sex of speaker. *Journal of Social Psychology*, **99**, 207–20.

ALLEN, D.E. and GUY, R.F. (1977) Ocular breaks and verbal output. *Sociometry*, **40**, 90–6.

BEATTIE, G.W. (1978) Floor apportionment and gaze in conversational dyads. *British Journal of Social and Clinical Psychology*, **17**, 7–15.

BEATTIE, G.W. (1981) A further investigation of the cognitive interference hypothesis of gaze patterns during conversation. *British Journal of Social Psychology*, **20**, 243–8.

BEATTIE, G.W. (1983) *Talk: an analysis of speech and non-verbal behaviour in conversation*. Milton Keynes: Open University Press.

BOOMER, D.S. (1963) Speech dysfluencies and body movement in interviews. *Journal of Nervous and Mental Disease*, **136**, 263–66

BROWN, B.L. and BRADSHAW, J.M. (1985) Towards a social psychology of voice variations. *In* H. Giles and R.N. St. Clair (eds.), *Recent Advances in Language, Communication, and Social Psychology*. London: Lawrence Erlbaum.

BROWN, B.L., STRONG, W.J. and RENCHER, A.C. (1975) Acoustic determinants of perceptions of personality from speech. *International Journal of the Sociology of Language*, **6**, 11–32

BULL, P. (1983) *Body Movement and Interpersonal Communication*. Chichester: Wiley.

CAMPBELL, A. and RUSHTON, J.R. (1978) Bodily communication and personality. *British Journal of Social and Clinical Psychology*, **17**, 31–6.

CARMENT, D.W., MILES, C.S. and CERVIN, V.B. (1965) Persuasiveness and persuasibility as related to intelligence and extroversion. *British Journal of Social and Clinical Psychology*, **4**, 1–7.

CASSOTTA, L., FELDSTEIN, S. and JAFFE, J. (1964) AVTA: a device for automatic vocal transaction analysis. *Journal for the Experimental Analysis of Behavior*, **7**, 99–104.

CEGALA, D.J., ALEXANDER, A.F. and SOKUVITZ, S. (1979) An investigation of eye gaze and its relation to selected verbal behaviour. *Human Communications Research*, **5**, 99–108.

CHAPMAN, A.J. (1975) Eye contact, physical proximity and laughter: a re-examination of the equilibrium model of social intimacy *Social Behaviour and Personality*, **3**, 143–155.

CHAPPLE, E.D. (1939) Quantitative analysis of the interaction of individuals. *Proceedings of the National Academy of Science*, **25**, 58–67.

CHAPPLE, E.D. and LINDEMANN, E. (1942) Clinical implications of measurements of interaction rates in psychiatric interviews. *Applied Anthropology*, **1**, 1–11.

CHAPPLE, E.D., CHAPPLE, M.F., WOOD, L.A., MIKLOWITZ, A., KLINE, N.S. and SAUNDERS, J.C. (1960) Interaction chronograph method for analysis of differences between schizophrenics and controls. *Archives of General Psychiatry*, **3**, 160–7.

COOK, M. (1969) Anxiety, speech disturbances and speech rate. *British Journal of Social and Clinical Psychology*, **8**, 13–21.

COPE, C.S. (1969) Linguistic structure and personality development. *Journal of Counselling Psychology*, **16**, 1–19.

COUTTS, L.M. and SCHNEIDER, F.W. (1976) Affiliative conflict theory: an investigation of the intimacy equilibrium and compensation hypothesis. *Journal of Personality and Social Psychology*, **34**, 1135–42.

DARBY, J.K. (1981) (ed.) *Speech Evaluation in Psychiatry*. New York: Grune & Stratton.

DARBY, J.K. (1985) (ed.) *Speech and Language Evaluation in Neurology: Adult Disorders*. New York: Grune & Stratton.

DAVITZ, J.R. (1964) (ed.) *The Communication of Emotional Meaning*. New York: McGraw-Hill.

DAVITZ, J.R. and DAVITZ, L.J. (1959) The communication of feelings by content-free speech. *Journal of Communication*, **9**, 6–13

DUNCAN, S.D. (1972) Some signals and rules for taking speaking turns in conversations. *Journal of Personality and Social Psychology*, **23**, 283–92.

DUNCAN, S.D. (1974) On the structure of speaker–auditor interaction during speaking turns. *Language in Society*, **2**, 161–80.

EDINGER, J.A. and PATTERSON, M.L. (1983) Nonverbal involvement and social control. *Psychological Bulletin*, **93**, 30–56.

EKMAN, P. (1985) *Telling Lies: clues to deceit in the market place, politics and marriage*. New York: Norton.

EKMAN, P. and FRIESEN, W.V. (1969) Nonverbal leakage and clues to deception. *Psychiatry* **32**, 88–105.

ELLIS, A. and BEATTIE, G. (1986) *The Psychology of Language and Communication*. London: Weidenfeld & Nicholson.

ELLSWORTH, P.C. (1978) The meaningful look. (Review of Argyle and Cook, 1976). *Semiotica*, **24**, 341–51.

ELLSWORTH, P.C. and LANGER, E.J. (1976) Staring and approach: An interpretation of the stare as a nonspecific activator. *Journal of Personality and Social Psychology*, **33**, 117–22.

ELLSWORTH, P.C., CARLSMITH, J.M. and HENSON, A. (1972) The stare as a stimulus to flight in human subjects: a series of field experiments. *Journal of Personality and Social Psychology*, **21**, 302–11.

ELLSWORTH, P.C. and LUDWIG, L.M. (1972) Visual behaviour in social interaction. *Journal of Communication*, **22**, 375–403.

ERLICHMAN, H. (1981) From gaze aversion to eye-movement suppression: an investigation of the cognitive interference explanation of gaze patterns during conversation. *British Journal of Social Psychology*, **20**, 233–41.

EXLINE, R.V. (1971) Visual interaction: the glances of power and preference. *Nebraska Symposium on Motivation*, pp. 163–206.

EXLINE, R.V. and WINTERS L.C. (1965) Effects of cognitive difficulty and cognitive style on eye to eye contact in interviews. *Paper to Eastern Psychological Association*, Atlantic City, April, Mimeo.

FELDSTEIN, S. (1972) Temporal patterns of dialogue: basic research and reconsiderations. *In* A.W. Siegman and B. Pope (eds.), *Studies in Dyadic Communication*. New York: Pergamon.

FELDSTEIN, S. and WELKOWITZ, J. (1978) Achronography of conversation: in defence of an objective approach. *In* A.W. Siegman and S. Feldstein (eds.), *Nonverbal Behavior and Communication*. Hillsdale, N.J.: Lawrence Erlbaum.

FELDSTEIN, S., KONSTANTAREAS, M., OXMAN, J. and WEBSTER, C.D. (1982) The chronography of interactions with autistic speakers: an initial report. *Journal of Communication Disorders*, **15**, 451–60.

FRIEDMAN, M., BROWN, A.E. and ROSENMAN, R.H. (1969) Voice analysis test for detection of behaviour pattern. *Journal of the American Medical Association*, **208**, 828–36

GLAISTER, J., FELDSTEIN, S. and POLLACK, H (1980) Chronographic speech patterns of acutely psychotic patients: a preliminary note. *Journal of Nervous and Mental Disease*, **168**, 219–23

GOFFMAN, E. (1963) *Behavior in Public Places*. Glencoe: The Free Press.

GOODWIN, C. (1981) *Conversational Organization*. New York: Academic Press.

HARGREAVES, C.P. and FULLER, M.F. (1984) Some analyses of data from eye contact studies. *British Journal of Social Psychology*, **23**, 77–82.

HARGREAVES, W.A., STARKWEATHER, J.A. and BLACKER, K.H. (1965) Voice quality in depression. *Journal of Abnormal Psychology*, **70**, 218–20

HARPER, R.G., WIENS, A.N. and MATARAZZO, J.D. (1978) *Nonverbal Communication: the state of the art*. Chichester: Wiley.

JAFFE, J. and FELDSTEIN, S. (1970) *Rhythms of Dialogue*. New York: Academic Press.

JURICH, A.P. and JURICH, J.A. (1974) Correlations among nonverbal expressions of anxiety. *Psychological Reports*, **34**, 199–204.

KASL, S.V. and MAHL, G.F. (1965) The relationship of disturbances and hesitations in spontaneous speech to anxiety. *Journal of Personality and Social Psychology*, **1**, 425–33.

KENDON, A. (1967) Some functions of gaze direction in social interaction. *Acta Psychologica*, **26**, 1–47.

KENDON, A. and COOK, M. (1969) The consistency of gaze patterns in social interaction. *British Journal of Psychology*, **69**, 481–94.

KRAUSE, M.S. and PILISUK, M. (1961) Anxiety in verbal behavior: a validation study. *Journal of Consulting Psychology*, **25**, 414–29.

LAZZERINI, A.J. and STEPHENSON, G.M. (1975) Visual interaction and affiliative-conflict theory. Unpublished. University of Nottingham.

MAHL, G.F. (1956) Disturbances and silences in the patients' speech in psychotherapy. *Journal of Abnormal and Social Psychology*, **53**, 1–15.

MAHL, G.F. and SCHULZE, G. (1964) Psychological research in the extralinguistic area. *In* T.A. Sebeok, A.S. Hayes and M.C. Bateson (eds.), *Approaches to Semiotics*. The Hague: Mouton.

MATARAZZO, J.D. and SASLOW, G. (1961) Difference in interview interaction behavior among normal and deviant groups. *In* I.A. Berg and R.M. Bass (eds.), *Conformity and Deviation*. New York: Harper & Row.

MATARAZZO, J.D. and WIENS, A.N. (1972) *The Interview: research on its anatomy and structure*. Chicago: Aldine-Atherton.

MATARAZZO, J.D., WIENS, A.M., SASLOW, G., DUNHAM, R.M. and VOAS, R.B. (1964) Speech durations of astronaut and ground communicator. *Science*, **143**, 148–50

MEHRABIAN, A. (1971) Nonverbal betrayal of feeling. *Journal of Experimental Research in Personality*, **5**, 64–73

MEHRABIAN, A. (1972) *Nonverbal Communication*. Chicago: Aldine-Atherton.

MORLEY, I.E. and STEPHENSON, G.M. (1969) Interpersonal and inter-party exchange: a laboratory simulation of an industrial negotiation at the plant level. *British Journal of Psychology*, **60**, 543–5.

MORLEY, I.E. and STEPHENSON, G.M. (1970) Formality in experimental negotiations: a validation study. *British Journal of Psychology*, **61**, 383–4.

MORLEY, I.E. and STEPHENSON, G.M. (1977) *The Social Psychology of Bargaining*. London: Allen & Unwin.

MOSCOVICI, S. (1967) Communication processes and the properties of language. *In* L. Berkowitz (ed.), *Advances in Experimental Psychology*, **3**, 225–70.

MOSCOVICI, S. and PLON, M. (1966) Les situations-colloques: observations théoriques et expérimentales. *Bulletin de Psychologie*, **247**, 702–22.

MULLER-SUUR, H. (1981) Spoerris descriptions of psychotic speech. *In* J.K. Darby (ed.), *Speech Evaluation in Psychiatry*. New York: Grune & Stratton.

MURRAY, D.C. (1971) Talk, silence, and anxiety. *Psychological Bulletin*, **75**, 244–60

NIELSEN, G. (1962) *Studies in Self Confrontation*. Copenhagen: Monksgaard.

OSTWALD, P.F. (1965) Acoustic methods in psychiatry. *Scientific American*, **212**, March, 82–91.

OSTWALD, P.F. (1981) Speech and Schizophrenia. *In* J.K. Darby (ed.), *Speech Evaluation in Psychiatry*. New York: Grune & Stratton.

PATTERSON, M.L. (1982) A sequential functional model of nonverbal exchange. *Psychological Review*, **89**, 231–49.

PATTERSON, M.L. (1983) *Non-verbal Behavior: a functional perspective*. Berlin: Springer.

PATTERSON, M. and HOLMES, D.S. (1966) Social interaction correlates of the MMPI extraversion-introversion scale. *American Psychologist*, **21**, 724–5.

PANEK, D.M. and MARTIN, B. (1959) The relationship between GSR and speech disturbances in psychotherapy. *Journal of Abnormal and Social Psychology*, **58**, 402–5.

PENNINGTON, D.C. and RUTTER, D.R. (1981) Information or affiliation? Effects of intimacy on visual interaction. *Semiotica*, **35**, 29–39.

POPE, B., BLASS, J., SIEGMAN, A.W. and RAHER, J. (1970) Anxiety and depression in speech. *Journal of Consulting and Clinical Psychology*, **35**, 128–33.

RAMSAY, R.W. (1966) Personality and speech. *Journal of Personality and Social Psychology*, **4**, 116–18.

RAMSAY, R.W. (1968) Speech patterns and personality. *Language and Speech*, **11**, 54–63.

RAY, M.L. and WEBB, E.J. (1966) Speech duration effects in the Kennedy news conference. *Science*, **153**, 899–901.

RICE, D.G., ABRAMS, G.M. and SAXMAN, J.H. (1969) Speech and physiological correlates of 'flat' affect. *Archives of General Psychiatry*, **20**, 566–72.

ROCHESTER, S.R. (1973) The significance of pauses in spontaneous speech. *Journal of Psycholinguistic Research*, **2**, 51–81.

RUBIN, A. (1970) Measurement of romantic love. *Journal of Personality and Social Psychology*, **16**, 265–73.

RUSSO, N.F. (1975) Eye contact, interpersonal distance, and the equilibrium theory. *Journal of Personality and Social Psychology*, **31**, 497–502.

RUTTER, D.R. (1973) Visual interaction in psychiatric patients: a review. *British Journal of Psychiatry*, **123**, 193–202.

RUTTER, D.R. (1976) Visual interaction in recently admitted and chronic long-stay schizophrenic patients. *British Journal of Social and Clinical Psychology*, **15**, 295–303.

RUTTER, D.R. (1977a) Speech patterning in recently admitted and chronic long-stay schizophrenic patients. *British Journal of Social and Clinical Psychology*, **16**, 47–55.

RUTTER, D.R. (1977b) Visual interaction and speech patterning in remitted and acute schizophrenic patients. *British Journal of Social and Clinical Psychology*, **16**, 357–61.

RUTTER, D.R. (1984) *Looking and Seeing: the role of visual communication in social interaction*. Chichester: Wiley.

RUTTER, D.R. (in press) Turn-taking in schizophrenic patients. In S. Feldstein, C. Crown and J. Welkowitz (eds.), *Speech Sounds and Silences: a social-psychophysical approach to clinical concerns*. Hillsdale, N.J.: Lawrence Erlbaum.

RUTTER, D.R. and O'BRIEN, P. (1980) Social interaction in withdrawn and aggressive maladjusted girls: a study of gaze. *Journal of Child Psychology and Psychiatry*, **21**, 59–66.

RUTTER, D.R. and STEPHENSON, G.M. (1972) Visual interaction in a group of schizophrenic and depressive patients. *British Journal of Social and Clinical Psychology*, **11**, 57–65.

RUTTER, D.R. and STEPHENSON, G.M. (1977) The role of visual communication in synchronising conversation. *European Journal of Social Psychology*, **7**, 29–37.

RUTTER, D.R. and STEPHENSON, G.M. (1979b) The functions of Looking: effects of friendship on gaze. *British Journal of Social and Clinical Psychology*, **18**, 203–5.

RUTTER, D.R., MORLEY, I.E. and GRAHAM, J.C. (1972) Visual interaction in a group of introverts or extroverts. *European Journal of Social Psychology*, **2**, 371–84.

RUTTER, D.R., STEPHENSON, G.M. and DEWEY, M.E. (1981) Visual communication and the content and style of conversation. *British Journal of Social Psychology*, **20**, 41–52.

RUTTER, D.R., STEPHENSON, G.M., LAZZERINI, A.J., AYLING, K. and WHITE, P.A. (1977) Eye-contact: a chance product of individual Looking? *British Journal of Social and Clinical Psychology*, **16**, 191–2.

RUTTER, D.R., STEPHENSON, G.M., AYLING, K. and WHITE, P.A. (1978) The timing of looks in dyadic conversation. *British Journal of Social and Clinical Psychology*, **17**, 17–21.

RUTTER, D.R., PENNINGTON, D.C., DEWEY, M.E. and SWAIN, J. (1984) Eye-contact as a chance product of individual looking: implications for the intimacy model of Argyle and Dean. *Journal of Nonverbal Behavior*, **8**, 250–8.

SACKS, H., SCHEGLOFF, E.A. and JEFFERSON, G.A. (1974) A simplest systematics for the organization of turn-taking for conversation. *Language*, **50**, 697–735.

SASLOW, G. and MATARAZZO, J.D. (1959) A technique for studying changes in interview behaviour. *In* E.A. Rubenstcin and M.B. Parloff (cds.), *Research in Psychotherapy*, Volume 1. Washington, D.C.: American Psychological Association.

SAXMAN, J.M. and BURK, K.W. (1968) Speaking fundamental frequency and rate characteristics ofadult female schizophrenics. *Journal of Speech and Hearing Research*, **11**, 194–203.

SCHERER, K.R. (1974) Acoustic concomitants of emotional dimensions: judging affect from synthesised tone sequences. *In* S. Weitz (ed.), *Nonverbal Communication*. New York: Oxford University Press.

SCHERER, K.R. (1979) Personality markers in speech. *In* K.R. Scherer and H. Giles (eds.), *Social Markers in Speech*. Cambridge: Cambridge University Press.

SCHERER, K.R. (1982) Methods of research on vocal communication: paradigms and parameters. *In* K.R. Scherer and P. Ekman (eds.), *Handbook of Methods in Nonverbal Behavior Research*. Cambridge: Cambridge University Press.

SCHERER, K.R. (1986) Vocal affect expression: a review and a model for future research. *Psychological Bulletin*, **99**, 143–65.

SCHERER, K.R., KOIVUMAKI, J. and ROSENTHAL, R. (1972) Minimal cues in the vocal communication of affect: judging emotions from content-masked speech. *Journal of Psycholinguistic Research*, **1**, 269–85.

SHORT, J., WILLIAMS, E. and CHRISTIE, B. (1976) *The Social Psychology of Telecommunications*. Chichester: Wiley.

SIEGMAN, A.W. (1978) The tell-tale voice: nonverbal messages of verbal communication. *In* A.W. Siegman and S. Feldstein (eds.), *Nonverbal Behavior and Communication*. Hillsdale, N.J.: Lawrence Erlbaum.

SIEGMAN, A.W. and POPE, B. (1965) Personality variables associated with productivity and verbal fluency in the initial interview. *In* B.E. Compton (ed.), *Proceedings of the 73rd Annual Convention of the American Psychological Association*, pp. 273–4. Washington, D.C.: American Psychological Association.

SIEGMAN, A.W. and POPE, B. (1972) (eds.), *Studies in Dyadic Communication*. New York: Pergamon.

SORRENTINO, R.M. and BOUTILLIER, R.G. (1975) The effect of quantity and quality of verbal interaction on ratings of leadership ability. *Journal of Experimental Research in Personality*, **11**, 403–11.

SPOERRI, T.H. (1966) Speaking voice of the schizophrenic patient. *Archives of General Psychiatry*, **14**, 581–5.

STANG, D.J. (1973) Effect of interaction rate on ratings of leadership and liking. *Journal of Personality and Social Psychology*, **27**, 405–8.

STARKWEATHER, J.A. (1967) Vocal behavior as an information channel of speaker status. *In* K. Salzinger and S. Salzinger (eds.), *Research in Verbal Behavior and Some Neurophysiological Implications*. New York: Academic Press.

STEPHENSON, G.M., AYLING, K. and RUTTER, D.R. (1976) The role of visual communication in social exchange. *British Journal of Social and Clinical Psychology*, **15**, 113–20.

STEPHENSON, G.M. and RUTTER, D.R. (1970) Eye-contact, distance, and affiliation: a re-evaluation. *British Journal of Psychology*, **61**, 385–93.

STEPHENSON, G.M., RUTTER, D.R. and DORE, S.R. (1973) Visual interaction and distance. *British Journal of Psychology*, **64**, 251–7.

STRONGMAN, K.T. and CHAMPNESS, B.G. (1968) Dominance hierarchies and conflict in eye contact. *Acta Psychologica*, **28**, 376–86.

SWAIN, J., STEPHENSON, G.M. and DEWEY, M.E. (1982) Seeing a stranger: Does eye-contact reflect intimacy? *Semiotica*, **42**, 107–18.

WAGNER, H., CLARKE, A.H. and ELLGRING, J.H. (1983) Eye-contact and individual looking: the role of chance. *British Journal of Social Psychology*, **22**, 61–2.

WEINSTEIN, M.S. and HANSON, R.G. (1975) Personality trait correlates of verbal interaction levels in an encounter group context. *Canadian Journal of Behavioural Science*, **7**, 192–200.

WIENER, M., DEVOE, S., RUBINOW, S. and GELLER, J. (1972) Nonverbal behavior and nonverbal communication. *Psychological Review*, **79**, 185–214.

ZUCKERMAN, M. DE PAULO, B.M. and ROSENTAL, R. (1981) Verbal and nonverbal communication of deception. *Advances in Experimental Social Psychology*, **14**, 1–59.

3

Outcome

TRANSMISSION OF INFORMATION AND PROBLEM-SOLVING

We come now to the two central chapters of the book. In Chapter 1 we surveyed the history and everyday uses of the telephone, and in Chapter 2 we moved on to consider a variety of theoretical issues. The most important feature of the telephone, I suggested, was the absence of social cues — or cuelessness, as we called it — and the result of cuelessness was a feeling of psychological distance. Psychological distance leads normally to task-oriented and depersonalised content, and that in turn leads to a style of speech which lacks spontaneity, and to outcomes which lack compromise. Necessarily, the discussion in Chapter 2 was very brief, and it is time now for a more detailed elaboration. Chater 3 will consider outcome, and Chapter 4 will consider process and its relationship with outcome.

Research on outcome has concentrated on two main issues: how effective is communicating by telephone; and how do the conclusions and perceptions which people reach differ from those they reach face-to-face. For everyday users, the main concern has been effectiveness, of course, and, as we saw in Chapter 1, the evidence suggests that the telephone is a perfectly satisfactory medium for a wide range of uses, not just in industry and at home but for interviews and surveys, crisis intervention and counselling, and even conferences and teaching. What did not emerge, however, was the answer to the second of our questions, and for that we must turn to the experimental literature, which has come mainly from the laboratory. Three main areas have been explored: transmission of information and problem-solving; persuasion, which includes negotiation and conflict, and attitude and opinion change; and person perception. From a theoretical point of view, the principle influence upon the literature, at least at first, was the Intimacy model, but gradually alternatives began to develop, especially the formality model of Morley and Stephenson, the Social Presence model of Short and his colleagues, and our own cuelessness model. How and when the new models evolved will emerge as we review the empirical findings.

Transmission of information and problem-solving have received much less attention than any other type of outcome. Most of the earliest research was concerned only with the former, and the question at issue was whether visual contact affects the ease and accuracy with which factual information is communicated. In this country, much of the work was conducted by the Communications Studies Group and a typical example was an experiment by Champness and Reid (1970). People were asked to convey the contents of a business letter face-to-face, over a sound-only link, or from behind an opaque screen, and the time they took, the accuracy with which the task was accomplished, and the subjects' perceptions of their accuracy were all measured. No significant differences were detected and, in general, the group's subsequent research produced very similar outcomes. Provided the information to be exchanged is purely verbal, so that it can be transmitted in writing or speech without graphics, differences between media are likely to occur only when social interaction is necessary. If one subject transmits, the other receives, and feedback is not required, almost any medium will be adequate.

Research on problem-solving, particularly co-operative problem-solving, has been rather more extensive, and here the findings are of more interest from a social-psychological point of view because there is social interaction. As Williams (1977) pointed out in his very useful review, an intriguing variety of tasks has been used, including locating the nearest doctor on a map, assembling machinery from a set of instructions, classifying newspaper articles by topic, identifying matching light sockets, drafting a college timetable, discovering variables which distinguish between profitable and non-profitable imaginary factories, and trying to solve an industrial relations problem — an old but loyal worker who is holding up a production line.

It was this last task which Champness and Davies (1971) used, in one of the earliest of the Communications Studies Group's experiments. Pairs of subjects were asked to hold their discussions either face-to-face or over a sound-only link, and the nature of the solution, whether or not subjects were satisfied with it, and the extent of agreement or disagreement between them were all measured. No significant differences were detected for outcome, but there were some marked effects upon process. Face-to-face the solutions concentrated upon the worker, and the conversation was generally equally divided between the two subjects; but in the sound-only condition there was less concern with the individual employee and a less equitable sharing of the floor.

In later experiments by the group (Davies, 1971a, 1971b), the emphasis moved to closed, deductive tasks, in which the quality of the solution could be measured objectively and precisely. Still, however, there were marked effects upon process, namely that face-to-face discussions were longer and a wider range of possible solutions was aired before the final choice was made. Whether the wider range of solutions caused or was caused by the length of the discussions was impossible to say, however, and there may, of course, have been no causal relationship at all.

Nevertheless, as we shall see later, similar effects were soon to be reported by Tysoe (1984), and in any case it is well established, at least for interviews, that telephone encounters are normally shorter than their face-to-face counterparts (Short, Williams and Christie, 1976). Expense and physical discomfort may be partly responsible in everyday-life, but the fact that the laboratory evidence was similar suggests that the process of social interaction is genuinely different.

Most of the other tasks identified by Williams (1977) came from the research of Chapanis and his colleagues in the U.S.A., and it is Chapanis who has probably made the most extensive contribution of all. Much of his work was concerned with communication between people and computers, but for comparative purposes many other types of media were included as well (e.g. Chapanis, 1971; Chapanis *et al.*, 1972; Weeks and Chapanis, 1976). In each of the tasks, the subject was given only part of the information needed to solve the problem, and the remainder had to be elicited from the partner. In the typical design, face-to-face, sound-only, teletypewriting, and remote handwriting were compared, and the main dependent measure was the time it took to reach the correct solution. Written modes together were generally slower than face-to-face and sound-only together, and the physical constraints were the obvious explanation. The strongest effect, however, was that sound-only subjects exchanged ten times more messages than those who communicated in writing, while face-to-face subjects exchanged more still, so that, while the media which were rich in cues produced the most social interaction, the others were in some respects more efficient. Thus, even though interpersonal factors were unimportant and social cues were of little significance for outcome, still there were effects to be detected upon process.

PERSUASION

Negotiation and Conflict

Morley and Stephenson (1969, 1970)

The first important work on negotiation and conflict, and indeed on outcome in general, was by Morley and Stephenson (1969, 1970a) as we saw in Chapter 2. The main setting for the research was plant-level negotiations between union and management, and a series of simulations was set up using male students assigned at random to the two roles. Each was given a detailed description of the dispute, which was based on a genuine case, but unknown to the two participants the accounts were

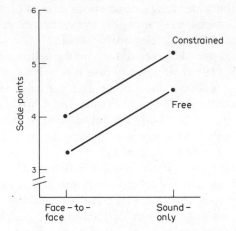

FIG. 3.1. Morley and Stephenson (1969, 1970a): Outcome of negotiations.
Note: Higher scores denote victories for stronger case. Range = 0 to 7.

carefully edited so that one side was given the stronger case — the management side in Morley and Stephenson (1969) and the union side in Morley and Stephenson (1970a). There were forty pairs of subjects altogether, twenty in each of the experiments, and the task was to spend 30 minutes trying to agree a settlement. Half the pairs negotiated face-to-face, and the other half communicated over a sound-only link in which subjects sat hidden from each other in separate rooms and spoke over a microphone–headphone intercom. In the absence of vision, it emerged, there were more settlements in favour of the side with the stronger case than the other side while, face-to-face, the most common outcome was compromise (Fig. 3.1). The effect was particularly noticeable when subjects were constrained to speak one at a time and were not allowed to interrupt. That is, the greatest difference was between the constrained sound-only condition and the unconstrained face-to-face condition.

It was now, to try to account for the findings, that Morley and Stephenson introduced their concept of formality, and it was thus right at the beginning of research in the area that the first of the models to which I have referred was set up. Formality, for Morley and Stephenson, meant lack or absence of social cues, where a social cue is any piece of behaviour, whether verbal or nonverbal, which tells us something about the person. Among the most important, it was assumed, were cues which were transmitted by vision. The sound-only condition was thus more formal in Morley and Stephenson's terms than face-to-face — especially when social cues were still further depleted by the constraint on interruptions — and the effect of formality was to disturb the normal processes of negotiation. Negotiations include both interpersonal and interparty dimensions (e.g.

Douglas, 1957, 1962; Stephenson, 1984), and it was the balance between them which formality influenced most, so that interpersonal considerations came to be disregarded, relatively speaking, and the interparty issues took over. Formality encouraged negotiators to behave impersonally, to ignore the subtleties of self-presentation, and to concentrate on putting their cases as thoroughly as possible and pursuing victory for their side. As the participants focused increasingly on the issues, the relative merits of the two cases came to the fore and were evaluated objectively, and the stronger case simply carried itself. Face-to-face, where the richness of cues made for a less formal setting, interpersonal considerations were less easy to disregard, the objective merits of the cases were less prominent, and the result was typically an outcome of compromise.

The formality model marked an important point of departure in the literature. There were perhaps three main reasons: it was one of the earliest attempts to move away from the Intimacy model of Argyle and Dean; it had something important to say not just about individual social cues but about the integration between them; and it had clear implications for applied research and practice as well as for traditional theoretical and empirical work. The 1969 and 1970a experiments were, however, only preliminary attempts to test the model, and a series of replications followed.

In the original experiments, each of the negotiators had been given a minimum point below which he was forbidden to settle, and it was so arranged that the two points were incompatible — one side necessarily "lost" if an agreement was made — but neither side knew the other's instructions. In the first of the replications, the procedure was modified: half the pairs were given compatible goals, while half were still not; and for half the pairs within each condition the other person's target was known, while for half it remained secret. The result, as unfortunately is often the case with replications, was that the original effect of strength of case disappeared, even in the condition which most closely resembled the orginal. There was, however, a confounding factor, for the material was more complex and detailed than before, and it was this, perhaps, which had produced the difference. If a second replication were set up, with more time to master the detail and prepare the case, the original pattern might perhaps return.

That, indeed, is precisely what happened, and moreover an extra finding emerged as well, one with considerable implications. Subjects were given the same material as in the first of the replications, but more time was allowed, and the original effect was confirmed: when subjects had incompatible goals and incomplete information about the other side's instructions, the sound-only condition gave a measurable advantage to the stronger case; but, and this was the important new finding, when subjects did know their opponent's target, the difference between face-to-face and sound-only was cancelled out and in fact was almost reversed. That is, when negotiators were told the point below which their opponent was forbidden to settle, the sound-only condition lost its advantage for the stronger case, and the trend emerged in the opposite direction instead. Exactly the same was to be found in a third replication, in which the original material was used once more. Thus, simply by giving the participants additional information about each other's goals, the authors had produced a significant change in outcome. What the mechanism might be was unclear — but, by implication, something had happened to the interpersonal/interparty balance.

Before we consider what that "something" might be, there is one final replication in the 1977 series to describe, and this time it was concerned not with the material or the instructions but the properties of the two media. As we saw in Chapter 2, one of the problems of comparing sound-only or telephone conditions with face-to-face is that one cannot be sure of the critical difference. As well as denying vision, the sound-only intercom means that subjects sit in separate rooms. Although Morley and Stephenson, like most other authors, did not seriously entertain the possibility that physical separation had any great significance, nevertheless it was essential for the purposes of experimental rigour and theoretical interpretation to devise some means of disentangling the variables.

The solution which Morley and Stephenson adopted was closed-circuit television. Subjects sat in separate rooms, each with a camera which conveyed their head-and-shoulders image to the other's monitor, so that visual contact was made possible — though not to quite the extent which face-to-face permits, of course, since looking and eye-contact could not occur. The 1969 and 1970a materials and procedures were used once again, and the original findings for face-to-face and sound-only were reproduced successfully. Moreover, just as the authors had anticipated, CCTV was significantly different in outcome from the sound-only condition and very similar to face-to-face. Formality, it was concluded — or now, more precisely, visual contact — had indeed been the crucial factor all along. If negotiators have incompatible goals and they do not know their opponent's target, the side with objectively the stronger case will probably win if the setting is formal; but if the settlement points are common knowledge, the advantage will probably disappear and may even be reversed. What still remained unclear, though, was why knowledge of the opponent's goals should have so much effect — but, as we shall see, an explanation was eventually to emerge, from the work of Short and his colleagues.

Short

Like Morley and Stephenson, Short based his investigation on simulated negotiations (Short, Williams and Christie, 1976) but, at the same time, other writers were using rather different approaches. Smith (1969), for example, set up a series of simulated law suits, in which litigants were assigned to communicate either face-to-face or in writing. Sometimes no settlement was reached at all but, when it was, it was usually face-to-face and the solutions were generally more various than in the other condition. The explanation, Smith argued, was that face-to-face gave greater scope for individuals' powers of persuasion. Wichman (1970) likewise moved away from simulated industrial negotiations and instead used the Prisoners' Dilemma, a mixed-motive game in which subjects may choose to adopt either a co-operative or a competitive strategy. There were four experimental conditions — no communication, vision without sound, sound-only, and face-to-face — and, as more cues were added, so co-operation became more common, to such an extent that, when the two vision conditions were combined and compared with the two no-vision conditions in combination, a large significant difference was revealed. Increasing the number of cues, Wichman argued rather like Smith, increased the feeling that the partner was capable of being influenced and so made co-operation seem more worthwhile. Similar findings, again based on the Prisoners' Dilemma, were to be reported by Laplante (1971) and Gardin *et al*. (1973), and there was thus good evidence that Morley and Stephenson's conclusions extended well beyond the industrial setting.

The solution to Morley and Stephenson's problem of interpretation, I suggested earlier, came eventually from Short, and it is Short in this country and Pruitt in the U.S.A. who have made the most important of the recent contributions. Both were concerned once more with experimental bargaining. Short first considered Morley and Stephenson's failure in some of their 1977 replications to reproduce their original findings and, like them, he suggested that the results might well be attributable to the lack of time which subjects were given to prepare their cases. In his first study, therefore, he attempted to replicate the first of Morley and Stephenson's follow-up experiments but allowing longer (Short, 1971a). Subjects were assigned at random to management and union roles, and half the pairs met face-to-face and half over a sound-only intercom. The union side was given the stronger case and, as in Morley and Stephenson's own second replication, the original 1970a findings were reproduced successfully: the sound-only condition gave a clear advantage to the stronger case. It also produced significantly more failures to reach agreement.

From the procedural question of time, Short next turned his attention to a conceptual issue: the definition of "strength of case". For Morley and Stephenson, a strong case was one in which a large number of supporting arguments was available to the negotiators, and the arguments were of good quality. Alternatively, Short argued, it might be preferable to measure whether the arguments produced a successful outcome, and on this index, of course there would be no difference between Morley and Stephenson's cases, since victories were evenly distributed between them.

Yet another definition would be that a strong case was simply one which the negotiator accepted and believed himself, one which gave him "the strength of his own convictions". If so, perhaps subjects in previous experiments who had been assigned a weak case had lacked the strength of their convictions, and this, rather than the objective merits of the material, had been responsible for the findings.

It was this last possibility which Short went on to test in Short (1974). The subjects were civil servants, and the discussions concerned depart-mental budget cuts. A variety of proposals were to be negotiated, and the proceedings were so arranged that one member of the pair was able to argue a case which was consistent with his or her beliefs ("consonant" condition), while the other had argued for a position which had nothing to do with his or her own views or might even be against them ("non-consonant" condition). The purpose of the manipulation was to emphasise interpersonal factors and to make them salient, and it was predicted that the individual who was personally involved would be relatively more successful face-to-face, while the other subject would be more successful in the sound-only condition.

The prediction was confirmed and, what is more, a condition in which subjects communicated by CCTV produced very similar results to face-to-face. Once again, therefore, the effects could be attributed with confidence to visual contact, and physical presence appeared to be unimportant. By manipulating the interpersonal dimension, Short had produced a very different pattern of findings from those reported originally by Morley and Stephenson. Interpersonal factors had been made salient at the expense of interparty considerations, and the earlier results had been reversed. Now face-to-face had become the favourable medium for the stronger side (Fig. 3.2.).

From strength of case, Short moved on to the concept of "conflict". This was to be the last experiment in the series and, although it was reported in Short (1971b), the data were collected some time after the experiment described in Short (1974) had been conducted. Conflict in negotiations, Short argued, could mean a number of things, and it was not to be regarded as a unitary concept. There can be a conflict of interests, a conflict of values, or a personal conflict, yet all three have typically been subsumed under "interpersonal" and "interparty". Suppose that the 1974 experi-ment were now to be repeated, but in such a way that the individuals' beliefs were disregarded and both negotiators were assigned to the "non-consonont" condition. Neither should have the strength of his or her con-victions any more, interpersonal factors should be relatively unimportant, and the only reliable conflict should be a conflict of interests. Differences in outcome between face-to-face and sound-only should therefore disappear — and indeed that is precisely what happened.

What we have in summary, then, is this. Negotiations include both interpersonal and interparty dimensions. If the setting is made formal,

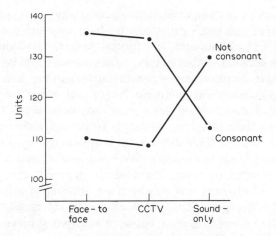

FIG. 3.2. Short (1974): Mean payoffs.

Morley and Stephenson argued, the normal balance is disturbed, interparty considerations predominate, and the side with objectively the stronger case generally prevails. However, if negotiators are given a little more information about each other, and are made aware of their opponents' targets, the effect disappears. As to why, Short's findings suggest an answer. If one subject is asked to negotiate a case to which he or she is committed, but the other is assigned at random, the person with the strength of his or her convictions will hold an advantage face-to-face and will probably win; but if neither subject is committed, there will be no difference between conditions. As Morley and Stephenson first suggested, the critical variable was the balance between interpersonal and interparty considerations. If the setting lacks visual cues and so can be described as formal, interparty factors will normally predominate, and the side with objectively the stronger case will prevail. If the experimenter intervenes, however, and changes the balance by increasing the salience of interpersonal considerations — by asking subjects to argue for their own beliefs, for example, or by giving them more information about the other person — the differences in outcome between formal and informal settings will be removed or even reversed. Increasing the salience of interpersonal considerations was precisely what Morley and Stephenson had done by telling subjects their opponents' targets — just as Short had done with his own manipulations — and the original balance, and so the findings, were destroyed. When the balance changes between interpersonal and interparty factors, the effects of formality change too.

Pruitt

In a rather different way, very similar arguments were proposed and confirmed by Pruitt, who, with Short, I suggested, has been the most important of the recent writers. Pruitt's interest was integrative bargaining, in which both sides can "win", since the opportunity exists for maximising joint profit so that one side's gain does not have to mean the other's loss. Pruitt *et al*. (1978) had found that, if negotiators were "accountable" to the people they represented — that is, their performance could be rewarded or punished by their constituents — the result was lower joint profit than when negotiators were not accountable. Negotiators were also found to use more "pressure tactics" when they were accountable — threats, firm committments to their positions, attempts to persuade the other to concede, and efforts to raise their status in their opponent's eyes — suggesting that accountability leads to a competitive "win/lose" frame of mind. In an unpublished follow-up, however, Pruitt had been able to find no effects of accountability — but there was an important difference in methodology, for while the 1978 negotiations had been conducted face-to-face, in the later sessions there was a screen between the two subjects, precluding visual contact. When other studies in the literature were reviewed (Carnevale *et al*. 1981), exactly the same pattern emerged: face-to-face produced effects of accountability, but more formal conditions, in which there was a screen or subjects communicated by written notes, did not. Accountability, Carnevale therefore predicted, will enhance pressure tactics and diminish joint profit when negotiators can see and hear each other, but will not when they can only hear.

The prediction, Pruitt acknowledged, was apparently quite at odds with the early findings of Morley and Stephenson, but nevertheless it was confirmed. Subjects were assigned the role of buyer or seller in a wholesale market, and their task was to agree prices for a range of electrical goods. The buyer was said to represent a large department store, and the seller a manufacturer. Each member of the pair was given priorities, which were not revealed to the other side, and they were so designed that both sides could profit if they chose to co-operate. There were three levels of accountability (high, low, and none), and two media of communication (face-to-face and screen). A variety of measures of both outcome and process were taken.

For outcome, it emerged, accountability and medium of communication interacted, with joint profits lower in the condition of high accountability and visual access than all the others. Process too produced significant effects, but this time they were rather more complex. While pressure tactics and understanding of the others person's priorities followed the same pattern as outcome — more pressure tactics and less understanding in the condition with high accountability and visual access — the most important of the remaining measures did not. For both the amount of information exchanged and for interpersonal atmosphere (measured objectively by the ratio of "we" and "I" references in the proceedings, and subjectively by ratings of co-operation), there were significant main effects, with the values for the screen condition greater than face-to-face (Fig. 3.3).

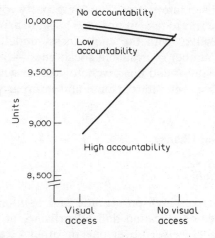

FIG. 3.3. Carnevale *et al*. (1981): Mean dyadic profit.

The key to interpreting the findings was the psychological set with which subjects entered the negotiations. High accountability, suggested Pruitt, leads individuals to adopt a set competition, and visual access enhances that set and encourages dominance — but why?

> "To answer this question, we must recall that bargaining tends to evoke a competitive definition of the situation, especially under high accountability. In such a context, we postulate that various elements of nonverbal behavior, such as staring, are employed in an effect to dominate and are interpreted as domineering behavior. When there is no visual access, such nonverbal tactics are not available. Hence, there is less temptation to try to dominate and less reason to view the other party as trying to dominate. The result is fewer pressure tactics and more cooperation. . . . Accountability produces dominance behavior that precludes negotiator understanding of the other party's priorities, resulting in the development of agreements involving low mutual gain."
>
> (Carnevale *et al*., 1981, p. 119)

Face-to-face, then, made social cues available, particularly because it gave subjects the opportunity to look and to stare (Lewis and Fry, 1977), and accountability increased the significance of the cues — and so made the setting personal and competitive — because subjects were able to use them to enhance their performance in the eyes of their constituents. In the screen condition, however, set was less personal and competitive, for there were fewer cues with which to dominate and compete and so to enhance one's rewards. For Morley and Stephenson and Short, the key to interpretation had been interpersonal and interparty considerations. What Pruitt had now done was to take us one step back, to *psychological set* — as we have done ourselves with the cuelessness model. Psychological set depends upon the number of available social cues — and a host of other variables too, no doubt — and it is psychological set which determines the particular balance between interpersonal and interparty considerations.

Attitude and Opinion Change

Communications Studies Group

Much of the early research on attitude and opinion change was concerned with mass communication and advertising, in which a "sender" tried to influence a "receiver" over one or other of a variety of media and there was no interaction between them. In the late 1970s, however, the field began to widen to include two-way communication, and once again some of the most interesting work was by Short and his colleagues at the Communications Studies Group (Short, Williams and Christie, 1976).

The first experiment was by Short (1972a). Most people, Short argued, believe that the best medium for persuasion is face-to-face since, to change someone's mind, we need personal contact so that we can make full use of our persuasive powers. The impersonal nature of the telephone — the limits it places on the skills we can use — is too restrictive. Opinion change should therefore be greater face-to-face than over a sound-only link, and CCTV, for example, should be somewhere in between. There were two discussion conditions in the experiment: "real disagreement", in which subjects were genuinely divided and were asked simply to reach an agreement; and "false disagreement", in which there was in reality no division of opinion but one subject was asked to play devil's advocate. Pairs met face-to-face, over a loudspeaker intercom, or over CCTV, and each underwent two of the three conditions.

Against Short's prediction, medium of communication had no effect upon agreements in either of the discussion conditions. However, it did have a significant effect on private opinions, which were recorded after the discussions had finished, but in the opposite direction to that predicted — more not less change in the sound-only condition than face-to-face, with CCTV in between but significantly different from neither. The effect on private opinions held for both the "real" and the "false" conditions, and for genuine and devil's advocate subjects alike, and the most common pattern was convergence towards the middle. Neither side could be said to have had the stronger case — even the devil's advocates, no doubt, were as strongly committed to their roles as the genuine subjects — and the literature on negotiation and conflict was thus apparently unable to explain the pattern.

To try to interpret the findings, Short went on to a series of replications. There were four experiments altogether, and three of them used very similar procedures to the original (Short, 1972b, 1973; Young, 1974b). The fourth, however, was rather different (Short, 1972c), in that subjects were asked to rank-order the seriousness of a number of social problems and then to try to reach an agreement on a final ranking. Agreements and private opinions were both recorded in all four experiments, and the original pattern was confirmed: while agreements were unaffected, private opinions changed more in the sound-only condition than face-to-face, with CCTV in between. For only two of the experiments, in fact, did the results reach statistical significance (Short 1972c, 1973), but when all five sets of data were combined, both sound-only and CCTV were found to have produced significantly more change than the face-to-face condition.

There were two possible interpretations, suggested Short. The first was that, face-to-face, irrespective of the objective merits of my arguments, I believe I can influence you by using my skill. Since you presumably can do the same to me, I have to be wary, and so I resist and try not to change my mind. In the sound-only condition, however, I believe there is less scope for our persuasive skills and I allow myself to relax and concentrate on the issues, with the result that I am more likely to be swayed by the straight-forward merits of your case. The second possibility was that, because the encounters were somewhat tense and embarrassing, people were more relaxed in the sound-only condition than face-to-face because it removed some of the more threatening and personal features of the confrontation. They were therefore able to concentrate better on the issues and devote more attention to the task, with the result that once again the objective merits of the case came to the fore and the outcome was greater opinion change.

The first interpretation, despite its attractions, was not supported by the data, for, when subjects who had changed their opinions were compared with those who had not, only the face-to-face and CCTV conditions showed a positive association between trusting one's partner and changing one's mind. The other condition revealed exactly the opposite and, although there was no obvious reason for the reversal, it nevertheless meant that the second interpretation was the more likely. The sound-only condition, Short argued, was less personal than face-to-face, and subjects were able to devote more attention to the task and so were more likely to be swayed by the arguments — in much the way that Morley and Stephenson had suggested for negotiations:

"Medium can affect the likelihood of reaching agreement, the side which is more successful, the nature of the settlement reached, the evaluation of the other side and the individual opinions after the discussion. Understanding these effects is therefore important. All the results can be reconciled with the underlying hypothesis that . . .

discussions over that medium [sound-only] are more task-orientated, less person-oriented than face-to-face discussions."

(Short, Williams and Christie, 1976, p. 109)

Recent research

For some years after the work of Short, there was little progress, but more recently a number of additional studies have been published, and three in particular deserve attention. The first was by de Alberdi (1982). The design made use of the four experimental conditions which we had used ourselves in Rutter, Stephenson and Dewey (1981) — face-to-face, CCTV, curtain, and sound-only — while the topics for discussion were based on the items which Short (1973) had introduced. De Alberdi's theoretical purpose was to test whether vision or physical presence was responsible for the difference between face-to-face and sound-only which he expected, but, unfortunately, the results were inconclusive. In all four conditions, the trend was for subjects to change their opinions back from the extremes in the direction of moderation, but visual contact and physical presence produced no significant main effects, and there was no interaction between them. Even a comparison between face-to-face and sound-only revealed no significant difference. The author could offer no explanation.

The second experiment was published by Tysoe (1984) and, like much of the earlier work, it was concerned with labour relations. The subjects, who were male students, first completed a questionnaire to determine whether their views were broadly pro-union or pro-management. Each was then assigned to the role of union negotiator or management negotiator, consistent with his beliefs and attitudes, and the task was to spend 30 minutes with another representative from his own side preparing for a later negotiation. The negotiation was to be about an industrial dispute, and there were to be a number of financial issues to resolve with the other side. The purpose of the planning session was to increase subjects' committment to their side, and so to maximise interparty considerations in what was to follow. The negotiations themselves, which lasted 50 minutes and were restricted to five specific issues, were held either face-to-face or over a sound-only intercom.

The results revealed an interesting pattern. The main dependent measure was changed between responses to the initial questionnaire and responses to the same questionnaire once the negotiations had been completed. Sound-only subjects, it emerged, showed no change on average, but face-to-face subjects showed a significant degree of polarisation, which was defined as movement towards more extreme positions. Some moved one way and some the other, and there was no obvious way of reconciling the findings with the previous literature. From an analysis of the process of the negotiations, however, there eventually emerged an explanation. Face-to-face the discussions were protracted and wide-ranging, but in the sound-only condition they kept much more to the specific issues, and agreement was typically reached in less than half the time allotted. When the discussions were task-specific, general beliefs and attitudes as measured by the questionnaire were unaffected; but when they were wider-ranging, and so perhaps included a consideration of the broader issues, changes did occur. Had change been measured for the specific issues — which more closely resembled Short's approach — the pattern might well have been reversed. What had appeared to be a contradiction with Short's findings in particular was thus, it seemed, resolved.

The third and final paper, by Rutter *et al*. (1984), brings us to an important theoretical issue. The early literature on outcomes, as we have seen, was mostly concerned with simulated industrial negotiations of one sort or another, and the main explanatory concepts were "interparty" and "interpersonal". As interest moved away to non-industrial settings and to attitude and opinion change — in fact, even with the work of Pruitt — "interparty" began to lose its relevance, for subjects were no longer representing sides or parties but were working for themselves. Instead, the concept of "interparty orientation" began to be replaced by "task-orientation". For Morley and Stephenson, task-orientation had been merely one index of interparty orientation, and what we might well expect to find, therefore, is that the relationship between "formality" and "task-orientated/interpersonal" will be weaker than between "formality" and "interparty/interpersonal". Indeed, if Morley and Stephenson's model is followed strictly, the relationship might disappear altogether. The transition from "interparty" to "task" had so far been implicit in the literature, and little if any attention had been paid to it — but now, with the paper by Rutter *et al*., it became an important point of theoretical concern.

Perhaps the central difference between this and the previous studies was that the issue which subjects were asked to debate was the very personal one of abortion. The discussions were held either face-to-face or behind cloth screens which precluded visual communication, and subjects met in pairs or groups of four — something which also distinguished the experiment from previous research, which had almost always restricted itself to pairs. Subjects completed a questionnaire about abortion some days before the discussions took place, and a variety of outcome measures were taken at the end, all of them based on differences between individuals' final positions and the responses they had given to the initial questionnaire. Group consensus, which subjects had been asked to try to reach by the end of the discussions, was excluded from the analysis because, even after the 20 minutes allotted for the debates, the majority of groups were dead-locked.

By the time the experiment was conducted, we had begun to consider the suggestions which our cuelessness model makes about the relationship between outcome and process, particularly content, and we therefore tested the following three predictions. First, in line with Short's findings, we expected that there would be more attitude change in the screen condition than face-to-face, because there were fewer social cues. Second, because in large groups it is harder to take account of each member as an individual person than in small groups — because there are so many cues that we become overloaded and psychological distance develops — we predicted that four-person groups would lead to more attitude change than pairs. An interaction with medium of communication was also anticipated, such that the greatest change would occur in the four-person screen groups and the least in the face-to-face pairs. However, and this was the important third prediction, the first two hypotheses would be supported only to the extent that verbal content was influenced by our manipulations. If content were task-orientated and depersonalised, there would be a considerable degree of attitude change but, if it were not, there would be very little.

The first two predictions were firmly rejected: there were no effects upon outcome of either medium of communication or group size, and only one of the measures produced a significant interaction between them. The third prediction, in contrast, did produce a number of significant effects, but they were quite different from those we had found in previous studies, and they were neither strong nor numerous. Task-orientation we had generally measured by discussion of outcomes (possible targets, points of agreement, and so on) and exchange of information which is relevant to the task (in this case, anything to do with abortion). Both *were* affected by medium — though only in two person encounters — but while "outcomes", as anticipated, were discussed more frequently the screen condition, "information" was more common face-to-face, the reverse of our normal pattern. Depersonalisation revealed no effects for medium of communication, but there were three effects for group size: more acceptance of partners' contributions in the pairs than the groups of four, and less rejection and criticism. Since attitudes have been expected to change only to the extent that content changed, and since content had *not* been greatly affected, the failure of the first two hypotheses was thus explained. The question, though, was why content had behaved in quite the way it had.

At the time the experiment was conducted — which was some years ago now, before our cuelessness model had been properly developed — there seemed to us to be three possible explanations. The first and second were methodological: that the beliefs and attitudes with which the discussions were concerned were so deep-seated and strongly held that a brief, superficial laboratory debate was unlikely to influence them; and that our manipulation of the setting was not sufficiently strong, since the cloth screens removed only visual signals and left the remainder intact.

Though both interpretations are consistent with the data, it is the third possibility, we believe, which is the most important, and the focus this time is the topic of the discussion, abortion. As we have seen even in the literature on negotiation, where the task is generally impersonal, differences between media can be cancelled out if the experimenter introduces personal considerations and so brings the subjects close together, psychologically. If those considerations are salient from the outset — the topic is personal, or subjects believe that they should behave in a personal way — psychological distance is replaced by psychological proximity, the "task"/"person" distinction breaks down, and the "normal" balance of behaviour is destroyed. Here, both task and role *were* personal, and it was the psychological proximity of face-to-face which produced the greater exchange of information — even though screen subjects were still in some ways more task-orientated since they were the more concerned with outcomes, an indication that they were following the experimenter's instructions closely and were trying to reach a consensus.

In these particular circumstances, the predictions we normally make from the cuelessness model — cuelessness leads to task-orientated, depersonalised content, and so to a style which lacks spontaneity and outcomes which lack compromise — are no longer appropriate. The key, however, is still psychological distance, for psychological distance, however it is produced, will continue to have the same effects upon process and outcome. Thus, in hotline counselling, for example, the whole point of the system is that the telephone *allows* and *encourages* the very psychological proximity and intimate content which is normally possible only face-to-face — but this time it is the *anonymity* which produces psychological proximity, and the role of cuelessness is to make that anonymity possible. Moreover, as we have acknowledged from the beginning, cuelessness is only one of the determinants of psychological distance and proximity. Task, role, and indeed the relationship between the subjects may well be others — and, though typically they will work together in the same direction, they will almost certainly have variable weightings, and they may sometimes even conflict. These are important issues to develop further, and we shall return to them in Chapter 4.

PERSON PERCEPTION

Person perception can be divided into two main areas: impression formation, and attribution. Although attribution theory has played an important part in recent models of looking and eye-contact, the literature on seeing has confined itself almost exclusively to impression formation. In general, there have been only two types of study: interaction studies, in which subjects interact; and observation studies, in which they observe other people interacting. In both cases, the partner or target is visible under some conditions but invisible under others, and the dependent measure is the impressions which subjects report at the end of the session.

The majority of studies have examined the evaluative quality of the impressions — whether people are perceived more or less favourably when they are visible than when they are not — but a number of attempts have also been made to explore the accuracy of the impressions and the confidence with which they are held. Despite the widespread belief that visual information ought to play an important part in impression formation (e.g. Argyle, 1978; Harper, Wiens and Matarazzo, 1978; Cook, 1979), the experimental literature, as we shall see, is far from conclusive.

Interaction Studies

Evaluative quality

Interaction studies began to appear around 1970, and almost all were concerned with the evaluative quality of impressions. Among the most popular paradigms was the Prisoners' Dilemma. A variety of studies were published, each including vision and no-vision conditions, and on balance the evidence suggested that visual contact increased co-operation (for example, Wichman, 1970; Gardin et al., 1973), and led to more favourable impressions of the other person. Sometimes, however, the effect of vision was simply to intensify whatever emotion was already being experienced (Laplante, 1971) — recalling the suggestions of Ellsworth and Patterson about gaze as a "non-specific activator", and the findings of Pruitt on the influence of vision on competitiveness in negotiations.

Another of the early approaches was concerned with the "observer-observed" effect. Manipulations of visions can sometimes be asymmetrical, so that more of one subject is visible than the other. The more exposed person will often regard himself or herself as the observed and the other person as the observer, and the effect of the asymmetry will be discomfort. The best known of the work was by Argyle and his colleagues (Argyle, Lalljee and Cook, 1968; Argyle and Williams, 1969), and the findings suggested that women typically feel more observed than men, interviewees feel more observed than interviewers, and young people feel more observed than old people when they talk together. Furthermore, subjects who look relatively little feel more observed than those who look more, and the whole effect, it appeared, was more the product of set than anything objective. Levine and Ranelli (1977), in contrast, concluded that asymmetry might sometimes be welcomed, for subjects who were made to watch a target "losing face" felt very uncomfortable when they too were visible and much preferred to be hidden. The important consideration, in other words, was the task which subjects were assigned.

More recent work has been rather more substantial, and once again some of the most interesting findings have come from the Communications Studies Group — not least because of the group's concern with everyday life beyond the laboratory. In the first of the studies, civil servants were asked to interview a "candidate" — actually a confederate — for a travel scholarship (Reid, 1970). The interviews were conducted either face-to-face or over the telephone, and no differences were detected in the way the candidate was perceived. Unfortunately, though, the same confederate was used for all the sessions, and the possibility could not be ruled out that he had varied his behaviour systematically from condition to condition. In a follow-up study, therefore, geniune interactions were monitored instead (Young, 1974a) — but once again there were no clear effects, even though face-to-face, CCTV, and a sound-only system were all included. Interestingly enough, a report by Klemmer and Stocker (1971) in the U.S.A. had also concluded that vision was not important, for impressions over Bell Laboratories' Picturephone were found to be almost identical to those over the ordinary telephone.

Given the widespread belief that visual information ought to make a difference to our impressions, the early results from the Communications Studies Group were both surprising and disappointing. According to Williams (1975a), however, there was an obvious explanation. and that was that the subjects' task had differed from experiment to experiment, just as Levine and Ranelli (1977) were to argue later. To test his suggestion, Williams recruited subjects, civil servants once more, to take part in two conversations, one a discussion about the problems of everyday life, the other a debate about how those problems should be rank-ordered for importance. Each conversation was with a different partner and over a different medium — face-to-face, CCTV, or telephone — and the subjects were asked to complete a series of forced-choice evaluations of their partners and their conversations. For both sets of ratings, the order of preference was face-to-face, CCTV, telephone, but only some of the comparisons reached statistical significance. A number of them, however, *were* affected by task, as Williams had anticipated. In the free discussion, partners were evaluated more positively over CCTV than the telephone, and the conversations produced a straightforward rank-ordering from face-to-face, to CCTV, down to telephone. In the debate, however, CCTV partners were preferred to those in either of the other conditions, and the same was true for the conversations. Task, it appeared, really was an important variable.

According to our cuelessness model, the central difference between media is the extent to which they encourage psychological distance. Psychological distance will generally lead to task-oriented, impersonal exchanges, while psychological proximity will have the opposite effect. In both cases, what produces that set will often be in part the number of available social cues. For the Communications Studies Group, however, the crucial concept was not cuelessness but *Social Presence*, a concept they introduced themselves. Social Presence is a phenomenological concept, and media which allow psychologically close encounters are those which are high in Social Presence while those which do not are low. Of the early alternatives to Morley and Stephenson's "formality", Social Presence was much the most significant concept, and I shall return to it in more detail in Chapter 4. For Williams, it was Social Presence, together with Argyle and Dean's Intimacy, which offered the most acceptable interpretation of his 1975a findings. Resolving a conflict, he argued. was an intimate task, and a medium which was rich in Social Presence, such as face-to-face, might lead to still greater intimacy and disturb the equilibrium. A medium with less Social Presence, such as CCTV, was therefore preferred, as were the partners in that condition. A free discussion, in contrast, was much less intimate and, for that reason, Social Presence was a benefit and face-to-face was therefore the medium of choice. What mattered most, in other words, was the interaction between Social Presence and task.

Despite its attractions, Williams' analysis could not, in fact, account for all the findings — for example, CCTV is intermediate between face-to-face and telephone in Social Presence but was not always intermediate in subjects' ratings — and the main problem was that the intimacy of the topic could seldom be judged in advance, so that interpretation was necessarily retrospective. In a further study, therefore, by Williams (1972) — for which the data were collected after those for Williams (1975a), despite the dates — intimacy was manipulated directly by comparing free discussion, debate, and persuasion (where persuasion was assumed to be the most intimate), and examining both strangers and friends (where friends represented intimacy). Only two media were included, sound-only and video-phone, and nothing conclusive, unfortunately, emerged from the results. There were no clear effects of intimacy — perhaps because, despite Williams' intentions, it was uncertain whether intimacy *had* been manipulated effectively — and, in any case, the experiment omitted a face-to-face condition for some reason. Williams' 1975a interpretation was still uncertain.

The remainder of the work by the Communications Studies Group was concerned with persuasion, and some aspects of the findings have been discussed already. Short (1972a), for example, asked subjects to try to persuade each other to their own points of view, either face-to-face, over CCTV, or over a sound-only link, and then to evaluate each other on Williams' scales. Five factors emerged altogether, but only the first, trustworthiness, distinguished between the conditions, with sound-only subjects perceived as more trustworthy than the other two groups. Williams (1973, 1975b), in two subsequent studies of his own, again found little to support his expectations, and the same was true of Tysoe (1984), though face-to-face did lead subjects to more favourable impressions of *themselves* in that particular study. Overall, therefore, the best summary of interaction studies continues to be that clear and consistent effects of vision have simply not been found for evaluative quality.

Accuracy and confidence

The remainder of the interaction studies have moved away from evaluation to accuracy and confidence. Very little research has been published, unfortunately, but the Communications Studies Group has again played a leading role. In the first of their experiments, by Reid (1970), people were asked to judge whether a speaker was telling the truth or lying. The speaker was a confederate who was programmed to lie and tell the truth alternately, and subjects either met him face-to-face or listened to him on a sound-only system. No significant effects were found. Accuracy was scarcely greater than chance in either of the conditions and, although face-to-face subjects reported greater confidence than sound-only subjects, the difference was not reliable statistically. In a second experiment in the same paper, however, Reid was more successful. Civil servants were asked to interview a candidate for a scholarship, as we saw earlier, and face-to-face interviewers were found to be significantly more confident than their sound-only counterparts that their impressions were accurate. Unfortunately, accuracy itself was not measured.

All the group's subsequent work on accuracy and confidence was conducted by Young, and his first experiment was an attempt to overcome the methodological problems in Reid's research (Young, 1974a). This time, civil servants interviewed genuine applicants, but again there were no differences in accuracy. It should be noted, however, that accuracy was measured by comparing interviewers' evaluations of the subjects with the subjects' evaluations of themselves — a method which has often been criticised in the past because, of course, it lacks an external criterion (Cook, 1979).

Young's other studies were concerned with metaperceptions — subjects' perceptions of their partners' perceptions (Young, 1974b, 1975). Weston and Kristen (1973) had reported that people deprived of visual contact found it difficult to gauge one another's responses, and often said that there was much misunderstanding in the discussions and little agreement on the issues. Young (1975) was able to confirm the result for perceived misunderstanding — though, when genuine accuracy was measured rather than perceived accuracy, the effects disappeared (Young, 1974b). Vision had no effect upon the discrepancy between genuine and perceived accuracy, and typically subjects' performance was in any case only slightly above chance. The literature on evaluation, I concluded earlier, has produced no clear pattern — and exactly the same, unfortunately, is true for accuracy and confidence.

Observation Studies

Evaluative quality

Observation studies began to appear a little earlier than interaction studies, in the mid-1960s. The earliest were concerned with evaluative quality, particularly impressions of emotion (Levitt, 1964; Williams and Sundene, 1965; Byrne and Clore, 1966), and by the early 1970s the literature had come to focus on warmth and empathy. Dilley, Lee and Verrill (1971), for example, arranged for practising therapists to meet their clients either face-to-face, through a "confessional" screen, or over a telephone, and then asked experienced counsellors to rate them for empathy, from audio tapes. No differences between conditions were found. In a later study, by Strahan and Zytowski (1976), students were asked to rate Carl Rogers from one of his training films, but while some were able to watch the film and listen to it in the normal way, there were a variety of other conditions in which verbal and visual information were removed. For women, verbal content was found to be especially important in producing a favourable impression of the target, while visual information was not, but for men there was no clear pattern. In one final study, by Berman, Shulman and Marwit (1976), warmth was used as the *independent* variable, and actors were asked to portray warm or cold experimenters. Observers then made judgements in sound, vision, or sound and vision together, but there was no obvious pattern, for a variety of significant interactions was revealed between actor and medium, suggesting that some actors conveyed emotion through sound predominantly while others relied on vision.

More recent experiments have moved away from warmth and empathy to a wider range of judgements (e.g. Ekman *et al.*, 1980; Krauss *et al.*, 1981; O'Sullivan *et al.*, 1985), and one particularly interesting development has been research in the courtroom. In both the U.S.A. and Britain there has been concern in recent years about whether the personal and emotive nature of legal proceedings may lead to injustices, and whether alternative procedures might be adopted. As a result, identity parades are now sometimes mounted without face-to-face contact (by means of one-way screens), and witnesses' testimony is sometimes given in the form of videotaped playback.

It was this latter issue, videotaped testimony, which concerned Williams *et al.* (1975) — not the Williams of the Communications Studies Group, it should be noted, or the Williams of Williams and Sundene (1965) — in one of the most extensive pieces of research in the area. After a thorough and helpful review of the legal literature, the authors set up a careful and detailed simulation of a civil case in which a landowner was seeking compensation for land which the state had purchased from him by compulsory order. "Simulation", in fact, is not quite the right word, since the case was a genuine one which had already been heard and settled, and the participants were all comparable to those in the original case — genuine lawyers, witnesses, jury, and so on.

The subjects were the jury members, and each jury observed the proceedings live, on colour tape, on black-and-white tape, on audio tape, or by listening to someone reading the verbatim transcript. The dependent measures, of which there were many, included evaluative ratings of the participants and the proceedings, and how much compensation subjects would award. Perceived competence, honesty, objectivity, and handsomeness of the participants, it emerged, were all unaffected by medium, but live participants were regarded as significantly more friendly than when they were seen in black-and-white, of better appearance than when they were merely heard or monitored from transcripts, and significantly calmer than in any other condition. There were no effects upon compensation. One of the most attractive features of the findings, apart from their theoretical value, was their obvious *practical* implications, and it is perhaps significant that the authors were a mixture of psychologists and lawyers. Similar research is to be found in the papers of Miller and his colleagues, from the Department of Communication at Michigan State University (Hocking, Miller and Fontes, 1978; Kaminski, Fontes and Miller, 1978; Boster, Miller and Fontes, 1978).

The literature so far on observation studies has been similar to the literature on interaction studies – except that the measures, of course, are from observers rather than interactants — but the remaining studies have all taken a very different approach, one which has produced some intriguing results. The pioneer was Mehrabian, in the U.S.A. (Mehrabian, 1971), and the purpose of the approach was to try to assess the relative importance of visual and verbal information by combining them in various ways, so that sometimes they were consistent but sometimes they conflicted. Mehrabian and Ferris (1967), for example, recorded speakers uttering a single neutral word ("maybe") in three tones of voice — positive, neutral, and negative. Facial expression was varied in the same way — positive, neutral and negative — and each subject was asked to decode all nine messages. Decoding consisted of making judgements as to what emotion was being expressed. Facial expression accounted for around 40% of the variance, vocal cues under 20% — even though vocal cues were themselves said to be more important than verbal content (Mehrabian and Wiener, 1967).

The paradigm was soon taken up in Britain, by Argyle and his colleagues (Argyle *et al.*, 1970), but this time the focus was how we form impressions of people's attitudes towards us. Three verbal messages were prepared — superior to the receiver, equal, and inferior — and each was delivered on videotape in three different nonverbal manners — superior, equal, and inferior again. Nonverbal information was found to carry much more weight than verbal content — so much so that when the two conflicted (a superios verbal message delivered in an inferior manner, for example), the observers were overwhelmed by the nonverbal information and all but ignored verbal content. The same was later found for hostility/friendship (Argyle *et al.*, 1971), and for confidence (Walker, 1977).

By the mid-1970s many similar studies had been published, and useful reviews are to be found in de Paulo *et al.* (1978) and Furnham, Trevethen and Gaskell (1981). The majority had arrived at much the same conclusions as Mehrabian and Argyle, but in recent years rather different findings have begun to emerge, and a number of criticisms have been levelled at the approach. Friedman (1978), for example, argued that the early studies had wrongly assumed that communicated meaning is unidimensional, and he went on to demonstrate that whether or not nonverbal cues carry the greater weight depends upon the particular response the observers are asked to make — that is, their task. Photographs of teachers with different facial expressions were paired with the words they were supposed to be saying to a student, and subjects were asked to make two judgements: how positive the teacher was towards the student, and what course grade he or she would award the student. Nonverbal information had a greater impact than words for the first question, but the reverse was the case for the second (Fig. 3.4). Verbal content was especially important, it was suggested by de Paulo, when the verbal/nonverbal discrepancy was particularly marked, for observers took large discrepancies to indicate deception, and in those circumstances retreated to the spoken word. As Friedman (1978) had already suggested:

> ". . . the present demonstration suggests what should be obvious: words do matter. . . . The prepotency of nonverbal cues is a myth. Even worse, the issue is a red herring. It will likely prove more profitable to ask not which cues matter more, but rather 'Which mean what, and when?'"
>
> (Friedman, 1978, p. 149)

The most influential of the more recent papers has probably been the excellent review, and experimental demonstration, by Furnham, Trevethen and Gaskell (1981). Two principal weaknesses, they suggested, were to be found in most of the previous studies. First, the stimulus material was often contrived, so that verbal and nonverbal components were made to carry equal weights — something which is uncommon in everyday life. Second, the comparisons were crude, and confined themselves to verbal against nonverbal, with little attempt to break down those two categories — vocal against visual, for example, in the case of nonverbal information. Moreover, the presentations were typically brief and unrealistic, arbitrary response measures were generally invented specially, and most of the

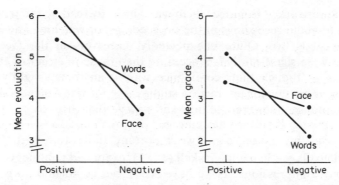

FIG. 3.4. Friedman (1978): Mean evaluations and grades awarded by type (verbal/non-verbal) and nature (positive/negative) of information.

studies used repeated measures, with all the attendant problems of demand characteristics. To generalise from study to study was therefore hazardous. In their own experiment, care was taken to avoid as many of the pitfalls as possible, and no clear pattern of results emerged. The previous literature, the authors argued, had simply been asking the wrong question:

> "It is not a case of whether verbal or nonverbal channels carry more information relative to each other, because they act differently in different situations depending on the nature of the message, the people communicating and the situational constraints of the social episode in which the communication occurs. . . . It may well be that verbal, vocal, and visual cues operate quite differently in different situations and are integrated in different ways depending on the nature of the interaction, wider aspects of the situation, the personal characteristics of the people being perceived and finally the personalities of the perceivers. It is completely misleading to maintain that non-verbal cues are more important than verbal cues in impression formation and attraction across all persons and all situations."
>
> (Furnham *et al.*, 1981, pp. 14 and 15)

Accuracy and confidence

From the evaluative quality of impressions, the remainder of the literature on observation has turned to accuracy and confidence. As we saw in the case of interaction studies, accuracy is seldom easy to assess, because it is difficult to find objective criteria. Most of the observation studies have suffered from exactly the same problem (e.g. Giedt, 1955; Cline, Atzet and Holmes, 1972; Burns and Beier, 1973), but there was one early experiment which did produce unambiguous results (Maier and Thurber, 1968). Students were asked to role-play lying or telling the truth, and observers were asked to judge which was which, by reading the transcripts, listening to audio recordings of the proceedings, or watching and listening to the sessions live. Quite unexpectedly, observers in the face-to-face condition were significantly *less* accurate than those in either of the other conditions — though their confidence was, if anything, slightly higher. Thus, just as we saw for interaction studies, even if visual signals do not in fact promote accuracy, people may still *believe* that they do.

The remaining literature has emerged as a response to the Mehrabian/Argyle paradigm, and there are two important studies to report. The first, by Furnham, Trevethen and Gaskell (1981), examined confidence (as well as evaluative impressions, as we have seen), but could find no consistent evidence of differences between conditions. The second, in contrast, by Archer and Akert (1977), was concerned with accuracy. Like Furnham and his colleagues, Archer and Akert were critical of the paradigm, and they chose instead to make videotape recordings of real everyday scenes and then to ask observers after each one to make a very simple judgement to which there was only one right answer. One of the episodes, for example, showed two women playing with a baby, and the question was which was the mother; another showed two men discussing a game of basketball they had just finished, and the question was who had won; and another showed a young woman on the telephone, and the question was whether the person at the other end was male or female. Half the subjects were played the recording in sound-and-vision, and half simply read the verbatim transcript. Sound-and-vision produced significantly more accurate responses than transcripts, it emerged; and, while sound-and-vision subjects performed significantly better than chance, subjects in the transcript condition were significantly worse than chance (Fig. 3.5).

Of all the findings on accuracy, Archer and Akert's were much the most convincing but, nevertheless, they have themselves come under recent attack from Roger Brown. Commenting on the whole Mehrabian/Argyle tradition in *Social Psychology: The Second Edition*, Brown (1986) argues that the paradigm distorts what happens in everyday-life. While it *may* be that emotions, attitudes and so on really are decoded through nonverbal behaviour rather than language, we cannot be sure.

> "The real question is whether the conclusions of Archer and Akert as well as those of Mehrabian and of Argyle are legitimate conclusions about what *can* be accomplished by linguistic and nonverbal means or what happened to be accomplished in particular circumstances. Archer and Akert, describing the rules they followed in extracting their short sequences from longer videotapes, write that 'since we did not want a simple test of audition, we avoided explicit mentions of the correct answer (e.g. "I won the game because . . .")' (p. 446). You might like to read the previous sentence again. Why would it be a

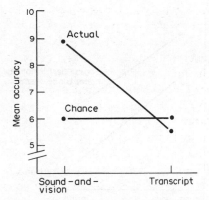

FIG. 3.5. Archer and Akert (1977): Mean accuracy of perceptions.

simple test of *audition* to include explicit mentions of the correct answer? It would not be a test of audition only, but, rather, a fair test of the powers of the linguistic channel. It would be a perfectly legitimate use of language if one of the two women playing with the baby were to say: 'This here is my baby.' By excluding such expressions, they deprived the linguistic channel of its usual power. Of course, if they had permitted such expressions, the videotape full-channel messages would have enjoyed no advantage whatsoever over the verbal transcripts. I believe that the correct answer to the question about the relative powers of the verbal and nonverbal channels is that language is a universal medium that can express anything that can be thought or felt, whereas the nonverbal channels are specialized to a restricted class of meanings."

(Brown, 1986, pp. 499–500)

Interaction versus Observation

Theoretical issues

By now it will be clear that neither interaction studies nor observation studies have produced conclusive evidence. There are, I should like to suggest, two main reasons, one theoretical, the other methodological. The theoretical reason is the role of task — which many writers have acknowledged, as we have seen, but few have investigated systematically — and the importance of the argument was highlighted once again in two of our own recent experiments.

In the first experiment, by Clark and Rutter (1985), our main interest was in trying to determine whether prior knowledge about the the targets would affect observers' impressions. Videotaped interviews were prepared, with a male or female confederate, and the topic was the British National

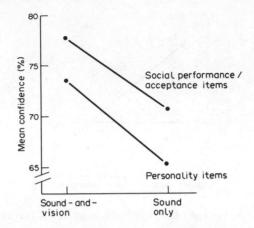

FIG. 3.6. Clark and Rutter (1985): Mean confidence of impressions.

Health Service. Subjects then monitored the confederates in either sound-and-vision or sound-only, and the prior information they were given was categorical, for the targets were described as either psychiatric hospital in-patients (high salience category), general hospital in-patients (marginal salience) or ordinary members of the public (low salience). Measures were taken of the targets' perceived personality, how well the observers thought they performed in the interview and expected them to perform in everyday life, and how socially acceptable they found them. Confidence ratings were taken as well. Visual information, it emerged, led to greater confidence but had no effects upon the quality of judgements, while categorisation had strong effects upon quality but was unrelated to confidence (Fig. 3.6). Confidence was on average some 10% higher when visual information was present than when it was absent, and the least favourable ratings of the targets were elicited when the high salience category was applied. Both visual information and categorisation thus did have effects, but where those effects lay depended upon what type of judgement was to be formed — in other words, the task.

The second experiment was reported by Elwell, Brown and Rutter (1984), and this information was examined in the context not of prior information but of vocal information, namely accent. Two videotape recordings were made of an Indian student apparently being interviewed for a job, and in one he used a standard English accent and in the other a non-standard, Indian, accent. The content was carefully scripted to remain constant. Subjects then monitored the tapes in sound-and-vision or sound-only, giving a two-by-two "matched guise" design, with accent (standard/non-standard) the first variable and medium (sound-and-vision/sound-only) the second. The dependent measures were a series of scales designed to tap personality, perceived similarity of target to subject,

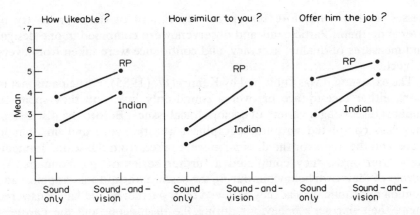

Fig. 3.7. Elwell *et al*. (1984): Mean ratings of target.

and what might be called intention ("How well would you get on with him?" and "How likely is it that you would offer him the job?"). The results were very straightforward, for both accent and vision had strong effects on almost all the measures: the standard accent led to more favourable impressions of the target than did the non-standard accent; and sound-and-vision produced more favourable ratings than did sound-only, so much so that the Indian accent in sound-and-vision often led to more favourable ratings of the target than did the standard accent without vision (Fig. 3.7). There was no interaction between vision and accent, and the findings thus confirmed that type of judgement, context, and the other available cues all affect the part which visual signals play.

Methodological issues

Theoretical problems, I suggested, were the first reason for the inconsistency of the literature on observation studies, and the second was methodological. A number of weaknesses have been touched upon already — short presentations of posed, unfamiliar stimulus material; repeated measures from small samples of subjects; limited and insensitive dependent variables — but there remain two overriding problems which we have not yet addressed. The first is that, although participants in interaction have been examined in one set of studies and observers in another, never have the two been combined in one design. The assumption has been that visual information will affect participants and observers similarly but, until they are compared directly, we cannot be sure. The second problem is that, while some studies have measured evaluative quality, others accuracy, and others confidence, there have been no attempts to measure all three togther. Both, we believe, are major weaknesses, and we therefore set up an experiment of our own to try to overcome them. Participants and observers were combined in one design, and measures of quality, accuracy, and confidence were taken from every subject.

The experiment was published by Kemp *et al*. (1985). Participants met in pairs, either face-to-face or over a sound-only link, and they spent 10 minutes discussing a variety of sociopolitical issues. Before the discussion, they had completed an autobiographical questionnaire and an opinion scale, and the items for the discussion were taken from the scale. Immediately afterwards, they completed a further series of questionnaires — ratings of their own behaviour during the session, the autobiographical and opinion questionnaires as they believed their partner would have answered them, their partner's behaviour during the discussion, and the partner's personality — and for every item they also recorded how confident they felt about their judgement. All the discussions were videotape recorded and were later monitored by observers in sound-and-vision, vision-only, and sound-only. Each observer was responsible for only one participant and, as soon as the playback had finished, observers were asked to complete the same questionnaires the participants themselves had answered: the autobiographical and sociopolitical questionnaires as they believed their speaker would have responded; and ratings of behaviour and personality. Confidence scales were once again included for every item.

Three sets of predictions were made; in comparison with observers, participants would form more accurate, qualitatively different, and more confidently held impressions; for observers, impressions would be more accurate, qualitatively different, and more confidently held under sound-and-vision than vision-only or sound-only; and impressions formed of face-to-face speakers would differ in accuracy, quality, and confidence from impressions formed of sound-only speakers. The first prediction received good support from the findings for confidence, but no support from the evaluative quality of the impressions or from accuracy — which was measured by discrepancies between participants' and observers' scores on the biographical and sociopolitical items. The significant results for confidence, which were restricted to the behavioural items, consistently showed that participants were more confident in their impressions than were observers.

The second prediction received mixed support for, although there were several differences between observation conditions for accuracy, quality, and confidence alike, the most important factor was the *type* of judgement to be made — in other words, the task. Observers who could hear the discussions, for example, were more accurate in gauging sociopolitical beliefs and more confident in rating influence than were observers with visual cues only, while observers who could see the discussions produced more positive evaluations of the speakers' personality characteristics than did those with sound cues only. Thus, to make judgements about beliefs and influence, people needed verbal content; but for impressions of personality, nonverbal information was the more salient.

For the third prediction there was no support. Taken together, therefore, and regardless of experimental condition, our results produced relatively few significant effects for either accuracy, quality, or confidence. In general, subjects were both accurate *and* confident in their judgements — though the two measures were not related in any consistent way — and the impressions they formed were mostly favourable. Visual information did not play the significant role which the literature had suggested, and task emerged once again as probably the most important variable of all. Visual cues led to more positive impressions of personality and to greater confidence in biographical judgements, but they were unimportant in judgements about sociopolitical beliefs. Verbal and nonverbal cues, we conclude, all play some part in impression formation, but their significance depends upon their availability, their salience for the particular situation (or "importance-in-context", as Warr and Jackson (1977) have called it), and the type of impression to be formed. Visual signals *are* important — but only in interaction with a host of other variables which are as yet only poorly understood.

REFERENCES

ARCHER, D. and AKERT, R.M. (1977) Words and everything else: verbal and nonverbal cues in social interpretation. *Journal of Personality and Social Psychology*, **35**, 443–9.

ARGYLE, M. (1978) *The Psychology of Interpersonal Behaviour* (third edition). Harmondsworth: Penguin.

ARGYLE, M., ALKEMA, F. and GILMOUR, R. (1971) The communication of friendly and hostile attitudes by verbal and non-verbal signals. *European Journal of Social Psychology*, **1**, 385–402

ARGYLE M., LALLJEE, M. and COOK, M. (1968) The effects of visibility on interaction in a dyad. *Human Relations*, **21**, 3–17.

ARGYLE, M., SALTER, V., NICHOLSON, H., WILLIAMS, M. and BURGESS, P. (1970) The communication of inferior and superior attitudes by verbal and nonverbal signals. *British Journal of Social and Clinical Psychology*, **9**, 222–31.

ARGYLE, M. and WILLIAMS, M. (1969) Observer or observed? A reversible perspective in person perception. *Sociometry*, **32**, 396–412.

BERMAN, H.J., SHULMAN, A.D. and MARWIT, S.J. (1976) Comparison of multidimensional decoding of affect for audio, video and audio video recordings. *Sociometry*, **39**, 83–9.

BOSTER, F.J., MILLER, G.R. and FONTES, N.E. (1978) Videotape in the courtroom. Part III. *Trial*, June 1978, 49–51.

BROWN, R. (1986) *Social Psychology: The Second Edition*. New York: Free Press.

BURNS, K.L. and BEIER, E.G. (1973) Significance of vocal and visual channels in the decoding of emotional meaning. *Journal of Communication*, **23**, 118–30.

BYRNE, D. and CLORE, G.L. (1966) Predicting interpersonal attraction toward strangers presented in three different stimulus modes. *Psychonomic Science*, **4**, 239–40.

CARNEVALE, P.J.D., PRUITT, D.G. and SEILHEIMER, S.D. (1981) Looking and competing: accountability and visual access in integrative bargaining. *Journal of Personality and Social Psychology*, **40**, 111–20.

CHAMPNESS, B.G. and DAVIES, M.F. (1971) The Maier pilot experiment. *Communications Studies Group* paper No. E/71030/CH.

CHAMPNESS, B.G. and REID, A.A.L. (1970) The Efficiency of Information Transmission: A Preliminary Comparison Between Face-to-Face Meetings and the Telephone. *Communications Studies Group* paper No. P/70240/CH.

CHAPANIS, A. (1971) Prelude to 2001: Explorations in human communication. *American Psychologist,* **26,** 949–61.

CHAPANIS, A., OCHSMAN, R.B., PARRISH, R.N. and WEEKS, G.D. (1972) Studies in interactive communication. I. The effects of four communication modes on the behaviour of teams during cooperative problem-solving. *Human Factors,* **14,** 487–510.

CLARK, N.K. and RUTTER, D.R. (1985) Social categorization, visual cues, and social judgements. *European Journal of Social Psychology,* **15,** 105–19.

CLINE, V.B., ATZET, J. and HOLMES, E. (1972) Assessing the validity of verbal and nonverbal cues in accurately judging others. *In* D.C. Speer (ed.), *Nonverbal Communication.* Beverly Hills: Sage.

COOK, M. (1979) *Perceiving Others.* London: Methuen.

DAVIES, M. (1971a) Cooperative problem solving. *Communications Studies Group* paper No. E/71159/DV.

DAVIES, M. (1971b) Cooperative problem solving. A follow-up study. *Communications Studies Group* paper No. E/71252/DV.

De ALBERDI, M. (1982) More opinion change over audio: process or pseudoprocess? *Annual Conference of Social Psychology Section of the British Psychological Society,* Edinburgh, September 1982.

De PAULO, B.M., ROSENTHAL, R., EISENSTAT, R.A., ROGERS, P.L. and FINKELSTEIN, S. (1978) Decoding discrepant nonverbal cues. *Journal of Personality and Social Psychology,* **36,** 313–23.

DILLEY, J., LEE, J.L. and VERRILL, E.L. (1971) Is empathy ear-to-ear or face-to-face? *Personnel and Guidance Journal,* **50,** 188–91.

DOUGLAS, A. (1957) The peaceful settlement of industrial and intergroup disputes. *Journal of Conflict Resolution,* **1** 69–81.

DOUGLAS, A. (1961) *Industrial Peacemaking.* New York: Columbia University Press.

EKMAN, P., FRIESEN, W.V., O'SULLIVAN, M. and SCHERER, K. (1980). Relative importance of face, body and speech in judgements of personality and affect. *Journal of Personality and Social Psychology,* **38,** 270–77.

ELWELL, C.M., BROWN, R.J. and RUTTER, D.R. (1984) Effects of accent and visual information on impression formation. *Journal of Language and Social Psychology,* **3** 297–9.

FRIEDMAN, H.S. (1978) The relative strength of verbal versus nonverbal cues. *Personality and Social Psychology Bulletin,* **4,** 147–50.

FURNHAM, A., TREVETHAN, R. and GASKELL, G. (1981) The relative contribution of verbal, vocal and visual channels to person perception: experiment and critique. *Semiotica,* **37,** 39–57.

GARDIN, H., KAPLIN, K.J., FIRESTONE, I.J. and COWAN, G.A. (1973) Proxemic effects on cooperation, attitude and approach avoidance in a prisoner's dilemma game. *Journal of Personality and Social Psychology,* **27,** 13–18.

GIEDT, F.H. (1955) Comparison of visual content and auditory cues in interviewing. *Journal of Consulting Psychology,* **19,** 407–19.

HARPER, R.G., WIENS, A.N. and MATARAZZO, J.D. (1978) *Nonverbal Communication: the state of the art.* Chichester: Wiley.

HOCKING, J.E., MILLER, G.R. and FONTES, N.E. (1978) Videotape in the courtroom. Part I. *Trial,* April 1978, 52–5.

KAMINSKI, E.P., FONTES, N.E. and MILLER, G.R. (1978) Videotape in the courtroom. Part II. *Trial,* May 1978, 38–42.

KEMP, N.J., RUTTER, D.R., DEWEY, M.E., HARDING, A., and STEPHENSON, G.M. (1984) Visual communication and impression formation. *British Journal of Social Psychology,* **23,** 133–45.

KLEMMER, E.T. and STOCKER, L.P. (1971) *Picturephone Versus Speakerphone for Conversation Between Strangers.* Unpublished company data.

KRAUS, R.M., APPLE, W., MORENCY, N., WENZEL, C, and WINTON, W. (1981) Verbal, vocal, and visible factors in judgements of another's affect. *Journal of Personality and Social Psychology,* **40,** 312–20

LAPLANTE, D. (1971) *Communication, Friendliness, Trust and the Prisoner's Dilemma.* M.A. thesis, University of Windsor.

LEVINE, J.M. and RANELLI, C.J. (1977) Observer visiblity and comfort in a surveillance situation. *Sociometry*, **40**, 343–50.

LEVITT, E.A. (1964) The relationship between abilities to express emotional meanings vocally and facially. *In* J.R. Davitz (ed.), *The Communication of Emotional Meaning*. New York: McGraw-Hill.

LEWIS, S.A. and FRY, W.R. (1977) Effects of visual access and orientation on the discovery of integrative bargaining alternatives. *Organizational Behavior and Human Performance*, **20**, 75–92.

MAIER, N.R.F. and THURBER, J.A. (1968) Accuracy of judgements of deception when an interview is watched, heard and read. *Personnel Psychology*, **21**, 23–30.

MEHRABIAN, A. (1971) Nonverbal communication. *Nebraska Symposium on Motivation*, 107–61.

MEHRABIAN, A. and FERRIS, S.R. (1967) Interference of attitudes from non verbal communication in two channels. *Journal of Consulting Psychology*, **31**, 248–52.

MEHRABIAN, A. and WIENER, M. (1967) Decoding of inconsistent information. *Journal of Personality and Social Psychology*, **6**, 109–14.

MORLEY, I.E. and STEPHENSON, G.M. (1969) Interpersonal and interparty exchange: a laboratory simulation of an industrial negotiation at the plant level. *British Journal of Psychology*, **60**, 543–5.

MORLEY, I.E. and STEPHENSON, G.M. (1970a) Formality in experimental negotiations: a validation study. *British Journal of Psychology*, **61**, 383–4.

O'SULLIVAN, M., EKMAN, P., FRIESEN, W. and SCHERER, K. (1985) What you say and how you say it. The contribution of speech content and voice quality to judgements of others. *Journal of Personality and Social Psychology*, **48**, 54–62.

PRUITT, D.G., KIMMEL, M.J., BRITTON, S., CARNEVALE, P.J.D., MAGENAU, J.M., PERAGALLO, J. and ENGRAM, P. (1978) The effect of accountability and surveillance on integrative bargaining. *In* H. Sauermann (ed.), *Contributions to Experimental Economics*. Tubingen: Mohr.

REID, A.A.L. (1970) Electronic person-person communications. *Communications Studies Group* paper No. P/70244/RD.

RUTTER, D.R., STEPHENSON, G.M. and DEWEY, M.E. (1981) Visual communication and the content and style of conversation. *British Journal of Social Psychology*, **20**, 41–52.

RUTTER, D.R., DEWEY, M.E., HARDING, A. and STEPHENSON, G.M. (1984) Medium of communication and group size: effects of cuelessness on the content, style, and outcome of discussion. Unpublished. University of Kent at Canterbury.

SHORT, J.A. (1971a) Bargaining and negotiation: an exploratory study. *Communications Studies Group* paper No. E/71065/SH.

SHORT, J. (1971b) Conflicts of interest and conflicts of opinion in an experimental bargaining game conducted over three media. *Communications Studies Group* paper No. E/71245/SH.

SHORT, J. (1972a) Medium of communication, opinion change, and the solution of a problem of priorities. *Communications Studies Group* paper No. E/72245/SH.

SHORT, J. (1972b) Conflicts of opinion and medium of communication. *Communications Studies Group* paper No. E/72001/SE.

SHORT, J. (1972c) Medium of communication and consensus. *Communications Studies Group* paper No. E/72210/SH.

SHORT, J.A. (1973) The effects of medium of communications on persuasion, bargaining and perceptions of the other. *Communications Studies Group* paper No. E/73100/SH.

SHORT, J.A. (1974) Effect of medium of communication on experimental negotiation. *Human Relations*, **27**, 225–34.

SHORT, J., WILLIAMS, E. and CHRISTIE, H. (1976) *The Social Psychology of Telecommunications*. Chichester: Wiley.

SMITH, D.H. (1969) Communication and negotiation outcome. *Journal of Communication*, **19**, 248–56.

STEPHENSON, G.M. (1984) Intergroup and interpersonal dimensions of bargaining and negotiation. *In* H. Tajfel (ed.), *Social Dimensions, Volume 2*, Cambridge: Cambridge University Press.

STRAHAN, C. and ZYTOWSKI, D.G. (1976) Impact of visual, vocal and lexical cues on judgements of counselor qualities. *Journal of Counseling Psychology*, **23**, 387–93.

TYSOE, M. (1984) Social cues and the negotiation process. *British Journal of Social Psychology*, **23**, 61–7.

WALKER, M.B. (1977) The relative importance of verbal and nonverbal cues in the expression of confidence. *Australian Journal of Psychology*, **29**, 45–57.

WARR, P.B. and JACKSON, P.R. (1977) Salience, importance and evaluation in judgements about people. *British Journal of Social and Clinical Psychology*, **16**, 35–46.

WEEKS, G.D. and CHAPANIS, A. (1976) Cooperative versus conflictive problem solving in three telecommunication modes. *Perceptual and Motor Skills*, **42**, 879–917.

WESTON, J.R. and KRISTEN, C. (1973) *Teleconferencing: A Comparison of Attitudes, Uncertainty and Interpersonal Atmospheres in Mediated and Face-to-Face Group Interaction*. Department of Communications, Canada.

WICHMAN, H. (1970) Effects of isolation and communication on co-operation in a two-person game. *Journal of Personality and Social Psychology*, **16**, 114–20.

WILLIAMS, E. (1972) Factors Influencing the Effect of Medium of Communication upon Preferences for Media, Conversations and Person. *Communications Studies Group* paper No. E/72227/WL.

WILLIAMS, E. (1973) Coalition Formation in Three-person Groups Communication via Telecommunications Media. *Communications Studies Group* paper No. E/73037/WL.

WILLIAMS, E. (1975a) Medium or message: Communications medium as a determinant of interpersonal evaluation: *Sociometry*, **38**, 119–30.

WILLIAMS, E. (1975b) Coalition formation over telecommunications media. *European Journal of Social Psychology*. **5**, 503–07.

WILLIAMS, E. (1977) Experimental comparisons of face-to-face and mediated communication: a review. *Psychological Bulletin*, **84**, 963–76.

WILLIAMS, F. and SUNDENE, B. (1965) Dimensions of recognition: visual vs. vocal expression of emotion. *Audio Visual Communication Review*, **18**, 44–52.

WILLIAMS, G.R., FARMER, L.C., LEE, R.E., CUNDICK, B.P., HOWELL, R.J. and ROOKER, C.K. (1975) Juror perceptions of trial testimony as a function of the method of presentation: a comparison of live, color video, black-and-white video, audio, and transcript presentations. *Brigham Young University Law Review*, **1975**, 375–421.

YOUNG, I. (1974a) Telecommunicated Interviews: An Exploratory Study. *Communications Studies Group* paper No. E/74165/YN.

YOUNG, I. (1974b) Understanding the Other Person in Mediated Interactions. *Communications Studies Group* paper No.E/74266/YN.

YOUNG, I. (1975) A Three Party Mixed-Media Business Game: A Progress Report on Results to Date. *Communications Studies Group* paper No. E/75189/YN.

4
Process

CONTENT AND STYLE OF CONVERSATION

From outcome we turn now to process. As we have seen in the previous chapter, the most important feature of the telephone from a social-psychological point of view is that it removes social cues. The fewer the social cues, in general the greater the feeling of psychological distance and, in turn, according to our cuelessness model, the more task-oriented and depersonalised the content of what people say, the less spontaneous their style and the less likely an outcome of compromise. Outcome, we know from Chapter 3, *is* affected in the way the model predicts, and we come now to the evidence for content and style.

Content: Exchanging Information

Early literature: impersonal negotiations

Among the earliest research on visual communication, as we have seen, was the work of Morley and Stephenson on bargaining and negotiation. Negotiations over a sound-only link, they found, were more likely than face-to-face negotiations to end in a victory for the side with the stronger case, and the explanation, it was suggested, lay with the *content* of the discussions. Interparty issues predominated at the expense of interpersonal considerations, the relative merits of the two sets of arguments became clearer and clearer as the negotiation developed, and the stronger case simply carried itself. Unfortunately, though, there was no *direct* evidence for the importance of content, because no analysis was conducted.

The first paper to report a content analysis was by Stephenson, Ayling and Rutter (1976), and the findings were described briefly in Chapter 2. Student subjects were asked to complete a questionnaire about union–management relations, and pairs were then formed with one member pro-union and the other pro-management. Each pair held a 15 minute discussion, either face-to-face or over a sound-only link, and the task was to discuss items from the questionnaire which had revealed disagreement. The sessions were tape-recorded, and transcribed and typed

Mode	Resource	Referent
1 Offer	*Structuring Activity*	0 No Referent
2 Accept	1 Procedure	1 Self
3 Reject	*Outcome Activity*	2 Person
4 Seek	2 Settlement point (a) initial (b) new	3 Other
	3 Limits	4 Party
	4 Positive consequences of proposed outcomes	5 Opponent
		6 Both persons
	5 Negative consequences of proposed outcomes	7 Both parties
	6 Other statements about outcomes	
	Acknowledgement	
	7 Acknowledgement + (a) own and both sides, (b) other side	
	8 Acknowledgement − (a) own and both sides, (b) other side	
	Other information	
	9 Information	

FIG. 4.1. Stephenson, Ayling and Rutter (1976): C.P.A. categories.

verbatim, and then they were analysed by a new coding system called Conference Process Analysis (CPA), devised by Morley and Stephenson (1977). Previous systems in the literature had generally concentrated on the *structure* of discussions, often using the whole utterance as their unit of analysis and simple categories as their unit of coding. The purpose of the new scheme, in contrast, was to examine the *functions* of what people said, and the unit of analysis this time was generally smaller than the utterance and was coded on not one but three dimensions: Mode, the means of exchange; Resource, what it was that was being exchanged; and Referent, whether anyone was referred to while the exchange was in progress. (Fig. 4.1).

The experiment incorporated two sets of predictions: sound-only discussions would be more task-oriented than face-to-face discussions; and they would be depersonalised. Task-orientation, it was expected, would result in greater discussion of task-relevant information and outcomes; and depersonalisation would result in more blame and less praise for the opponent, fewer self references, more party references, and greater disagreement. Both predictions, in the event, received some measure of support, but rather less than we had anticipated. While offers of "information" discriminated successfully between conditions, "outcomes" did not; and though two of the five measures of depersonalisation (praise for opponent, and party references) produced significant differences between conditions, the remainder revealed no more than trends (Table 4.1).

Many other findings emerged, about which predictions had not been made, and the most important was that medium of communication interacted with union–management status. In each case, the union subjects

TABLE 4.1. *Stephenson, Ayling and Rutter (1976): Depersonalisation and task-orientation.*

		Means	
		Face-to-face	Telephone
(a)	Depersonalization		
	Blame for opponent	2.00	2.17
	Praise for opponent	0.92	0.25*
	"Self" references	7.58	7.25
	"Party" references	7.67	11.17*
	"Rejects" (disagreement)	0.67	1.08
(b)	Task orientation		
	Outcome	1.75	1.25
	Offers of information	48.56	55.53*
	"Union" offers of information about opponent's party	1.60	3.10*

F values for Face-to-face versus Telephone with df = 1,20 *$P < 0.05$

were more task-oriented in the sound-only condition than face-to-face, while management subjects tended in the opposite direction. In the mid-1970s, we argued, when the experiment was conducted, the climate of industrial relations in Britain was such that unions were widely held to be stronger than managements. To that extent, the union subjects came armed with the "stronger" case even before the sessions began, and their behaviour was thus consistent with Morley and Stephenson's prediction: concentration on interparty issues and disregard for interpersonal considerations.

The implication from our findings was that the results of the earlier outcome studies indeed *were* attributable to the effects of the experimental conditions upon content. To try to clinch the argument, Morley and Stephenson (1977) went on to make a content analysis of their own 1970a material. The outcome findings, it will be recalled, has been impressive — seven of the ten negotiations held in the sound-only condition had resulted in a clear victory for the stronger side, against none of the ten conducted face-to-face. The content analysis, however, was disappointing, for only one significant effect was revealed, and even the non-significant trends were sometimes in the "wrong" direction. The findings were thus much weaker than those reported by Stephenson, Ayling and Rutter (1976), but there was, according to Morley and Stephenson, a simple explanation. There had been a "ceiling effect".

> "Apparently, C.P.A. can detect differences in behaviour of the predicted sort (Stephenson, Ayling and Rutter, 1976), and the failure to find face-to-face/audio differences (in Morley and Stephenson, 1970a) cannot be attributed to the inadequacy of the category system

per se. Rather, we are inclined to suggest that differences between
the two situations were due to the differences in the task used. We
used a formal negotiation task . . . whereas Stephenson, Ayling and
Rutter did not. Furthermore, the latter authors gave subjects greater
freedom to control the content of the 'agenda' than did the former.
The implication is that in Morley and Stephenson (1970) the task
was so highly structured that the expected behavioural differences
could not emerge."

(Morley and Stephenson, 1977, pp. 223–4)

Despite the ceiling effect, Morley and Stephenson did succeed in finding
one important difference between the sound-only and face-to-face discussions. Stephenson, Ayling and Rutter (1976) had reported as part of
their subsidiary results that the two conditions differed in what they called
"responsiveness" — that is, the tendency for one subject to take the lead
and the other to respond. In the sound-only condition there had been a
clear initiative–response–initiative–response pattern, but face-to-face
there had not. Sound-only, in other words, encouraged greater role
differentiation, with an obvious leader and an obvious follower, and the
greater the role differeniation, Morley and Stephenson argued, the easier it
ought to be to tell which speaker was which. Accordingly, if randomly
selected passages from the transcripts were given to "blind" observers, the
union speaker and the management speaker should be identified more
frequently in the sound-only condition than the face-to-face condition. The
prediction was confirmed, and the authors were able to conclude that, even
when the removal of social cues had relatively little direct effect upon
content, there were nevertheless clear effects upon role differentiation
(Fig. 4.2).

Almost the opposite conclusion, it seemed, was later to emerge from a
study of leadership, by Strickland *et al*. (1978) — though, interestingly
enough, the number of available social cues was once again invoked as the
most likely theoretical explanation. Groups of students met face-to-face or
over a video conference network to try to solve a number of human
relations problems. Each group met five times, and in the video condition
there was much *less* role differentiation than face-to-face, with a weaker
pattern of correlations. The reason, the authors suggested, was that the
relative lack of social cues over the video link meant that individuality was
less salient than face-to-face. Since leadership *requires* individuality, role
differentiation was thus less readily achieved, and potential leaders simply
had less opportunity for the quality of their contributions to be recognised.

In one final experiment on bargaining and negotiation, conducted by
Tysoe (1984), the focus was once again union–management negotiations.
In contrast to Morley and Stephenson, Tysoe was able to report marked
differences between sound-only and face-to-face. This time, subjects
argued in line with their own views and were not assigned to the roles at

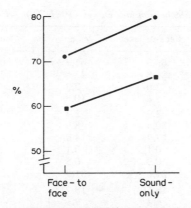

FIG. 4.2. Role identifiability: mean proportion (%) of speeches attributed to correct speaker.

random. The sessions were analysed by CPA as before and, although there was no evidence of depersonalisation in the absence of visual cues, the sound-only condition was noticeably more task-oriented than face-to-face, with much greater emphasis on specific outcomes, as the experimental task required — trying to reach agreement on particular issues. The most important finding was a clear relationship between content and outcome. Face-to-face, the discussions were wide-ranging but, in the sound-only condition, they kept to the specifics of the immediate task. In consequence, the sound-only sessions were generally shorter, and there were marked differences between conditions in attitude change. Sound-only subjects were less likely than face-to-face subjects to change their attitude to union–management issues in general during the discussion (because they had not discussed them), but they were more likely to emerge from the experiment with a low opinion of themselves (because the discussions had been short and task-specific and there had been little opportunity to make a full and satisfactory contribution).

Later literature: personal discussions

Reasearch on industrial settings accounts for almost all the early literature on content, but the later literature has turned to *personal* discussions. In the first of our own more recent reports, by Rutter, Stephenson and Dewey (1981), we presented two such experiments, one conducted with sighted people, the other with blind people. The experiment on sighted people was described in Chapter 2. Because we were just beginning to develop the cuelessness model in detail, we were concerned to include

TABLE 4.2. *Rutter, Stephenson and Dewey (1981) Expt. II: Content.*

	Face-to-face	Video	Curtain	Audio
Offer	60.3	61.7	64.2	64.7
Accept	26.8	23.6	24.2	20.7
Reject	2.0	2.3	0.9	1.3
Seek	8.8	10.8	9.3	12.1
Procedure	2.9	2.4	2.2	7.1**
Information	30.4	38.0	37.6	31.0
Irrelevant information	27.7	14.0	21.9	19.6
Positive acknowledgement	0.1	0.1	0.5	0.1
Negative acknowledgement	0.9	0.5	0.3	0.3
Outcomes	21.6	31.9	24.7	27.9
Self	18.5	18.2	19.3	21.2
Others excluding speaker	6.4	7.1	6.0	8.3
Persons present including speaker	0.4	1.4	1.1	1.6**
Third parties	8.2	12.2	8.8	7.6
No referent	66.5	61.0	64.8	61.2

t values for Face-to-face versus Audio with df = 20
**$P < 0.01$

conditions we had not used before, so that the number and type of social cues could be manipulated more thoroughly. Two intermediate conditions were therefore added to face-to-face and sound-only, one in which subjects sat in separate rooms and communicated over a closed-circuit television link, the other in which they sat in the same room and spoke through a curtain which precluded visual communication. The task was to discuss a variety of social and political issues, and the sessions were analysed by CPA.

The comparison between face-to-face and sound-only produced a number of differences — significantly more discussion of procedures for conducting the debate, and more reference to the people taking part, presumably about the procedures they were to follow, as well as trends towards more discussion of outcomes and less introduction of irrelevant material (Table 4.2). The most important finding, however, was that, whenever a significant difference between sound-only and face-to-face emerged, the CCTV and curtain conditions lay *between* them. It was for that reason that the experiment led us for the first time to conclude that the *aggregate* of social cues was what mattered most, and not just visual cues. The same conclusion was to be reached in a replication by Kemp and Rutter (1982), in which a comparison was made between face-to-face, sound-only, and a third condition in which a small wooden screen was placed on the table between the subjects.

The other experiment reported in our 1981 paper, the one which examined blind people, was designed as a "naturalistic" pilot study of the cuelessness model, and in subsequent research we have gone on to examine blind people in more detail. The most important of our studies was conducted by Kemp and Rutter (in press) and consisted of a comparison of blind-blind pairs, blind-sighted pairs, and sighted-sighted pairs. When both people were blind, we argued, the number of available social cues would be small, and the content of the conversations would therefore be task-oriented and depersonalised. Sighted-sighted conversations, in contrast, would be rich in social cues, leading to content which was much less task-oriented and more personal. Blind-sighted conversations, we predicted, would be intermediate. The experimental sessions took place in the laboratory, and once again the subjects' task was to discuss a number of sociopolitical issues. The sessions were analysed by CPA.

For the first prediction, the results were quite unexpected. Indeed, for task-orientation, they were the opposite of what we had predicted, for there was almost eight times as much discussion of "irrelevant" information in blind-blind conversations as sighted-sighted conversations, as well as a trend towards less discussion of outcomes — both of which indicated greater task-orientation in the *sighted-sighted* pairs. For depersonalisation there were no effects, except that the category, "accept", occurred most frequently in the blind-blind pairs, an indication that here too there had been a reversal. Other findings revealed more discussion of "procedures" in blind-blind conversations than sighted-sighted conversations (though "procedures" accounted for only 2% of what was said in total), but less offering of information and fewer incomplete utterances (Table 4.3).

The second prediction, in contrast, received good support, and it was the finding that blind-sighted pairs *were* intermediate which led us eventually to a possible interpretation. Because the blind-blind conversations were

TABLE 4.3. *Kemp and Rutter (1986): Content*

Category	Blind–blind Mean	Blind–sighted Mean	Sighted–sighted Mean	d.f.	F
Mode 0	3.9	3.6	4.1	2,24	<1
Offer	54.0	58.6	63.7	2,24	5.5**
Reject	1.0	1.0	0.9	2,24	<1
Accept	32.3	29.5	24.5	2,24	3.2*
Seek	8.9	7.1	6.5	2,24	1.7
Resource 0	12.6	15.9	18.1	2,24	6.6**
Procedure	2.0	1.5	0.5	2,24	3.9*
Information	36.4	33.9	44.7	2,24	1.6
Irrelevant information	18.7	18.6	2.4	2,24	3.5*
Acknowledgement +	0.8	0.1	0.2	2,24	1.9
Acknowledgement −	1.5	1.1	0.7	2,24	<1
Outcome	28.1	28.8	33.5	2,24	<1
Referent 0	69.4	65.6	69.8	2,24	2.0
Self	13.8	15.3	14.5	2,24	<1
Others excluding speaker	4.0	3.9	3.2	2,24	<1
Others including speaker	1.2	0.7	0.7	2,24	2.0
Third parties	11.3	14.6	11.8	2,24	1.6

*P < 0.05; **P < 0.01.

lacking in social cues, subjects found themselves without the information they needed about their partners, and they simply asked for it in words. More time was therefore spent on personal information, which was supposedly irrelevant to the task — and less time on the task itself — and it was precisely because so few cues were available, we realised eventually, that the subjects behaved in that way. Sighted people faced with cuelessness over an experimental sound-only link, for example, or a real telephone, have comparatively little relevant experience, and their way of coping is to avoid and ignore personal information. Blind people, however, do have that experience and, far from avoiding the personal dimension, they confront it directly and ask for the missing information in words. For both groups of people, cuelessness creates psychological distance — but while sighted subjects *remain* distant because they lack the experience to change, blind people simply call upon the skills they have had to develop in everyday social interaction and quickly turn distance into proximity. In a similar way, I suggested in Chapter 3, cuelessness also leads to psychological proximity over telephone hotlines.

A related issue, it will be recalled, emerged at the end of the experiment by Rutter *et al.* (1984), in which the topic of conversation was abortion. Subjects held their discussions either face-to-face or from behind screens, and this time it was face-to-face which produced apparently the more task-oriented conversations, for there was considerably more discussion of relevant information in that condition than in the screen condition (Table 4.4). As we have seen even in the literature on negotiation, where the task is typically impersonal, differences between media can be cancelled out

TABLE 4.4. *Rutter* et al. *(1984): Content*

	Face-to-face		Screen				
	2	4	2	4	FF/S	2/4	Interaction
Offer	61.0	63.5	63.7	63.1	0.3	0.2	0.5
Accept	28.6	22.3	25.4	21.2	2.8	16.4***	0.7
Reject	1.0	2.8	1.3	3.1	0.2	5.8*	0.0
Seek	8.4	10.3	9.0	11.6	0.4	2.1	0.1
Procedure	0.9	1.4	1.1	1.1	0.0	0.2	0.2
Information	44.9	36.1	31.6	37.5	5.0*	0.3	7.7*
Irrelevant information	3.1	1.2	0.9	1.0	0.9	0.5	0.7
Praise	0.0	0.1	0.1	0.0	0.2	0.2	1.8
Blame	0.0	0.9	0.1	0.3	1.0	6.4*	2.2
Outcomes	36.6	41.8	49.5	43.9	13.4**	0.0	7.0*
Self	14.7	16.0	16.4	16.8	0.8	0.4	0.1
Others excluding speaker	3.3	5.9	3.9	3.4	0.8	0.8	1.9
Others including speaker	2.2	2.4	1.6	3.2	0.0	1.1	0.7
Third parties	10.8	9.1	11.2	8.1	0.1	2.4	0.2
No referent	68.9	66.6	67.0	68.6	0.0	0.1	1.6

*$P < 0.05$; **$P < 0.01$; ***$P < 0.001$.

if the experimenter introduces personal considerations and so brings the subjects closer together psychologically. If, as here, those considerations are salient from the outset — the topic is personal, or subjects believe they should behave in a personal way — the distinction between "task" and "person" breaks down, and the two become one. Cuelessness this time will lead to psychological distance in the "normal" way, but "task" and "person" will be indistinguishable.

Among the remaining literature on content, the best-known study is probably one reported by Wilson and Williams (1977). It consisted of an analysis of the Watergate tapes from the transcripts published in the *New York Times* in 1974, and it confirmed the "normal", traditional predictions of our model. The Watergate experiment remains, so far as I know, the only published study of content which has made use of the real telephone and not a laboratory analogue. All the recordings, it will be recalled, included the then President Nixon, and as far as possible the design was balanced so that each member of staff who was recorded with Nixon over the telephone was also recorded with him face-to-face. The main findings were that the telephone conversations were shorter on average than face-to-face, included fewer greetings and ritualised sequences but more disagreements, and were apparently altogether less "intimate" and "pleasant". It does have to be remembered, of course, that both the tapes and the transcripts were highly edited, but, nevertheless, the pattern of findings was just as the cuelessness model would predict: the telephone created a feeling of psychological distance, and psychological distance led in turn to task-oriented and depersonalised content.

Style: Synchronising Conversation

Early research: vision

While research on content began as an attempt to explain why differences between media should produce differences in outcome, research on style began as a separate, identifiable body of work in its own right. Most of the research has concentrated on one particular aspect of discourse, the synchronisation of transitions from speaker to speaker. The earliest studies, however, which were conducted by Moscovici and his colleagues (Moscovici, 1967), were concerned as we saw in Chapter 2 with the formal, grammatical properties of spoken language. Subjects were observed in a variety of conditions — face-to-face, face-to-face with a screen between them, back-to-back, or side-by-side — and, while the first two resulted in speech which resembled ordinary everyday spoken language, the output of the others was much closer to written text. The crucial variables, argued Moscovici, were familiarity and formality. Familiar, informal settings produced one particular set of "psychosociological connotations" —

unfamiliar, formal settings another — and it was psychosociological connotations which in turn affected speech.

The main concern of the subsequent literature has been turn-taking, and the first major study was by Cook and Lalljee (1972). The experiment consisted of a straightforward comparison between face-to-face and sound-only, and was designed to clarify the group's earlier work, published by Argyle, Lalljee and Cook (1968). Pairs of students were assigned at random to one or other condition to "make each other's acquaintance", and 10 minutes of conversation were tape-recorded from each pair and subsequently transcribed. Verbal substitutes would compensate for the lack of visual cues in the sound-only condition, it was predicted, but the flow of conversation would sometimes break down nevertheless because the verbal substitutes would be less effective than visual cues. There would also be fewer changes of speaker and consequently longer utterances because the difficulty of exchanging the floor would result in fewer attempts to take over. There might also be more anxiety in the sound-only condition, and therefore more speech disturbance.

In the event, the results were disappointing, for there were only two significant effects: more very short utterances in the sound-only condition than face-to-face; and more frequent interruptions face-to-face. Both findings were against prediction. There was no evidence of verbal substitutes for visual signals; nor was there anything to suggest that synchronisation had broken down, for the overall structure of the conversations was remarkably similar in two conditions. The authors were unable to offer any firm interpretation of their results, but they pointed to three possibilities: that verbal signals do substitute for visual cues, but the experiment had concentrated on the wrong ones; that the removal of a single set of cues has little effect, because much of everyday communication is redundant; and that there *had* been difficulties in synchronisation, despite the overall appearance of smoothness.

The critical measure for this last point was interruptions, and the argument was as follows. Because it is difficult to decide when to interrupt in the absence of visual cues since interruptions are a potential source of disruption, people were reluctant to take the risk at all. In general, therefore, the speaker was simply allowed to continue, and the reduced incidence of interruptions in the sound-only condition was the result. The frequency of short utterances in the absence of visual cues was not explained, but it may, perhaps, have come from the slightly raised incidence of questions, or from brief interpolations coded as "proper" utterances when in fact they functioned as acknowledgement signals.

The next experiment was by Rutter and Stephenson (1977), and it consisted of an analysis of the material used by Stephenson, Ayling and Rutter (1976). Like Cook and Lalljee (1972), we expected that turn-taking would be less successfully negotiated in sound-only conversations than face-to-

TABLE 4.5. *Rutter and Stephenson (1977): Style.*

	Face-to-face		Audio			
	Mean	SD	Mean	SD	d.f.	F
No. occurrences simultaneous speech	14.7	4.6	9.0	3.9	1,20	12.1**
Duration simultaneous speech (seconds)	18.7	4.7	9.4	3.0	1,20	40.8***
Duration mutual silence (seconds)	18.9	9.3	14.4	7.0	1,20	1.8
Length utterances (words)	25.7	7.4	34.3	11.5	1,20	4.7*
No. utterances	18.2	4.7	15.3	3.5	1,20	3.0
No. floor changes	28.7	8.4	25.3	6.5	1,20	1.2
Duration speech (seconds)	145.0	4.8	142.3	4.3	1,20	1.8
Total no. words	431.3	4.5	455.4	54.7	1,20	1.3
Noun-verb ratio	1.5	0.1	1.5	0.1	1,20	<1
Speech rate (words/second)	3.0	0.3	3.2	0.3	1,20	2.6
No. questions†	5.3	1.3	4.9	2.0	1,20	<1
No. utterances ending as question	2.5	1.0	2.5	1.6	1,20	<1
% utterances ending as question	13.6	3.0	15.4	7.4	1,20	<1
% floor changes preceded by question	20.4	4.5	21.1	8.3	1,20	<1
No. attention signals††	6.1	2.2	4.3	3.3	1,20	2.9
Filled pause ratio (per 100 words)	2.4	2.0	3.3	2.1	1,20	2.0
Speech disturbance ratio (per 100 words)	6.3	2.3	8.2	2.6	1,20	4.6*

†The number of questions includes questions which occur in mid-utterance.
††Attention signals contribute to the word count but not to the utterance count or number of occurrences of simultaneous speech.
*$P < 0.05$; **$P < 0.01$; ***$P < 0.001$.

face, and we made two predictions: there would be more interruptions and silences in the sound-only condition; and the structure of the conversations would differ as the sound-only subjects compensated for the lack of visual signals. Compensation, we expected, would appear as a slower rate of speech and longer utterances, a grammatically more formal structure, more questions, more acknowledgement and attention signals, and more filled pauses. There might also be more speech disturbance because of anxiety (Table 4.5).

The first of our two hypotheses received no support. Once again it was the face-to-face condition and not sound-only which produced the greater simultaneous speech — both frequency and duration — and there was no difference between the conditions in silence. The second hypothesis, in contrast, received some measure of support, though relatively little: utterances were longer on average in the sound-only condition than face-to-face; and their overall distribution differed, with the majority of very short utterances face-to-face (the opposite of what Cook and Lalljee had found) and the majority of very long utterances in the sound-only condition. The possible influences of sex and time were also explored, and though there were a number of main effects for both the variables, there were no interactions with medium of communication. Men used more filled pauses than women (against what Feldstein, Brenner and Jaffé, 1963, and Lalljee

and Cook, 1973, had reported); and they produced more speech disturbance but fewer acknowledgement and attention signals. For men and
women alike, the number of filled pauses fell steadily as the conversations
progressed — as subjects became less attentive, perhaps, and felt less need
to plan their utterances carefully — but speech disturbance fluctuated from
period to period and showed no clear pattern.

Despite the lack of support for our predictions, visual contact, we argued
at the time, *was* an important factor in the synchronisation of conversations
— though its precise role was rather different from the one we had
anticipated. The most important measure for our interpretation was interruptions. Interruptions, we suggested, indicated not a breakdown in
sychronisation but spontaneity, and, when visual cues were present, subjects felt able to interrupt at will because their nonverbal behaviour
indicated that they were simply acting spontaneously and were not threatening the continuity of the proceedings. Interruptions without visual
signals might well lead to a breakdown, and for that reason they were made
less frequently.

Later research: cuelessness.

By the late 1970s the conclusion was emerging that visual cues were
rather less important for turn-taking and synchronisation than had been
thought originally, and research in other traditions was pointing in the
same direction. Duncan, for example, had been arguing for some time in
favour of intonation, linguistic structure, and gestures (e.g. Duncan, 1972;
Duncan and Fiske, 1977; Duncan, Brunner and Fiske, 1979) and Sacks
had drawn attention to the role of semantics (Sacks, Schegloff and Jefferson, 1974) which were to be echoed in later experimental research by
Beattie (1983) and Slugoski (1984).

Beattie's work was based on university tutorials and, later, television
interviews with politicians. The most important of Duncan's signals, it
emerged, was completing a clause, and change of pitch and drawling on the
final or stressed syllable were the most frequent accompaniments. Many
speaker-switches, however (around 13% in the tutorial studies), were
negotiated without any detectable signals from the speaker, and it was
clear that something was missing from traditional accounts. According to
Slugoski (1984), anticipation by the listener, based on the semantic content
of the speaker's utterance, was the key. Passages were produced experimentally, in such a way that semantic cues to completion were pitted
against intonation contour and speech rhythms, and "listeners" were asked
in a reaction-time design to note the point at which they felt the new
speaker could take over. Semantic cues were confirmed as the more
important when the two sets of cues conflicted, but the effects were not
entirely straightforward since an additional source of variance was the
nature of the conversation.

Our own attempts to disentangle vision — from physical presence, in particular — began with the work of Rutter, Stephenson and Dewey (1981), as we have seen, but already there existed two other reports. The first was by Jaffé and Feldstein (1970). Subjects were recruited to take part in three conversations designed to try to resolve differences in racial attitudes. Half of each conversation took place face-to-face and then, for the other half, the two subjects were separated by an opaque screen, so that visual communication was made impossible but physical presence was retained. Unfortunately, the results varied considerably from experiment to experiment. For one of the three, however, simultaneous speech was longer face-to-face than in the screen condition; for two of the three, so were pauses between speakers; and for one of the three, so too were pauses overall. Though the findings were thus relatively weak, the lack of visual cues again had little effect on meshing, and the more important finding was the spontaneity and loose structure face-to-face.

The second paper was by Siegman and Pope (1972), and it reported two experiments of interest. Just as Moscovici had argued that the relationship between medium and process is mediated by "psychosociological connotations", so Siegman and Pope suggested that, in the absence of visual feedback, people become uncertain about how their partners are responding and so experience what they called "relationship ambiguity". In the first experiment, subjects took part in two interviews, one held face-to-face, the other from behind an opaque screen. The screen condition, it was found, led to shorter utterances, slower speech rate, and more filled pauses, while speech disturbance, latency of response to questions, and duration of silences overall were unaffected. In the second experiment, subject and interviewer sat back-to-back and the results were similar to those of the screen condition. Both manipulations, the authors argued, had led to uncertainty about how the interviewer was responding — "relationship ambiguity" — and it was that which in turn had led to the differences in style.

Our own 1977 paper was soon followed by a report from the Communications Studies Group, by Williams (1978). It consisted of a stylistic analysis of conversations which Williams (1975) had recorded in his work on the formation of coalitions. From face-to-face, sound-only, and CCTV brainstorming sessions, three dependent measures were taken: the duration of simultaneous speech, the duration of mutual silence, and the length of utterances lasting 0.4 seconds or more (that is, "proper" utterances, and not acknowledgement signals or brief interpolations). Both simultaneous speech and silence produced significant effects, for both were longer face-to-face than in either of the other conditions, which in turn were equivalent. Once again, therefore, interruptions were more common face-to-face than in the cueless conditions, but the equivalence of CCTV and sound-only indicated that the effects could not be attributed to visual

TABLE 4.6. *Rutter,Stephenson and Dewey (1981) Expt. II: Style.*

	Face-to-face	Video	Curtain	Audio
No. simultaneous speech	8.3	8.9	8.1	5.8
Duration sim. speach (seconds)	12.7	9.9	11.7	7.6*
Duration mutual silence (seconds)	11.5	12.8	11.4	20.2
No. utterances	9.7	12.4	9.4	10.7
Mean word-length utterances	32.7	27.3	38.3	31.5
No. floor changes	15.9	21.7	14.4	18.3
Duration speech (seconds)	90.6	88.6	90.2	83.7
Total no. words	280.6	297.3	289.2	260.8
Noun–verb ratio	37.9	36.9	36.8	38.8
Speech rate (words/second)	3.2	3.4	3.3	3.2
Percentage utterances ending as question	14.4	21.5	17.9	22.9*
Percentage floor changes preceded by question	16.7	23.9	22.0	27.4*
No. attention and acknowledgement signals	7.2	4.7	5.8	3.6*
Filled pause ratio (per 100 words)	2.5	2.8	3.6	2.8
Speech disturbance ratio (per 100 words)	7.4	8.4	9.3	9.6*

t values for Face-to-face versus Audio with df = 20.
*$P < 0.05$.

signalling alone. In the only other laboratory study published at the time, by Butterworth, Hine and Brady (1977), hesitations and pauses were measured in sound-only, opaque screen, and transparent screen conditions, but there was no detectable pattern.

Our own experiment, as we saw in the section on content, examined four conditions: face-to-face, sound-only, CCTV, and a condition in which subjects conversed through a curtain (Rutter, Stephenson and Dewey, 1981). Simultaneous speech, we found, lasted significantly longer in the face-to-face condition than the sound-only condition, and acknowledgement and attention signals were more frequent; but new turns face-to-face were less often preceded by a question from the old speaker, and there was less speech disturbance (Table 4.6). In every case, what is more, the CCTV and curtain conditions lay in between, and the evidence was therefore very strong that the *aggregate* of social cues was indeed the critical variable. The findings for questions were especially interesting, since asking a question at the end of one's utterance is a powerful way of resolving the ambiguity and throwing the onus upon the other person. The findings for acknowledgement signals, which paralleled those for interruptions, added further support to our suggestion that the role of social cues is to produce spontaneous, relaxed conversation and that, despite previous interpretations, interruptions have little to do with "breakdown" or "desynchronisation".

In two subsequent experiments, we were able to investigate factors which we expected might interact with medium of communication in its effects on style. First we examined time (Kemp and Rutter, 1982), and then we turned to group size (Rutter *et al.*, 1984). In Kemp and Rutter (1982), a comparison was made between face-to-face, sound-only, and a wooden screen condition. While the frequency and duration of simultaneous speech and the number of filled pauses all produced significant differences between face-to-face and sound-only, with the wooden screen condition in between, only the frequency of simultaneous speech produced a significant interaction between medium of communication and time. As we had anticipated, the values for the two cueless conditions converged upon those for face-to-face as time went on, indicating a degree of adaptation to cuelessness, with a resulting increase in spontaneity. The effect was not, however, particularly strong, but since the conversations lasted only fifteen minutes, the opportunity for adaptation was limited.

In the study of group size, by Rutter *et al.* (1984), there were only two significant findings to report. Groups of four, we suggested, would lack spontaneity because, although more social cues are available than in pairs, fewer can be used from each individual for reasons of attention and information overload, and the setting will therefore be more, not less, cueless than in two-person conversations. The topic of conversation, it will be recalled, was abortion, and the experiment has already been discussed at length in the sections on the outcome and content. As for style, there were only two effects: significantly fewer acknowledgement signals in four-person groups than pairs; and significantly more filled pauses in the screen condition than face-to-face. While acknowledgement signals, we suggest, indicate spontaneity, filled pauses — which are normally regarded as an index of planning (Maclay and Osgood, 1959; Rochester, 1973; Beattie, 1983) — indicate the opposite. Both findings were therefore consistent with our prediction. There were, however, no interactions between size of group and medium of communication.

In one final study, we went on to examine blind people (Kemp and Rutter, in press). Blind-blind, blind-sighted, and sighted-sighted pairs of people were compared, in discussions of a variety of sociopolitical issues, and the usual range of stylistic measures was taken. From our analysis of content it had emerged that blind people dealt with the psychological distance which their blindness created by asking the other person directly, in words, for the personal information which cuelessness denied them. To that extent the "normal" pattern for cuelessness was reversed, and our prediction was therefore that style too should be reversed since content leads to style.

That, indeed, is precisely what emerged. Simultaneous speech in blind-blind pairs lasted in total almost twice as long as in sighted-sighted pairs, with blind-sighted pairs in between; and presumably for that reason (that is, the frequency with which utterances were interrupted), the number of utterances followed a corresponding pattern, with the lightest frequency in

TABLE 4.7. Kemp and Rutter (1986): Style

	Blind–blind		Blind–sighted		Sighted–sighted		d.f.	F
	Mean	SD	Mean	SD	Mean	SD		
No. occurrences of simultaneous speech	8.0	6.5	7.2	7.2	4.8	5.0	2,24	1.2
Duration of simultaneous speech (seconds)	34.8	12.4	27.8	18.0	18.6	6.9	2,24	4.1*
Duration of mutual silence (seconds)	15.3	9.8	11.0	9.3	15.4	17.3	2,24	<1
Length utterances (words)	27.5	14.6	43.6	25.5	48.1	35.9	2,24	3.0
No. utterances	20.6	7.2	14.6	7.5	13.3	6.3	2,24	4.1*
No. floor changes	13.2	6.6	8.7	4.3	9.7	5.7	2,24	2.7
Duration of speech (seconds)	159.6	46.3	158.3	45.4	151.7	36.6	2,24	2.9
Total no. words	443.3	145.4	459.7	126.7	441.3	112.9	2,24	<1
Speech rate (words per second)	2.8	0.5	3.0	0.5	2.9	0.5	2,24	<1
Percentage utterances ending as question	13.0	12.1	15.6	13.6	13.4	13.1	2,24	<1
No. attention signals	12.8	9.8	15.0	11.2	10.3	8.6	2,24	1.4
Filled pause ratio (per 100 words)	2.7	1.6	3.6	2.0	2.7	1.5	2,24	1.2
Speech disturbance ratio (per 100 words)	3.7	2.1	3.5	1.7	4.0	1.9	2,24	<1

*$P < 0.05$

blind-blind pairs and the lowest in sighted-sighted pairs. Through the content of their conversations, blind people were able to convert psychological distance into psychological proximity, and the findings for spontaneity of style simply followed suit (Table 4.7).

Earlier, in the section on content, I made the point that almost all the research had restricted itself to the laboratory, and very little had been reported on real-life telephone conversations. Exactly the same, unfortunately, is true of research on style, but there are, however, two published exceptions with which to conclude. The first is the Watergate experiment by Wilson and Williams (1977). Although the *New York Times* transcripts did not allow simultaneous speech to be examined, the authors were able to take four other measures: the duration of each meeting, the word-length of each utterance, the length of each "act" (where acts corresponded approximately to Bales's 1970 definition), and the number of acts in each utterance. In every case the telephone values were lower than those for face-to-face. The telephone conversations were shorter, the authors suggested, because they were less pleasant; and acts and utterances were shorter because speakers were uncertain how they were being received because of the relative lack of feedback. There was no evidence of verbal substitution.

The other study was by Beattie and Barnard (1979), and consisted of an analysis of Directory Enquiry calls. A "representative sample" of eighteen calls was selected from an initial total of over seven-hundred — though how and why so few were picked out was not explained — and they ranged in length from 28 to 492 words. For a comparison, the authors made use of material from face-to-face university tutorials, on which they had first reported in Beattie (1977). Subscribers, it was found, were more likely than operators to begin their utterances with an "er" or an "um", and filled pauses were more frequent in the telephone calls than in the tutorials. There were no differences in simultaneous speech or speaker-switch latencies between telephone and face-to-face conversations or between subscribers and operators; and, just as in the laboratory literature, there was nothing to indicate that meshing broke down in absence of visual communication. Apart from a suggestion that filled pauses were used to fend off interruption and so to retain the floor, there were no signs of verbal substitution for visual signals. Moreover, the similarity between subscribers and operators suggested that linguistic style was relatively unaffected by the skill and experience of the speakers.

THEORETICAL MODELS OF PROCESS AND OUTCOME

Formality: Information

The first model to have any significant impact on the literature was the "formality" model of Morley and Stephenson (1969). The purpose of the model was to provide a theoretical interpretation of the authors' finding that the outcomes of simulated negotiations were effected by medium of communication. It was based explicitly on the *information* each medium made available — rather than the subjects' *perceptions* of the medium, for instance — and formality was defined "in terms of the numbers of social cues available" (Morley and Stephenson, 1969, p. 543). The fewer the cues, the more formal the setting, so that sound-only was more formal than face-to-face, for example, and a constrained discussion in which subjects were not allowed to interrupt was more formal than one in which they were. The predictions which the model made for content, style and outcome were apparently identical to those which the later cuelessness model typically makes, but there was one important difference in the mechanisms: while the cuelessness model invoked the mediation of psychological distance, the formality model did not. The links between formality and content, style and outcome were not specified.

Social Presence: Phenomenology

The Social Presence model was devised by the Communications Studies Group, and a detailed account is to be found in Short, Williams and Christie (1976). Information-based models, it was argued, were inadequate, for they failed to consider the encounter as a whole: nonverbal cues were examined one at a time in isolation; language was seen as separate; and a variety of issues were disregarded altogether, particularly that subjects might adapt their behaviour when cues were removed, that a given set of cues might change its meaning from medium to medium or from conversation to conversation, and that much of the system of everyday communication might in any case be redundant. What mattered most about a medium was not its physical characteristics or the amount and type of information it made available but the way subjects perceived and construed it. The most important outcome of those perceptions and constructions was an attribution of high or low Social Presence, where Social Presence denoted the extent to which a medium was perceived to allow psychologically close, interpersonal communication.

"We regard Social Presence as being a quality of the communications medium. Although we would expect it to affect the way individuals preceive their discussions, and their relationships to the persons with whom they are communicating, it is important to emphasize that we are defining Social Presence as a quality of the medium itself. We hypothesize that communications media vary in their degree of Social Presence, and that these variations are important in determining the way individuals interact. We also hypothesize that the users of any given communications medium are in some sense aware of the degree of Social Presence of the medium and tend to avoid using the medium for certain types of interactions; specifically, interactions requiring a higher degree of Social Presence than they perceive the medium to have. Thus we believe that social presence is an important key to understanding person-to-person telecommunications. It varies between different media, it affects the nature of the interaction and it interacts with the purpose of the interaction to influence the medium chosen by the individual who wishes to communicate . . . we conceive of the Social Presence of a medium as a perceptual or attitudinal dimension of the user, a 'mental set' towards the medium. Thus, when we said earlier that Social Presence is a quality of the medium we were not being strictly accurate. We wished then to distinguish between the medium itself and the communications for which the medium is used. Now we need to make a finer distinction. We conceive of Social Presence not as an objective quality of medium, though it must surely be dependent upon the medium's objective qualities, but as a subjective quality of the medium. We believe that this is a more useful way of looking at Social Presence than trying to define it objectively . . . in understanding the effects of tele-communications media, we believe that it is important to know how the user perceives the medium, what his feelings are and what his 'mental set' is."

(Short, Williams and Christie, 1976, pp. 65–6)

Having established their model, Short and his colleagues went on to conduct a series of laboratory and field studies to determine how the most commonly used media were rated. In the typical design, subjects held a series of conversations over a variety of media, and were asked at the end of each one to complete a questionnaire which included items about Social Presence. The most frequent finding was that face-to-face had the greatest Social Presence and business letters the least, with video links, the telephone, and other types of audio arrangement in between (Fig. 4.3). An impressive body of evidence was amassed, with apparently consistent findings — but there were, in fact, a number of difficulties with the approach, both methodological and conceptual.

The principal methodological problem was that all subjects typically underwent all conditions. Although individuals thus acted as their own controls, the more important effect was that they almost certainly rated the media comparatively, so that their evaluation of one coloured their evaluation of the next. Sometimes, indeed, they were asked to rate all the media they had experienced in one questionnaire at the end of the entire session. Ratings from independent groups might well have produced a different pattern of findings.

The other main problem was that, since subjects rated the medium at the

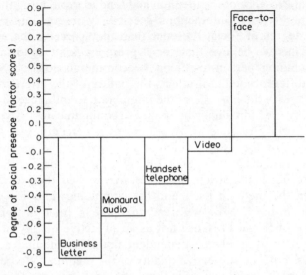

FIG. 4.3. Short, Williams and Christie (1976): The relative social presence of five communications media.

end of the discussion, their perceptions reflected not just the medium itself but the proceedings as well. The way in which the medium was evaluated was therefore confounded with whatever effects it may have upon the discussion, with the result that any attempt to use the ratings to account for what had happened in the discussion was of little value because it was circular. Social Presence was therefore a "pure" rating of neither the medium nor the proceedings. Potential relationships between medium, process, and outcome could not be disentangled.

As for the conceptual problems with the model, here the central issue was definition. In the quotation I cited earlier, Social Presence appeared to mean the extent to which a medium was perceived to allow psychologically close, interpersonal communication. The question which remained, however, was how subjects *arrived* at that perception. In rejecting information-based models, Short and his colleagues had argued that there was much more to media effects than the simple cues which subjects were permitted or denied; but, at the same time, still it was social cues, apparently, which underpinned the model.

"We would suggest that non-verbal communication only has effects on the outcomes of mediated interactions to the extent that it determines feelings of Social Presence. Social Presence is a phenomenological variable more complex than the relatively simple variations in, say, amount of gaze. It is affected not simply by the transmission of single non-verbal cues, but by whole constellations of cues which affect the 'apparent distance' of the other. In turn, it is more useful than any simple knowledge of the functions of non-verbal cues in predicting which tasks would be affected by medium of communication, and which would be unaffected."

(Short, Williams and Christie, 1976, p. 157)

What seems to be the case, then, is that a medium's Social Presence *was* at least in part, a product of the number and type of nonverbal cues it made available, and that the link between the physical features of the medium on the one hand and process and outcome on the other was the "apparent distance" which subjects perceived between them. Something else one might expect, therefore, is that the particular task the subjects were to perform, or the relationship between them, might have effects too. Short and his colleagues acknowledged that that might be the case, and they therefore extended their definition still further. Just as a given medium might *offer* more or less Social Presence, so a given task might *require* more or less Social Presence.

"Our prediction regarding differences in the Social Presence of various media is *not* simply that some media will be 'better' or more 'effective' than others. On the contrary, we hypothesize that the suitability of any given communications medium for a specified type of interaction will depend upon two things: the degree of Social Presence of the medium, and the degree of Social Presence required by the task. In particular, we would expect to observe the greatest distortions compared with face-to-face communication when a medium having a low degree of Social Presence is used for a type of person-to-person interaction requiring a high degree of Social Presence ... where the task does not require a high degree of Social Presence, we would not expect the Social Presence of the communications medium to be important. Thus, we would predict that in tasks where the emphasis is not on the people involved, and where the outcome does not reflect on the personal qualities of the individuals communicating, the outcome will be unaffected by the degree of Social Presence of the medium. Such tasks would include, for example, information transmission and simple problem-solving tasks."

(Short, Williams and Christie, 1976, pp. 75–5; authors' emphasis)

In one final extension to their definition, Short and his colleagues acknowledged that the mediating link in the model, apparent distance, would also be influenced by the number and type of media the participants had available.

"For example, if a person uses his telephone to speak to someone in an adjacent office when it would be just as convenient to go and see him, an impression of 'distance' and non-immediacy is likely to be created, especially if the person making the call is the other's superior. However, the non-immediacy associated with the use of the telephone in this instance is less likely to be replicated when the two parties are separated by considerable physical distances. In these cases, where face-to-face communication is not practicable, the use of the telephone does not carry the same connotation. Although immediacy varies in these two kinds of situation, the Social Presence afforded by the telephone will be the same (unless, of course, the quality of the sound is affected by the distances involved; if so, Social Presence will be *greater* not less, when the two parties are in adjacent offices)."

(Short, Williams and Christie, 1976, p. 73; authors' emphasis)

Cuelessness: Information and Phenomenology

The concept of cuelessness first appeared in the late 1970s, in a paper by Rutter and Stephenson (1979), and at that time were quite clear about its status. It was an information-based concept, not a phenomenological one, and its basis was straightforwardly the aggregate number of social cues which were available to subjects: the fewer the social cues, the greater the cuelessness. Since then, however, as our research findings have led us to develop the model, we have introduced a number of refinements. There have been two main issues: the definition of cuelessness; and the mechanism by which cuelessness has its effects upon process and outcome.

The first issue, how to define cuelessness, arose from the experiment by Rutter *et al.* (1984), in which, for the first time, we went beyond dyads and examined groups of four. The problem was that, although there were now more cues *available* than in dyads, people seemed unable to make full use of them. In social interaction, as in anything else, one's capacity to process information is limited, and the addition of extra participants meant that less and less information could be absorbed from each individual, even though more information was available in total. The crucial measure, we now believe, therefore, is not *available* cues but *usable* cues. As the aggregate number of usable cues decreases, cuelessness increases.

Despite the new definition, a variety of conceptual problems remain. First of all, though we are confident that the distinction between "available" and "usable" is an important one, we acknowledge that we cannot yet properly quantify it. More important still, perhaps, the concept of cuelessness itself remains imprecise, and as yet we can do little more than rank-order our experimental conditions. Thus, while we can say that CCTV is more cueless than face-to-face but less so than sound-only, we cannot say with any precision which are the most important cues it offers, nor how they function together or what happens when they are removed.

A related question concerns the quality of information. So far, we have argued as if all that matters is the *amount* of information in any setting, but might it be that the *quality* of that information is equally important? Sound-only, for example, removes some cues altogether, notably those conveyed by vision, but others, such as speech quality, are merely degraded. Degradation, perhaps, may sometimes matter to participants more than absolute removal, and cues should perhaps in any case be weighted to acknowledge that some are more salient than others. Perhaps, too, the salience of a particular cue might change from encounter to encounter or as given encounter develops — the stare, or the suppressed laugh, or the whispered "aside" which alters the whole course of the encounter. Furthermore, if cues do vary in salience, perhaps people attend only to the most important and simply ignore the remainder, making much of the available information redundant. Each of these isses, it is only fair to acknowledge, is still some way from resolution.

Apart from the issues of definition and conceptualisation, the other main question is the mechanisms by which cuelessness has its efffects upon process and outcome. When the model was first presented, we suggested that cuelessness has a *direct* effect upon behaviour, and that the first thing to be influenced is the content of what people say. Content in turn affects style and outcome. If, for example, a wooden screen is placed between participants, visual cues are removed altogether, and all that remains, apart from smell, heat, and touch, is auditory cues, themselves probably degraded to some extent. The problem, of course, was that it was difficult to imagine how cues such as heat and smell could, in fact, influence speech directly, and we were therefore compelled to revise the model. What we now believe, as I hope has become clear from the discussion already is that the relationship between cuelessness and behaviour is *indirect*, and that mediating the variable is *psycological distance*. At the start of the encounter, participants make use of whatever social cues they can to form an impression of psychological proximity or psychological distance — a feeling that their partner is "there" or "not there" — and it is this which in turn influences the content of what is said and so the style and outcome of the encounter. Cuelessness remains firmly an informational concept, but the link between cues and behaviour is phenomenological.

The introduction of psychological distance may at first appear to be a small step, but there are two important implications which deserve attention. The first is that psychological distance may be influenced by a host of variables, quite apart from the number of social cues. In the discussion of hotline counselling in Chapter 3, for example, I suggested that task, role and even the relationship between the people may all be implicated. Moreover, though typically they work together in the same direction, it is more than likely that they will have variable weightings, and may sometimes even conflict. Each is likely to have its own independent effects upon psychological distance, but those effects will probably change with time, and the variables will in any case interact.

The other implication concerns the relationship between cuelessness and Social Presence. As I have suggested already, though it is certainly true that the models have grown closer as they have developed, important and fundamental differences remain. There are three in particular to highlight. First, while our model explicity separates social cues from the "set" of psychological distance, Social Presence apparently does not — though, as we have seen, it is extremely difficult to discern precisely what the Social Presence model does say, and so to test it. For us, cuelessness merely *influences* set, but, for Short and his colleagues, Social Presence *is* that set. Second, while at least in principle we can specify and quantify in advance what produces psychological distance or psychological proximity, the Social Presence model cannot, for the Social Presence of a medium is measured only at the end of the encounter and there is no way of knowing how the judgement is reached or how it is underpinned. Finally, and this is perhaps the most important point, the models have from the outset had quite different purposes. The Communications Studies Group were funded by the British Post Office, and the overriding priority throughout their work was the everyday practical problems of telecommunications. Our own model and research, in contrast, have always been concerned first and foremost with theoretical and empirical issues in social psychology. Cuelessness, I hope I have demonstrated, is able to integrate a wide variety of previously disparate findings — from content, style and outcome alike — in a way which the Social Presence model has scarcely even attempted.

RELATIONSHIPS BETWEEN PROCESS AND OUTCOME

The cuelessness model makes two main predictions: content, style and outcome will vary according to the aggregate number of usable cues; and content, style and outcome are inter-related. The first of those predictions has been examined in detail in this and the previous chapter. The findings from what might be called our "early" experiments (Morley and Stephenson, 1969, 1970a; Stephenson, Ayling and Rutter, 1976; Rutter and Stephenson, 1977, Rutter, Stephenson and Dewey, 1981; Kemp and Rutter, 1982), in which the task was to debate social and political issues, suggested three main conclusions: that content in the absence of social cues was generally more task-oriented than when cues were plentiful, and also depersonalised; that style lacked spontaneity; and that outcomes lacked compromise. In our more recent studies, however (Rutter *et al.*, 1984; Kemp and Rutter, in press), in which the encounter was designed to be personal — discussion of abortion in the former, and conversations involving blind people in the latter — the "traditional" pattern was overturned. Cuelessness this time produced content which was *less* task-oriented and *more* personal, and a style which was *more* spontaneous. Outcomes showed little effect. As we have seen already, it was largely the difference between the early "task" experiments and the later "personal" experiments which led us to argue for the importance of psychological distance.

What concerns us now is the relationship between process and outcome. Task-oriented, depersonalised content should lead to a style of conversation which lacks spontaneity, and to outcomes which lack compromise. What is more, even if cuelessness had different effects on content from experiment to experiment — the "task" experiments compared with the "personal" experiments, for example — still the relationships between content on the one hand and style and outcome on the other should remain the same. If they do — we have not been able to examine the "personal" data in detail before — our model will be greatly strengthened.

The analyses which follow are based on four sets of data: Rutter, Stephenson and Dewey (1981) Experiment II; Kemp and Rutter (1982); Rutter et al. (1984) dyads; and Kemp and Rutter (in press). The first two studies examined sighted people in face-to-face and cueless conditions as they debated sociopolitical issues; and the latter two were our more recent "personal" experiments. The conditions to be examined from each of the four experiments will be face-to-face and sound-only from Rutter, Stephenson and Dewey (1981) and Kemp and Rutter (1982); face-to-face and screen from Rutter et al. (1984); and all three from Kemp and Rutter. (in press), that is, blind-blind, blind-sighted, and sighted-sighted.

Task-oriented content, it will be recalled from our discussion of CPA in previous sections, most commonly appears as a concern with outcomes and avoidance of information which is irrelevant to the task. Impersonal content, I have suggested, is marked by an avoidance of references to oneself, to other people in the discussion, and to third parties outside the discussion, with the result that many units of speech have no referent at all. Antagonistic content, the third and final dimension, most frequently appears as rejection of what the other person says and an unwillingness to accept his or her contributions, together with a tendency to criticise and to offer little praise.

The first of our analyses was concerned with the relationship beween those three dimensions of content and spontaneity of style, where spontaneity was measured by the frequency and duration of interruptions which occurred as simultaneous, overlapping speech. The prediction was that task-oriented, impersonal, and antagonistic content would be associated with unspontaneous style.

The analyses were based on correlation, and the results are given in Table 4.8. For task-orientation, first of all, the findings were very clear, and were exactly what we had predicted. For "outcomes" all eight correlations were negative, and for "irrelevant information" all eight were positive. Thus, every single correlation was in the expected direction, and many reached statistical significance. It is particularly important to note that the

TABLE 4.8. Correlations (r) between content and style

	Simultaneous speech duration				Simultaneous speech number			
	Rutter, Stephenson and Dewey (1981) Exp. II	Kemp and Rutter (1982)	Rutter et al. (1984), dyads	Kemp and Rutter (in press)	Rutter, Stephenson and Dewey (1981) Exp. II	Kemp and Rutter (1982)	Rutter et al. (1984), dyads	Kemp and Rutter (in press)
Outcome	−43*	−38*	−57*	−34*	−28	−18	−67**	−54**
Irrelevant information	+39	+27	+18	+40*	+20	+10	+39	+26
Self	+12	−19	−29	+02	+10	−16	−29	−25
Others exclud. speaker	−35	−08	+02	+33*	−11	+08	+27	−01
Others includ. speaker	−28	−12	+09	+29	−13	−25	+07	+11
Third parties	−28	−32	+12	−12	−33	−16	+08	+02
No referent	+32	+46**	+11	−04	+21	+25	+09	+11
Reject	+01	+31	−15	+01	+27	+13	+22	−12
Accept	+54**	+49**	+35	+62**	+16	+65**	+17	+26
Praise	+45*	+05	−29	+27	+42*	+06	−35	+56**
Criticism	+23	+07	−09	+42*	+18	+10	+14	+60**

*$P < 0.05$; **$P < 0.01$.
Decimal points omitted.

"task" and "personal" experiments produced almost identical patterns, even though the effects of cuelessness upon content had been quite different. Out model was thus supported (Table 4.8).

From the "impersonal" dimension of content, the results were much less clear, and indeed it was hard to detect any pattern. A total of forty correlations was calculated, but only two reached statistical significance, much as one would expect if chance alone were responsible. There was, however, a straightforward explanation, for in all four experiments around two-thirds of the units of speech had no referent and, apart from "self", the remaining categories were used hardly at all. Given such low frequencies, there was very little opportunity for significant correlations to emerge.

The final dimension was "antagonism", and this time the findings were once again strong and reliable, and generally consistent with our prediction. The most encouraging were for "accept", where all eight correlations were positive, as predicted, four of them significant beyond the 1% level. For the remaining categories, "reject", "praise", and "criticism", no particular pattern emerged, and there were few significant effects — though the infrequency of the categories may well again be the major factor. The most important point to note, as with task-orientation, was that "task" and "personal" experiments produced very similar findings, despite the marked differences between them in the effects of cuelessness upon content.

For the sake of completeness, we concluded our analysis of style by examining the correlations between content and all the other indices we had collected in the four experiments. Although, as we expected, there was no pattern overall, there were a number of interesting consistencies, of which two in particular deserve attention. The first was that task-orientation correlated with conciseness, in both the "task" experiments and the "personal" experiments. The second was that both "reject" and "accept" revealed strong correlations with acknowledgement signals. Acceptance one might expect to produce such a pattern, but the results for rejection were a little puzzling — unless, of course, people gave frequent, earnest acknowledgements during the other person's contributions, only to reject them as soon as they took over themselves. Once again, the "task" and "personal" experiments produced similar findings. The correlations were fewer than for simultaneous speech — as our model would lead us to expect — but when they did occur, they were to be found in both types of experiment. Thus, the model again received strong support.

Content and Outcome

From the relationships between content and style, we turned next to content and outcome. This time, data were available only from the study by Rutter *et al.* (1984), in which subjects met in dyads or four-person groups

TABLE 4.9. *Rutter* et al. *(1984): Correlations* (R) *between content and outcome*

	Two-person groups				Four-person groups			
	M	P	SP	A	M	P	SP	A
Outcome	+10	+05	−07	+08	+13	+45	+32	−05
Irrelevant information	−06	+34	+12	+01	−38	+02	00	+48
Self	−61*	−05	+56*	−05	−41	−32	+08	−21
Others excluding speaker	+62*	+26	−54*	+02	−21	+12	+52*	−49*
Others including speaker	−04	+29	+13	+01	+35	+12	−19	+59*
Third parties	+25	−47	−43	−18	−22	+08	+05	+35
No referent	+15	+36	+03	+23	+51*	+05	−42	+02
Reject	+42	+19	−30	−14	−18	−09	+33	−43
Accept	−42	+18	+44	−01	+41	+41	−07	−04
Praise	+20	−04	−38	+30	−19	+13	+40	−36
Blame	+89*	+15	−75**	−11	−07	−11	+12	−46

*$P < 0.05$; **$P < 0.01$.
M = movement; P = polarisation; SP = social progression; A = agreement.

to discuss abortion. Outcomes were measured in the form of opinion change, and there were four indices altogether: movement, which was the overall amount of change, in whatever direction; polarisation, which was movement in the direction of one or other extreme; social progression, which was polarisation in the direction of the extreme nearest which the subject had started; and agreement, which, unlike the other three, was a group measure, and represented the variability or lack of variability among the members of the group. It will be recalled from Chapter 3 that cuelessness had almost no effect on any of the measures but, nevertheless, it remained possible that there would be relationships between content and outcome. All our measures of content were therefore correlated with all our measures of opinion change.

The results are given in Table 4.9. For task-orientation there were no significant effects either for dyads or for four-person groups. For the "impersonal" dimension, however, there were several effects for both. In dyads, the more subjects referred to themselves the less movement and the more social progression they showed, while correlations for reference to others present apart from the speaker showed the opposite pattern. In four-person groups, reference to others excluding the speaker was associated with more social progression but less group agreement, while reference to others including the speaker correlated positively with group agreement. The less people referred to anyone, the greater the movement overall. For "antagonism", subjects in dyads showed a positive association between criticism and movement, and a negative association between criticism and social progression, but for subjects in four-person groups there were no significant correlations at all (Table 4.9).

In summary, though the results indicated that content and outcome certainly did correlate, there was no obvious pattern of the sort we might have anticipated — task-oriented, impersonal, antagonistic content leading to the greatest opinion change. In dyads, concentrating the discussion on oneself seemed to be associated with moving towards the pole one favoured originally, while reference to other people and antagonism towards them were associated with movement back from the pole towards the centre. In four-person groups, where there were in any case fewer significant effects, the only finding to reproduce the pattern for dyads was the negative association between agreement and references to other people excluding the speaker. The most important point to remember throughout, however, is that the very small effects of cuelessness on opinion change meant that there was little opportunity for significant correlations to emerge in *either* condition. To speculate about the data, therefore, would be extremely hazardous. What the literature needs above all is a proper experimental comparison between "task" and "personal" encounters but, as yet, so far as I know, there have been no published studies of that sort.

Style and Outcome

In one final analysis, to round off our findings, we explored the possibility that *style* might be related to outcome. According to our model, there should be no significant correlations at all, since outcome is the result not of style but of content. The only data we had available were those from dyads and four-person groups in Rutter *et al*. (1984). All our measures of style were correlated with all our measures of outcome, for the dyads and four-person groups separately, giving two 8 × 4 matrices — and not one of the sixty-four values reached statistical significance. Thus, while content predicted both style and, to some extent, outcome, the latter were unrelated, just as our model would lead one to expect. As yet, of course, we cannot say that content is causal, despite the temptation, for our experimental designs have not allowed us to establish cause-effect relationships. In Chapter 5, however, I shall present further data which I hope will strengthen the argument. The data will come from our examination of teaching by telephone.

REFERENCES

ARGYLE, M., LALLJEE, M. and COOK, M. (1968) The effects of visibility on interaction in a dyad. *Human Relations,* **21,** 3–17.

BALES, R.F. (1970) *Personality and Interpersonal Behaviour.* New York: Holt, Rinehart & Winston.

BEATTIE, G.W. (1977) The dynamics of interruptions and the filled pause. *British Journal of Social and Clinical Psychology,* **16,** 283–4.

BEATTIE, G.W. (1983) *Talk: an analysis of speech and non-verbal behaviour in conversation.* Milton Keynes: Open University Press.

BEATTIE, G.W. and BARNARD, P.J. (1979) The temporal structure of natural telephone conversations (Directory Enquiry Calls). *Linguistics,* **17,** 213–29.

BUTTERWORTH, B., HINE, R.R. and BRADY, K.D. (1977) Speech and interaction in sound-only communication channels. *Semiotica*, **20**, 81–99.

COOK, M. and LALLJEE, M.G. (1972) Verbal substitutes for visual signals. *Semiotica*, **3**, 212–21.

DUNCAN, S.D. (1972) Some signals and rules for taking speaking turns in conversations. *Journal of Personality and Social Psychology*, **23**, 283–92.

DUNCAN, S.D., BRUNNER, L.J. and FISKE, D.W. (1979) Strategy signals in face-to-face interaction. *Journal of Personality and Social Psychology*, **37**, 301–2.

DUNCAN, S.D. and FISKE, D.W. (1977) *Face-to-face Interaction: Research, Methods, and Theory*. New Jersey: Erlbaum.

FELDSTEIN, S., BRENNER, M.S. and JAFFÉ, J. (1963) The effect of subject sex, verbal interaction, and topical focus on speech disruption. *Language and Speech*, **6**, 229–39.

JAFFÉ, J. and FELDSTEIN, S. (1970) *Rhythms of dialogue*. New York: Academic Press.

KEMP, N.J. and RUTTER, D.R. (1982) Cuelessness and the content and style of conversation. *British Journal of Social Psychology*, **21**, 43–9.

KEMP, N.J. and RUTTER, D.R. (in press) Social interaction in blind people: an experimental analysis. *Human Relations*.

KEMP, N.J., RUTTER, D.R., DEWEY, M.E., HARDING, A.G. and STEPHENSON, G.M. (1984) Visual communication and impression formation. *British Journal of Social Psychology*, **23**, 133–45.

LALLJEE, M. and COOK, M. (1973) Uncertainty in first encounters. *Journal of Personality and Social Psychology*, **26**, 137–41.

MACLAY, H. and OSGOOD, C.E. (1959) Hesitation phenomena in spontaneous English speech. *Words*, **15**, 19–44.

MORLEY, I.E. and STEPHENSON, G.M. (1969) Interpersonal and inter-party exchange: a laboratory simulation of an industrial negotiation at the plant level. *British Journal of Psychology*, **60**, 543–5.

MORLEY, I.E. and STEPHENSON, G.M. (1970) Formality in experimental negotiations: a validation study. *British Journal of Psychology*, **61**, 383–4.

MORLEY, I.E. and STEPHENSON, G.M. (1977) *The Social Psychology of Bargaining*. London: Allen & Unwin.

MOSCOVICI, S. (1967) Communication processes and the properties of language. In L. Berkowitz (ed.), *Advances in Experimental Social Psychology*, **3**, 225–70.

ROCHESTER, S.R. (1973) The significance of pauses in spontaneous speech. *Journal of Psycholinguistic Research*, **2**, 51–81.

RUTTER, D.R. and STEPHENSON, G.M. (1977) The role of visual communication in synchronising conversation. *European Journal of Social Psychology*, **7**, 29–37.

RUTTER, D.R. and STEPHENSON, G.M. (1979) The role of visual communication in social interaction. *Current Anthropology*, **20**, 124–5.

RUTTER, D.R., STEPHENSON, G.M. and DEWEY, M.E. (1981) Visual communication and the content and style of conversation. *British Journal of Social Psychology*, **20**, 41–52.

RUTTER, D.R., DEWEY, M.E., HARDING, A. and STEPHENSON, G.M. (1984) Medium of communication and group size: effects of cuelessness on the content, style, and outcome of discussions. Unpublished. University of Kent at Canterbury.

SACKS, H., SCHEGLOFF, E.A. and JEFFERSON, G.A. (1974) A simplest systematics for the organisation of turn-taking for conversation. *Language*, **50**, 697–735.

SHORT, J., WILLIAMS, E. and CHRISTIE, B. (1976) *The Social Psychology of Telecommunications*. Chichester: Wiley.

SIEGMAN, A.W. and POPE, B. (1972) (eds). *Studies in Dyadic Communication*. New York: Pergamon Press.

SLUGOSKI, B. (1984) Semantics versus intonation as bases for anticipation in turn-taking. *Bulletin of the British Psychological Society* **37**, February, A21.

STEPHENSON, G.M., AYLING, K. and RUTTER, D.R. (1976) The role of visual communication in social exchange. *British Journal of Social and Clinical Psychology*, **15**, 113–20.

STEPHENSON, G.M., RUTTER, D.R. and DORE, S.R. (1973) Visual interaction and distance. *British Journal of Psychology*, **64**, 251–7.

STRICKLAND, L.H., GUILD, P.D., BAREFOOT, J.C. and PATTERSON, S.A. (1978) Tele-conferencing and leadership emergence. *Human Relations*, **31**, 583–96.

TYSOE, M. (1984) Social cues and the negotiation process. *British Journal of Social Psychology*, **23**, 61–7.

WILLIAMS, E. (1975) Coalition formation over telecommunications media. *European Journal of Social Psychology*, **5**, 503–7.

WILLIAMS, E. (1978) Visual interaction and speech patterns: an extension of previous results. *British Journal of Social and Clinical Psychology*, **17**, 101–2.

WILSON, C. and WILLIAMS, E. (1977) Watergate words: a naturalistic study of media and communication. *Communication Research*, **4**, 169–78.

5

Teaching and Learning by Telephone

TEACHING BY TELEPHONE IN THE U.S.A. AND BRITAIN

The University of Wisconsin-Extension

Teaching by telephone began in the 1930s, in Iowa. Initially, it was intended as a substitute for face-to-face teaching, for people who were geographically isolated, or handicapped in other ways, so that face-to-face contact was impossible. Today, however, it has become commonplace and widespread in its own right, so much so that a number of universities now mount entire degree courses by telephone, notably the University of Wisconsin-Extension in the U.S.A. and the University of Lund in Sweden. The most frequent approach has been to use the medium for relaying lectures, almost as if the lines were a radio network, but with the essential difference that students and teachers can interact, since the system is two-way, with microphones and loudspeakers at both ends. The other main use has been for tutorial classes, sometimes as a substitute for face-to-face, and sometimes as part of a package based on radio or television broadcasts and correspondence material.

Of all the systems in the U.S.A., much the most sophisticated is the one at the University of Wisconsin-Extension (UWEX). Wisconsin is the size of England, but with a population of 5 million confronted with harsh winters which last six months or more. UWEX was founded to provide off-campus education for the whole state, and its staff now exceeds those of many conventional American universities and almost all their British counterparts. The basis of the UWEX system is the Educational Telephone Network (ETN), which links the centre, in Madison, to over 200 study centres — or "remote classrooms", as they are known — all of which in turn are linked together by dedicated two-way lines. The network is open some 15 hours a day from Monday to Friday, though less at the weekends, and around three-quarters of transmission time is devoted to relaying lectures, both live and prerecorded. Normally the lectures are given from Madison but, in principle, they can come from any one of the points in the network. Since students can interact with the lecturer — during "live" transmissions, at least — and indeed with anyone else who is listening, the network has sometimes been likened to a giant party line.

The ETN was opened in 1965, to provide continuing education for doctors, but now it is in operation throughout the university. Continuing education remains the major user, however — around 90% of time and resources — not least because the State of Wisconsin obliges many people to continue their studies after normal graduation if they wish to retain their professional recognitions. ETN's enrolment today is well over 30,000, even though by 1970 a second network had been developed for courses which made use of graphics. The new system was called Statewide Engineering Education Network (SEEN) — because it was designed for engineering courses — and its graphic displays were made possible by the Electrowriter, an electronic "blackboard" which was a precursor of the slow-scan video and computer-controlled systems which have all but replaced it. SEEN is much smaller than ETN, with about one-third the budget and transmission hours and only one-tenth the number of students, and it provides a more specialist service, concentrating on engineering, business studies, and courses on real estate.

Apart from ETN and SEEN, there are three other systems at UWEX. The first is DIAL-ACCESS, a library of cassette tapes which was introduced in 1974. In older versions, subscribers telephoned the librarian, who by hand would load whichever of the catalogued recordings was requested, but today there is direct dialling with automatic retrieval and loading. Once again, the system was devised originally for continuing education — in this case, for practising doctors who needed easy access to specialised reference material in emergencies — but it now includes a wide variety of disciplines with over 4000 tapes and over 100,000 calls each year.

The second system, Administrative Teleconference Network (ATN), was set up in 1977, mainly as a private conference call arrangement for administrative staff, as the name suggests. The third of the services, MEET-ME, was established a year later, again as a conference call network, but this time for linking private domestic telephones, as many as twenty at a time. MEET-ME is especially suited to small-group tutorial and seminar work, and it has the obvious attraction that participants can speak from their homes. Many detailed reports of MEET-ME and all the other UWEX systems are available — though many, unfortunately, only as internal papers — and an excellent summary and commentary are to be found in Reid and Champness (1983).

The Open University

Teaching by telephone in Britain is much less developed than in the U.S.A., for obvious geographical reasons, but there is one institution which makes extensive use of it, the Open University. The Open University was founded in the late 1960s, for people who wished to study for degrees but had not followed traditional routes into higher education. It is a "university of the air", and its students are working adults who live at home and study in their spare time. The current enrolment is around 70,000, and a wide range of conventional university degree courses is offered, as well as a variety of non-degree courses. There is a central administrative headquarters, but no campus, and most of the teaching is done by television and radio, and by printed course material which is sent direct to the student's home. In addition, there are tutorials and counselling sessions with local staff, who are co-ordinated through the thirteen Regional Offices and often work for the university part-time. Though staff are available at almost any time for individual consultations — whether face-to-face or over the telephone — students and tutors normally meet in groups only five or six times a year. The only other personal contact is at summer schools.

Since television and radio are the principal media at the Open University, the main use for the telephone has been tutorial work. Tutorials are seen as "remedial", an opportunity for students to raise problems they have encountered with their course work and assignments, and to discuss them with their tutor and fellow students. Normally, they are held at special Study Centres, of which there are some 250 throughout Britain. Tutorials by telephone were offered originally only to students who were geographically isolated or disadvantaged in some other way, but, with the proliferation of courses, some regions now offer them routinely.

The most common arrangement is the "conference call", in which up to eight or ten students and their tutor are bridged together on an open line through their own domestic telephones, so that everyone can hear and speak to everyone else. The main alternative has been the loudspeaking telephone, which is an ordinary telephone coupled with an amplifier and loudspeaker, designed to allow a group of students to sit together in one centre and speak to their tutor at another. The most promising development, however, is the Open University's recent invention, CYCLOPS (Read, 1978; McConnell, 1982).

CYCLOPS is a computer-based machine, which allows visual information, notably graphics, to be transmitted at the same time as speech. It is typically used to link two study centres together, each with perhaps three or four people grouped round a monitor and loudspeaking telephone. Pre-recorded graphics can be presented from a cassette player, and material can be added "live" by means of a light-sensitive pen applied direct to the screen, or a special pen and "scribble pad". All the information appears on both monitors, and both groups of participants can transmit — and, indeed, change or even erase whatever the other group has presented. In some regions, especially the East Midlands where the system was pioneered. CYCLOPS is now regarded as the principal form of telephone teaching, and it has virtually replaced the conference call and loudspeaking telephone. Like the other systems, it is based at present on ordinary public telephone lines, and there are no dedicated networks like those at UWEX.

Early Evaluation Research

UWEX

Evaluation research at UWEX has concentrated almost exclusively on staff, in particular the programme makers. One of the most extensive studies, by Parker and Zornosa (1979), was based on interviews with ETN and SEEN programmers, as well as a further group who, though eligible to use the networks, had never done so. In general, satisfaction was high. Over 30% of ETN programmers, however, were unable to relay their productions at times they considered most appropriate to their audiences, and almost 50% made no use of the support and advisory services the university offers centrally. Of those who chose to use neither of the networks, only a minority, it emerged, believed their material could not be adapted, but there was no satisfactory explanation as to why they were reluctant to try.

As to the views of students, very little indeed has been published, since as many as 70% of staff do not collect routine feedback (Parker and Zornosa, 1979), and those who do are often reluctant to reveal the outcome. A handful of studies do exist, however — a total of seven between 1968 and 1976, according to Parker and Monson (1980) — but, though their results were generally favourable, the rapid advances in technology have quickly overtaken them.

As well as programme makers, administrators too have been canvassed about the successes and failures of UWEX (Parker and Zornosa, 1980). The major problem identified this time was once again competition for prime times, for a single programme occupies the entire network of remote classrooms. The staff have therefore begun to consider alternatives, including the possibility of dividing the networks into "mini networks", which would normally run in parallel but could be joined together whenever it was necessary. The main alternative is to introduce new "delivery systems" — that is, to move away from traditional telephone lines to other types of link. Optical fibres have not found support, because the cost would mean forsaking dedicated lines and sharing with commercial enterprises, and because the very people who need them most, those who are isolated in remote geographical locations, would almost certainly be the last to receive them. Satellites too have been rejected for reasons of cost – though they *have* been debated as a serious option — and the most likely candidate appears to be microwave delivery. Microwaves travel through the air, like radio waves, and the new technology would allow two-way transmission just as before, though, in principle, of a much higher quality.

Whatever developments may occur in the future, the present system at UWEX remains the most advanced in the world. The evidence from student feedback, such as it is, and from programme-makers and central administrative staff, suggests that it *is* successful, and the high student enrolment suggests the same. According to Reid and Champness (1983), one important reason for the success is the university's choice of a well-defined "market" on which to concentrate, namely "professional" continuing education. In addition, the networks are well designed and maintained, and special efforts are made by the university centrally to provide the programme makers with proper support services. Above all, though, the success of UWEX is attributable to its organisation. The various networks are an integral part of the university — indeed, in some respects, they *are* the university — and the university in turn is an integral part of the state. Without that integration, the development of telephone teaching at UWEX would have been quite different, if, indeed, it had started at all.

Open University

While research at UWEX has concentrated on staff satisfaction, the focus at the Open University has been the *processes* of teaching and learning, and satisfaction and outcome have been regarded as secondary. Almost all the published literature has concentrated on tutorials (see the reviews by Hammond, Young and Cook, 1978; Robinson, 1981; McConnell and Sharples, 1983; Rutter, 1984), and the first point of interest has been how to define their functions.

One of the most detailed of the early papers was by Murgatroyd (1980), and its purpose was to report a content analysis of thirty face-to-face tutorials recorded in Wales. Four major categories emerged: clarification by the tutor; development by the tutor; critical comments about the course; and attempts by the tutor to encourage students to participate. There was little evidence that tutors were following any particular model of teaching, and almost 60% of the time was taken up with their own contributions, leaving each student an average of only 8 minutes to speak in each 2-hour session. Tutors spent most of the time on explication and remedial help and, indeed, it was "chalk and talk" which students appeared to want most. Similar conclusions were later to be reached by L'Henry-Evans (1982).

Apart from Murgatroyd's work, there have been only two attempts to examine Open University tutorials in any systematic way. One is our own, which will be reported later in the chapter, and the other was by Hammond, Young, and Cook (1978), who had previously been members of the Communications Studies Group. Holloway and Hammond (1975) had already published a pilot study on tutors' and students' reactions to tutorials by conference call and LST 4, and the purpose of the new project was to extend the research to content and style as well as outcome. The experiment was conducted in the London and East Anglia regions of the Open University, which were the most prolific users of the telephone at the time, and there were four main issues: are telephone tutorials an effective substitute for face-to-face, and do they fulfil the same functions and satisfy the participants; are there certain ways of organising and conducting telephone tutorials which are more successful than others, and do they differ from successful face-to-face methods; do participants adapt to the constraints of the telephone as time goes on and, if so, might training accelerate the process; and what are the financial costs of telephone tutorials to the Open University, to the student, and to the tutor?

Since the main purpose of a tutorial, according to the Open University, is remedial, a "successful" session will be one which concentrates on the students' academic problems and is "student centred". However, as Murgatroyd's 1980 study revealed, students themselves appear to want something quite different. To try to measure success objectively, therefore, Hammond, Young and Cook concluded — by how much students learned and remembered, for example, or by how much support they received from the tutor — would be quite inappropriate, and instead they chose to define a successful tutorial as one which led to satisfaction, leaving the research project itself to reveal the components of success and the processes which led up to it.

The data for the authors' analyses came from thirty-three telephone and thirty-two face-to-face tutorials, all of them tape-recorded, as well as almost three hundred questionnaires from the tutors and students together with a number of supplementary interviews. A variety of disciplines was represented, even mathematics and music, and each tutorial was part of the planned programme for the region, so that every session was built into the annual schedule as a normal provision. In general, two meetings were examined from each class, one early in the academic year and another later.

Two main analyses were conducted, and the first was concerned with participants' views about the functions of tutorials and how well they had been fulfilled. The first thing to emerge was that students expected telephone tutorials to meet exactly the same criteria as face-to-face tutorials. Their most important requirement was that tutors should provide guidance on the significant academic areas to be covered; the second was that they should summarise the printed course material for them; and the third was that they should provide remedial help with their academic problems. For both the first and third of the functions the telephone was seen as *more* successful than face-to-face, while for the second there was no difference. The function which was said to be fulfilled the most successfully *face-to-face* was moral support from the tutor (Table 5.1).

TABLE 5.1. *Hammond, Young and Cook (1978): Tutorial functions ranked for importance by tutors, telephone students, and face-to-face students.*

	Tutors	Tel students	F-F students
Students' academic problems	1	3	3
Guidance on important areas	2	1	1
Students discuss own ideas	3	5	4
Tutor summarises O.U. texts	4	2	2
Moral support from tutor	5	4	6
Mutal support from students	6	6	5
Study techniques	7	7	7
Students' personal problems	8	9	8
Administrative problems	9	8	9

Note: 1 = most important; 9 = least important.

The pattern of findings for the tutors was rather different, and supported the suggestion made in Murgatroyd's paper that there is often a "mismatch" between students and tutors in what is regarded as the main purpose of tutorial teaching. According to the tutors, the most important function was to help students with their academic problems — consistent with the objectives of the Open University centrally. Guidance as to what were the important academic areas came second, and students' discussion of their own ideas third. One other important finding was that tutors, unlike their students, saw no particular advantage in one medium over the other. Indeed, tutors were generally much less satisfied *overall* with the sessions than were the students, and the difference held for telephone and face-to-face alike.

The second set of analyses examined the content and structure of the sessions, and were based on objective measures scored directly from the tape recordings. Only two significant effects emerged, however, and both were concerned with the students' discussion of their own ideas: more time proportionately spent talking about their ideas over the telephone than face-to-face, but in shorter utterances. To the extent that one of the objectives of a tutorial is to give students an opportunity to present their own ideas, the telephone thus appeared again to be *more* successful than face-to-face. Furthermore, face-to-face tutorials can easily be dominated by a verbose minority but, over the telephone, tutors can more readily encourage an equitable distribution of the available time, and they often do so by calling upon each student in turn. Questions to particular individuals were indeed more numerous over the telephone than face-to-face, Hammond, Young and Cook found, as were acknowledgements or agreements by the tutor, but questions to the group as a whole were less numerous than face-to-face. Participants remained consistent in their behaviour over time, with no evidence of adaptation.

The remaining analyses examined satisfaction. Students found the telephone tutorials "more interesting" than the face-to-face tutorials, it emerged, but there was no difference between conditions in either their overall satisfaction or how much they believed they had understood. The main advantage of the telephone, they said, was the efficient use of time, but almost half believed face-to-face meetings would have been more successful, though there were no complaints about the *social* limitations of the telephone. There were no differences between the disciplines, and there were no effects for tutors' teaching style. Tutors who were successful face-to-face, according to the students, were also successful over the telephone.

Like the students, the tutors reported no difference between conditions in their overall satisfaction, though almost two-thirds believed their face-to-face sessions were the more successful. In both telephone and face-to-face meetings, tutors reported significantly less satisfaction than their students, as we have seen already, and the two sets of ratings correlated negatively, so that the more satisfied the students the less satisfied the tutor. Though the authors could offer no explanation, the findings confirmed once again the mis-match to which Murgatroyd (1980) was to draw attention.

At the end of their project, Hammond, Young and Cook were able to conclude that teaching by telephone at the Open University, just as at UWEX, was a success. Their only serious reservations concerned the technical quality of the lines and the expense of mounting the sessions.

> "... what this research has emphasised is not only the relative adequacy and viability of telephone tutorials, but also the fact that in most of the ways in which they can be criticised, the criticism is equally valid and serious for the face-to-face tutorials. ... One major exception to this has been the crucial importance of good technical reception during telephone tutorials; the importance of this factor cannot be overlooked and technical problems must be overcome before telephone teaching can be successfully carried out in areas where students are widely dispersed. ... The future development of telephone teaching would appear to be limited not by the results it can achieve educationally so much as by the more practical considerations of costs and the quality of technical equipment."
>
> (Hammond, Young and Cook, 1978, p. 142)

TUTORIAL TEACHING BY TELEPHONE: AN EXPERIMENTAL INVESTIGATION

Conference Calls

In the late 1970s we began a project of our own. Until then, almost all the research on the Open University had been concerned with practical issues, and there had been little attempt to integrate the findings theoretically. Though we too hoped to make practical recommendations, our overriding concern remained as always theoretical. Our main objective was to make use of the new setting to test how our model of cuelessness would stand up outside the laboratory and to help us make refinements. Initially we confined ourselves to conference call tutorials but later, as we shall see, we were able to contribute to the Open University's evaluation of Cyclops.

Rutter and Robinson (1981)

The first of our experiments on conference calls took place in the East Midlands region of the Open University, and detailed reports are to be found in Rutter and Robinson (1981) and Rutter (1984). Almost all the region's teaching at that time was done face-to-face, but within our study there was provision to invite a number of groups to hold substitute sessions over the telephone. Five groups were included in total, all of them from the Personality and Learning course in the Faculty of Education, and each was examined twice, once over the telephone and once face-to-face. The sessions were tape-recorded and transcribed verbatim (Figs. 5.1 and 5.2), and analyses were conducted of content and style. Content was scored by

---

T   When you say their comfort is pandered to, what do you mean?

M_1 Well, I think in the first stages of childhood, before they're able to express their needs clearly, perhaps we are over-indulgent towards . . .

M_2 Oh (laughs) . . .

F_1 Why do you say that?

M_1 Er . . .

F_1 Because he's (laughs) . . .

M_1 I mean obviously we can make them comfortable if they mess their nappies. But when a child can't complain it's got earache, for example, it's no good just picking it up and just patting it on the back because you're not getting through to what's wrong with it. I think perhaps in some ways we do try to over-encourage children in the first stages to get all they want, and then later on when we start socialising them we say no you can't have what you want all the time. Perhaps that's why they become . . .

F_1 There's very little they do want, is there, when they're . . .

M_2 (Laughs). Well, perhaps there is but they can't express it.

F_1 Yes, but I still don't know how you can then over-indulge. If a child has an earache and he's crying and you pick it up and you think it's hungry and then it rejects the milk or whatever you're giving it – what is over-indulging about that? You're just misunderstanding it . . .

M_1 I think as I say – yes, but are we misunderstanding a child later on in its life when, after it's had its tea, it says it's still hungry?

T   Ah well, if people eat, and eating doesn't satisfy their hunger, of course a Freudian would jump up and down with delight.

T = Tutor; M_1/M_2 = Male students; F_1 = Female student.
. . . = interrupted utterance.

FIG. 5.1. Rutter and Robinson (1981): Extract from a face-to-face transcript.

T	What would you say is the basic similarity between the Chicago theory and Durkheim's theory, because the author of the unit lumps them together in the first section, doesn't he?
F_1	Yes. Well, Durkheim reckons that crime's always there, doesn't he?
T	Right.
F_1	And, really, the Chicago school is saying that in many places it's bound to be there because of the sort of society that there is.
T	Yes, or, to be more precise, because of the actual changes which are always taking place . . .
F_1	Yes, it's changes, yes. And they both link it to changes in society.
T	That's right, yes, and disorganisation, because I think the title of this section's pretty important. Crime is seen as an aspect of disorganisation. Right, any other views about that section of the unit? John?
M_1	Well, only to – I think some of the things that they were supposed to have discovered were in fact things that didn't really need discovering. They were already quite apparent and all they did really was to make a study of them. This business of certain areas where certain types of crime take place, I mean that had been apparent for many years before they ever mentioned it.
T	But is it – would that be a true sort of description of crime in the first place?
M_1	Sorry, what . . .
T	Would that be an accurate picture of the actual incidence of crime initially?
F_2	Well, officially, yes.

T = Tutor; M_1 = Male student; F_1/F_2 = Female students.
. . . = interrupted utterance.

FIG. 5.2. Rutter and Robinson (1981): Extract from a telephone transcript.

Conference Process Analysis (Fig. 5.3), and style was examined by means of our normal system. In addition, participants kept a tape-recorded diary of their impressions of each tutorial, to give us an index of outcome. Some of the measures were responses to a printed check-list, and the remainder were open-ended comments.

The first of the analyses examined content, and we predicted that telephone tutorials would be more task-oriented than face-to-face and perhaps depersonalised. In the event, however, not one of the comparisons produced a significant difference, either for tutors or for students. Irrespective of medium, all five groups maintained a high level of task-orientation throughout their sessions — academic substance accounting for almost 80% of tutors' speech and almost 90% of students' speech — and there was little personal content of any sort. What had occurred, in other words, was a ceiling effect, and there was simply no room for differences between conditions. What did distinguish between the media, however, was the way in which the task was approached — that is, the structuring of the sessions. Over the telephone, tutors sought contributions from the students significantly more than face-to-face, and students responded with correspondingly more offers, while seeking by students and offering by tutors showed the opposite pattern (Fig. 5.4). Tutors were more likely over the telephone than face-to-face to nominate particular individuals to speak and, in their replies, students were more likely than face-to-face to refer to themselves.

Mode	0	unclassifiable
	1	offer
	2	accept
	3	reject
	4	seek
Resource	0	unclassifiable
	1	procedure
	2	procedure for topic (academic)
	3	procedure for course (OU)
	4	evaluation (academic)
	5	evaluation of course (OU)
	6	information (academic)
	7	information about course (OU)
	8	information (relevant)
	9	information (irrelevant)
	10	praise
	11	blame
Referent	0	unclassifiable/no referent
	1	self
	2	student (or students as individuals)
	3	students as a group
	4	tutor
	5	tutor + student (or students as individuals)
	6	tutor + students (as a group)
	7	third party (academic)

FIG. 5.3. Rutter and Robinson (1981): C.P.A. categories.

The second analysis was concerned with style, and our prediction, as usual from the cuelessness model, was that the telephone sessions would be less spontaneous than face-to-face, with noticeably fewer interruptions. The prediction was confirmed (Table 5.2). Students interrupted almost twice as frequently face-to-face as over the telephone, and tutors responded in the same way, though not significantly so. Both types of participant used more filled pauses over the telephone, no doubt because they were planning more carefully what to say, and there were other differences too. Students gave more acknowledgement signals face-to-face than over the telephone, and asked more questions of their own whilst devoting fewer of their utterances to answering questions from the tutor. Tutors meanwhile said much more over the telephone than face-to-face, but there was no difference for students. The entire pattern, in summary, was one of task-orientation in *both* types of tutorial, but with greater structuring over the telephone and greater spontaneity face-to-face.

The third and last of our analyses examined outcome but, unfortunately, many participants failed to complete their diaries, and a proper statistical analysis was therefore not possible. The most frequent comments, however, were that the telephone was more "businesslike", "structured", and "formal" than face-to-face, and was more efficient at covering the

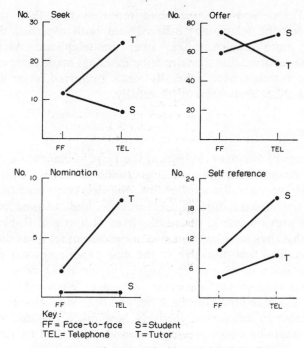

Key:
FF = Face-to-face   S = Student
TEL = Telephone   T = Tutor

FIG. 5.4. Rutter and Robinson (1981): Structuring of content.

TABLE 5.2. *Rutter and Robinson (1981): Style*

	Face-to-face		Telephone			
	Mean	SD	Mean	SD	d.f.	t
Tutor						
No. utterances	157.2	33.4	148.0	30.5	4	0.7
No. words	748.0	1071.5	4942.2	755.5	4	5.4**
Word length of utterances	50.0	18.4	33.5	8.0	4	2.0
No. interruptions	17.8	11.1	12.0	7.1	4	1.2
No. questions	48.6	12.4	69.0	19.8	4	2.0
No. acknowledgement signals	86.6	46.1	100.6	52.3	4	0.5
Filled pause ratio (% words)	2.5	1.4	4.9	2.8	4	3.3*
Students						
No. utterances	186.4	47.4	173.4	38.9	4	0.5
No. words	3990.0	678.0	4706.0	857.0	4	2.7
Word length of utterances	23.1	9.9	28.5	9.1	4	1.7
No. interruptions	33.4	20.0	17.6	10.2	4	2.9*
No. questions	36.4	12.4	20.0	8.0	4	5.0**
Percentage utterances which = response to tutor question	23.2	4.9	36.4	10.0	4	2.8*
No. acknowledgement signals	68.0	29.5	41.0	17.3	4	3.2*
Filled pause ratio (% words)	1.9	0.6	3.4	0.6	4	14.0**

*$P<0.05$ (two-tailed); **$P<0.01$ (two-tailed).

material. Tutors and students alike reported that they spent longer preparing for the telephone sessions, and both regarded the tutor as necessarily more "chairman-like" over the telephone. Almost all the respondents reported that the telephone meetings made them anxious, and face-to-face tutorials were generally much preferred, even if they were regarded as the less effective academically.

Rutter (1984)

From these preliminary findings in the East Midlands, we were able to go on to a second, more ambitious, experiment. There were three principal issues which we wished to explore, and the first concerned our measures. While our traditional indices of content, style, and outcome had served us well in our previous work, the results from Rutter and Robinson (1981) suggested that they were less sensitive in the case of teaching than we might have hoped. The first objective of the new experiment was therefore to develop and test a number of alternatives, in particular measures of tutors' strategy and measures of discourse structure. We would then be in a position to examine how content, style, and outcome fitted together, since we hoped also to measure objectively how much the student had ben- efited — something which previous research had failed to achieve, as we have seen.

The second issue we were able to explore in the new study was whether our preliminary findings would generalise across a more extensive sample of disciplines and tutorial groups. The third and final issue was whether we would find evidence of adaptation to the telephone as time went on. So far, in common with most other writers, we had examined the two media cross-sectionally, and our hope for the new investigation was to set up a longitudinal design.

The experiment took place in the South-East region of the Open University, and five Education and five Social Science groups were included, all of them from full-year post-foundation courses. Most of the region's teaching is done face-to-face, and there were no scheduled tele- phone sessions for any of the groups. Each of them was therefore invited to hold two supplementary meetings at the project's expense, over a confer- ence call link, towards the middle of the academic year. A limit of eight students was imposed for each session, and it was left to the group to decide who they would be. Most of the tutors, like the students, were inexperienced at telephone teaching — though some had used conference calls occasionally on previous courses — but they had all had at least a little training from the Open University. Training normally consists of a half-day seminar, based on role-playing and guidelines like those from UWEX (Robinson, 1979).

In the event, a full longitudinal design proved impossible, since all ten groups were to have a mixture of telephone and face-to-face meetings. Instead, we decided to tape-record all the telephone sessions, together with a number of face-to-face meetings from every group, and our eventual analyses were based on four recordings from each of the ten — the two telephone sessions, and the face-to-face sessions which immediately preceded and followed them — giving face-to-face, telephone, telephone, face-to-face for each group. The face-to-face tutorials generally lasted around 90 minutes, the telephone tutorials 45, and the data in each case were taken from the middle half-hour. Verbatim typescripts were prepared, and analyses were conducted of content, style, and structuring. To examine outcome, we used questionnaires, and the participants were asked to complete and post them to us immediately after the session. The response rate was 81% for tutors and 77% for students for the telephone sessions, and 93% and 72% for the face-to-face sessions.

The first of our analyses examined content, and our prediction was that, in comparison with face-to-face tutorials, telephone tutorials would be noticeably more task-oriented and perhaps depersonalised. The analysis was based on a further modified form of Conference Process Analysis, in which the Modes from the original version were retained and the Resources were amended and extended, but the Referents were abandoned altogether. It was also possible with the new system to code a number of Resources without Modes (Fig. 5.5). Since it soon became clear that many of the categories were used very seldom, we chose to base our

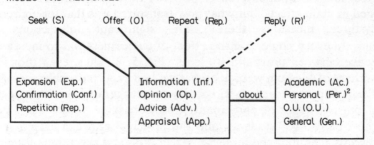

MODES AND RESOURCES

Seek (S)   Offer (O)   Repeat (Rep.)   Reply (R)[1]

| Expansion (Exp.) Confirmation (Conf.) Repetition (Rep.) | Information (Inf.) Opinion (Op.) Advice (Adv.) Appraisal (App.) | about | Academic (Ac.) Personal (Per.)[2] O.U. (O.U.) General (Gen.) |

1. Reply may be coded alone or with a resource

2. Personal is divided into Personal-procedure (Per.Proc.), Personal-example. (Per.Eg.), and Personal-irrelevant (Per.Irrel.)

Resources coded without modes

Agreement (Ag.)	Exclamation (!)
Disagreement (D)	Apology (Ap.)
Procedure (Proc.)	Praise (Pr.)
Academic procedure (Ac.Proc.)	Laugh (L)
Acknowledgement (Ack.)	Uncodable (U.C.)

FIG. 5.5. Rutter (1984): C.P.A. categories.

Seek	Offer	Reply	No mode
Exp.	Inf. Ac.	Inf. Ac.	Ag.
Conf.	Inf. Per. Proc.	Inf. Per. Proc.	Proc.
Inf. Ac.	Inf. Per. Eg.	Inf. Per. Eg.	Ac. Proc.
Inf. Per. Proc.	Inf. O.U.	Op. Ac.	Ack.
Inf. Per. Eg.	Op. Ac.	Reply (no resource)	
Op. Ac.	Op. O.U.		
	Adv. O.U.		
	App. Ac.		

FIG. 5.6. Rutter (1984): Principal C.P.A. categories.

statistical analysis on just twenty-three (Fig. 5.6), which together accounted for over 90% of the units of speech we recorded. Each of the categories was examined by analysis of variance with Faculty (Education/ Social Science), Medium (telephone/face-to-face), Occasion (first/second), and Participant (tutor/student) the independent variables.

Two principal findings emerged. The first was that only four of the measures produced a significant main effect of Medium, and, in every one of the four cases, the effect was against our prediction — more offering of academic information face-to-face, less responding with personal examples and personal accounts of study methods, and less acknowledgement.

The second finding concerned the interaction between Medium and Participant, and it was here that the most important effects were to be revealed. Many overall differences between tutor and student had already emerged as main effects, but what now transpired was that for eight of the twenty-three measures there were significant interactions with Medium. In every single case the effect of cuelessness was to increase the difference between tutor and students (Fig. 5.7). Thus, even though the main effects of Medium were not what we had expected, cuelessness had a significant impact nevertheless, namely to exaggerate the differences between the two types of participant. Tutors became "more like" tutors, students "more like" students, and the principal effect of cuelessness, in other words, was upon the subjects' perceptions and execution of their role — just as we had found in Stephenson, Ayling and Rutter (1976) and Rutter and Robinson (1981). There were few effects of Occasion, it should be added finally — suggesting once again that participants do not adapt to the telephone as time goes on — and there were no differences at all between the Education and Social Science groups.

The second of our analyses examined style and structuring, and there were two predictions: that telephone tutorials would be less spontaneous than face-to-face tutorials, and that they would be more noticeably structured by the tutor. To measure spontaneity, our first approach as usual was to examine interruptions, which this time were broken down into four

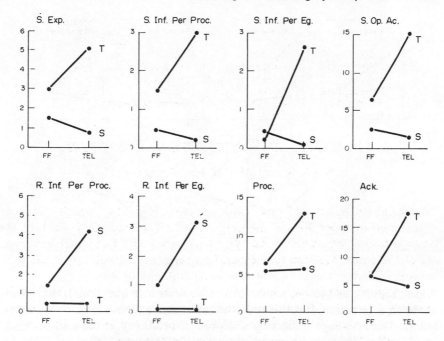

Fig. 5.7. Rutter (1984): Interactions between medium and participants for content.

categories: successful interruptions, unsuccessful interruptions, and any other interruptions which occurred without simultaneous speech.

For all four indices the pattern was as predicted, with fewer interruptions over the telephone than face-to-face, but the effect reached statistical significance for successful interruptions only — those which led to a change of speaker. Students in general interrupted more than tutors, and for two of the measures there was a significant interaction with Medium, so that the greatest frequency of all was for students face-to-face, especially students interrupting other students. Apart from interruptions, the only other measures to produce significant effects were laughter, acknowledgement signals, and filled pauses. Laughter was significantly more frequent among students than tutors, especially face-to-face; acknowledgement signals showed the same pattern; and filled pausing was considerably more common over the telephone, especially among students (Fig. 5.8).

For our examination of structuring by tutors, and discourse structure overall, a variety of measures was analysed. The first was the types of question tutors asked (Fig. 5.9). For both direct questions (those aimed at named individuals) and general questions (those for the group at large), the values were greater for tutors than for students, as was to be expected, but, more importantly, in both cases the difference was especially marked over the telephone. For question tags, in contrast ("isn't it?", "didn't I?",

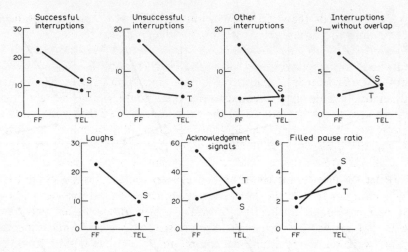

FIG. 5.8. Rutter (1984): Style.

"don't they?", and so on, which turn statements into questions), there was again an interaction, but this time the greatest frequency was for students face-to-face, perhaps indicating a degree of hesitancy at the end of what would otherwise have been straightforward assertions.

The other important measure to produce a significant effect was the links between utterances. As Fig. 5.9 suggests, the effect was very pronounced, for, while the telephone produced a rigid tutor–student–tutor–student pattern, the face-to-face condition did not and there were just as many exchanges between student and student as student and tutor. The only other significant finding concerned the amount said, for tutors, it emerged,

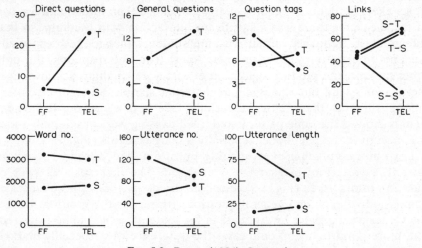

FIG. 5.9. Rutter (1984): Structuring.

spoke more words than students, in longer but less frequent utterances, and this time the differences were most noticeable face-to-face.

The third of our analyses examined outcome. So far, the pattern of results had confirmed what we had found in Rutter and Robinson (1981). In both types of tutorial, there was a very high level of task-orientation, with relatively little time devoted to personal matters, and the telephone sessions were highly structured by the tutors and lacked the spontaneity of face-to-face. As to what would emerge from the outcome measures, however, there was little guidance from the previous experiment since, on that occasion, we had been able to collect relatively little data.

This time, there were two sets of measures to analyse, both of them from the questionnaires. The first was a variety of open-ended questions about what had happened during the tutorial — how many issues had been raised, had anything unexpected been discussed or anything expected omitted, were there any additional comments the subject wished to make, and so on. It was these items, we hoped, which would enable us to say something "objective" about the sessions. The second set of measures was a checklist of twenty-four five-point adjective scales, intended to tap perceptions of task-orientation, depersonalisation, spontaneity, and the subject's overall evaluation. In the event, however, most of the participants made relatively few responses to the open-ended questions, except to list the topics which had been raised, and our analysis was therefore restricted to just that one item from the first part of the questionnaire and the twenty-four items from the second. Four-hundred-and-twelve question-naires were examined altogether, including 178 from the sessions which had not been used for the analyses of content, style, and structuring.

Two main findings emerged, and the first was that the number of discussion points recalled was significantly greater in the face-to-face condition than the telephone condition, for both students and tutors. Unfortunately, though, it is unclear whether the difference reflects the participants' memories or the actual number of points discussed, since the face-to-face tutorials were generally the wider-ranging. The second set of findings came from the five-point scales, and nine of the twenty-four items produced statistically reliable effects (Fig. 5.10). Face-to-face was regarded as more "spontaneous", "humorous", and "light-hearted" than the telephone condition, but less "formal" and "tense"; and tutors saw the proceedings as more "formal", "tutor-dominated", "tense", "light-hearted", "tiring", and "anxiety-provoking" than students, but less "democratic" and "spontaneous". For "tiring", the only measure to pro-duce an interaction between Medium of Communication and Participant, the lowest rating of all was for students face-to-face.

In summary, then, there were noticeable differences in outcome percep-tions between telephone and face-to-face tutorials and, once again, tutors were generally less satisfied than students, irrespective of medium. For

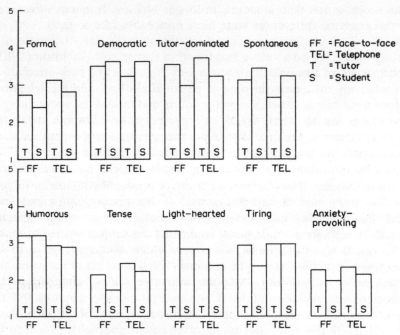

Note: scores are measured on seven-point scales

FIG. 5.10. Rutter (1984): Outcome.

	VP
Content	
1. Tutor seeking and commenting	3.5
2. Offering and replying with academic information	2.3
3. Open University	2.2
4. Offering and replying with personal information	1.9
5. Agreeing/offering opinions	1.6
6. Seeking/offering academic information and confirmation	1.6
7. Replying with opinions and personal examples	1.3
Style and structuring	
1. Spontaneity	5.8
2. Speech quantity	1.8
3. Questioning	1.1
Outcome	
1. Evaluation	3.4
2. Anxiety	3.0
3. Interaction/democracy	2.8
4. Structure	2.1
5. Personal evaluation	1.7
6. Academic relevance	1.4

Note: VP is a measure of variance explained.

FIG. 5.11. Rutter (1984): Content factors.

both groups of participants, the perceptions recorded in the questionnaires were often accurate reflections of what the analyses of content and style had demonstrated already, and the ratings were generally positive and strong for both types of meeting. Telephone and face-to-face tutorials alike were considered to be a success.

The fourth and last of our analyses was concerned with the way content, style, and outcome were related. According to our model, the only direct effect of cuelessness is upon content, and style and outcome are influenced indirectly, through the *mediation* of content. The technique we used to examine the relationships was multiple regression, but first we had to reduce the measures to a manageable number. We therefore conducted a factor analysis, and seven factors emerged for content, three for style and structuring, and six for outcome (Fig. 5.11). For each of the factors we then took the variable which loaded the most heavily, and it was those measures which we used finally in the multiple regressions.

The first analysis examined style, and all three of the measures were found to be predicted very strongly by content (Table 5.3). Moreover, the main relationship was exactly as our model predicted — the less task-oriented and the more personal the content, the more spontaneous the style (Factor 1). Both speech quantity and questioning, moreover, were also predicted strongly, and the evidence overall for relationships between content and style was among the most persuasive we had found.

The second analysis examined outcome, and this time there was less support for our predictions. The more task-oriented the tutorial — or, to be more precise, the more closely it followed the typical pattern of question and answer — the less favourable the overall evaluation, and the greater the reported anxiety. Beyond that there were no significant relationships.

The third analysis again examined outcome, but this time using style rather than content as the predictor. According to our model, there should be no relationship at all, since outcome and style are independent, and that is exactly what emerged. There was no single significant effect, and the average variance explained by the analyses was less than 5%. Thus, style and outcome were independent, but both were predicted by content, just as our model suggests.

Our analyses were now complete. The experiment had begun with three principal objectives, it will be recalled, the first of which was to refine and extend our measures and to examine the relationships between them. Tutor strategy, discourse structure, and the relationships between content, style, and outcome had all been examined, and the findings in general offered good support for our model — indeed, often much stronger support than in our earlier laboratory research. The second objective was to explore how far the findings would generalise, especially across faculties and across courses within faculties, and what emerged was very strong generalisation indeed. The important sources of variance were Medium of

TABLE 5.3. *Rutter (1984): Relationships between content and style*

	Cumulative MR	Cumulative MR²	Simple r	Standardised Beta	F
Factor 1: spontaneity	MR 0.83	MR² 0.69			21.6***
Step 1 Factor 5 – Agreeing and offering opinions	0.67	0.45	0.67	0.77	96.2***
Step 2 Factor 6 – Seeking and offering ac. info. and confirmation	0.75	0.57	−0.08	−0.34	18.6***
Step 3 Factor 4 – Offering and replying with personal info.	0.81	0.66	0.39	0.33	22.3***
Factor 2: speech quantity	MR 0.79	MR² 0.63			16.2***
Step 1 Factor 2 – Offering and replying with ac. info.	0.53	0.28	0.53	0.43	24.2***
Step 2 Factor 4 – Offering and replying with personal info.	0.66	0.43	0.40	0.41	29.1***
Step 3 Factor 6 – Seeking and offering ac. info. and confirmation	0.72	0.52	0.40	0.24	7.7**
Step 4 Factor 3 – Open University	0.76	0.57	0.30	0.29	12.0***
Step 5 Factor 1 – Tutor seeking and commenting	0.77	0.60	0.26	0.20	5.0*
Step 6 Factor 7 – Replying with opinions and personal eg's	0.79	0.62	−0.17	0.15	2.9
Factor 3: questioning	MR 0.75	MR² 0.56			12.3***
Step 1 Factor 1 – Tutor seeking and commenting	0.73	0.54	0.73	0.79	68.2***

$*P < 0.05$; $**P < 0.01$; $***P < 0.001$.

Communication and Participant, and especially the interaction between them, for, the more cueless the setting, the more the participants retreated into traditional forms of role behaviour. The third and last of our objectives was to examine whether people might adapt to cuelessness as time went on and, as the previous literature has suggested already, they did not, for there were few effects of Occasion and no interactions at all with Medium of Communication. The most likely explanation, we believe, is simply that people are already well used to the telephone, and there is little adaptation left for them to do.

Cyclops

The first published description of Cyclops was by Read (1978). Experimental trials began in the East Midlands region of the Open University, in 1981, with funding from British Telecom for a two-year evaluation. Cyclops terminals were installed in sixteen study centres across the region, and up to nine could be bridged together at any one time. The bridging equipment was rented from British Telecom, and is housed at the regional headquarters, from which it is operated by the Open University's own staff. The operator's role is to connect the lines, to be the host who introduces the participants at the start of the tutorial, to monitor the equipment and the lines throughout the session, and to make reconnections if the transmission deteriorates. The tutor, normally, will be alone in one centre, or perhaps with one or two students, and each of the other centres will have up to three students gathered round one machine — television monitor and microphone, DORIC loudspeaking telephone, and light-sensitive pen for writing and drawing on the screen (Fig. 5.12). In the centres which are used the most, there will also be a "scribble pad", which is a metal pad of A4 size, through which high-resolution graphics can be presented on the screens by means of another special pen. Courses from all six faculties were taught by Cyclops during the experimental period, and the criteria were that the number of students on the course should be small and they should be widely scattered geographically. The tutorials were not supplementary to face-to-face or telephone meetings, but were scheduled as part of the routine programme of teaching from the start of the academic year.

Probably the most important questions to ask about Cyclops are whether it is acceptable to tutors and students, and whether it is effective educationally. As part of its two-year experiment, the Open University set up its own evaluation to examine those and a variety of other questions, and the preliminary report, by McConnell and Sharples (1983), will be considered later in the chapter. Our own research, in contrast, was concerned with process rather than outcome, and its objective was to examine the content and style of Cyclops tutorials in comparison with telephone and face-to-face tutorials. Predictions were difficult to make, unfortunately, because,

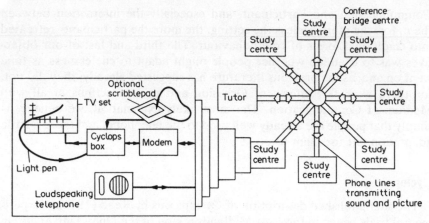

FIG. 5.12. A Cyclops network.

although Cyclops may appear to be intermediate between face-to-face and telephone from the point of view of cuelessness – more cues are available than over the telephone because the light-pen allows for interactive exchanges — the most important feature of the system may be its unfamiliarity. Cyclops makes special physical and procedural demands on the participants, and the possible effects of cuelessness may well be outweighed.

The data for our analyses came from nine Cyclops tutorials from a variety of disciplines. The recordings were made and selected for us by Open University staff, and the criteria for inclusion were that the recordings should come from as early as possible in the experiment and that they should be of sufficient technical quality for accurate transcription. The sessions generally lasted 90 minutes, and our analyses were based on the middle half-hour. The number of students ranged from two to eight, and there was always a technician/host present as well as the tutor.

To make our comparison, we used the data from Rutter (1984) on conference calls. Each of the ten groups in that particular study, it will be recalled, was examined twice face-to-face and twice over the telephone. To make the data as comparable as possible with the new Cyclops material, we therefore selected the first face-to-face session and the first telephone session from each group. Content, style, and structuring were measured in the same ways as before, and the effects of Medium of Communication, Participant, and the interaction between them were examined by analysis of variance.

The first of the analyses was concerned with content, and, of our twenty-three measures, only three produced significant effects of Medium of Communication: Procedure, Reply, and Acknowledgement. For Procedure and Acknowledgement, there were also interactions between Medium and Participant and, in all three cases, the greatest difference

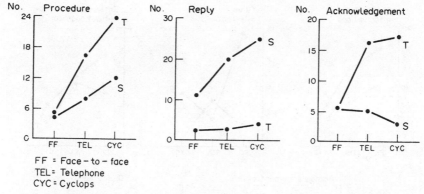

FF = Face – to – face
TEL = Telephone
CYC = Cyclops

Fig. 5.13. Cyclops experiment: Content.

between tutor and student was in the Cyclops condition (Fig. 5.13). The unusually high level of procedural comments suggests that the unfamiliarity of Cyclops indeed did have a considerable effect, and the overall appearance was one of even greater role differentiation between tutors and students in the Cyclops condition than we had found for the telephone. For the remaining measures of content, however, there were no significant effects for Medium, and only occasional interactions with Participant. There was no evidence, in summary, that Cyclops was intermediate between the other two conditions, and the simplest account of the findings is that unfamiliarity played the most important part.

The second of our analyses examined style and structuring, and this time there were five significant effects of Medium, three of them for interruptions of one sort or another (Fig. 5.14). Again, as for content, the findings for Cyclops were often even further from face-to-face than those for the telephone. For the most part, tutors and students behaved similarly in the Cyclops condition, and the only significant exception was for direct questions, which were much more likely to be asked by tutors than students. Direct questions, as we saw earlier, are an index of structuring and, just as we had found for telephone tutorials, the typical pattern of discourse for Cyclops was tutor question–student answer–tutor question–student answer, and so on. Only 10% of exchanges, on average, were from student to student. Cyclops tutorials were thus highly structured and lacking in spontaneity — even more so, on occasion, than telephone tutorials — and a large part of the explanation, we concluded, was once again the unfamiliarity of the medium.

From our own attempt to examine the process of teaching and learning by Cyclops, we turn finally to the work of McConnell and Sharples (1983). McConnell and Sharples were members of the Open University's project team, and their paper provides the most important summary to date of what Cyclops has achieved. The aims of the project were two-fold: to

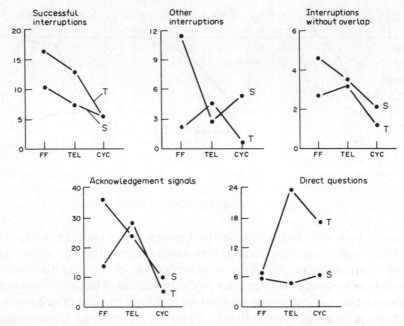

FIG. 5.14. Cyclops experiment: Style and structuring.

evaluate the effectiveness of Cyclops as a distance-teaching medium; and to examine the ergonomics of the light-pen and scribble pad. The methods the authors used included questionnaires, visits to study centres to observe tutorials "live" and to interview participants, tape-recordings of sessions for process analysis, special day meetings for interviewing and debriefing tutors, and detailed case studies of selected groups.

The first finding to emerge was that, of the twenty-two tutors originally assigned to teach by Cyclops, four dropped out, two because the screen was redundant to their needs, they said, another because he found the sessions unduly anxiety-provoking, particularly because there was no face-to-face contact with the students, and the last because he found the screen and light-pen inadequate for his particular course, which was in mathematics. The remaining eighteen, according to McConnell and Sharples, were "very favourable towards Cyclops", and used it for a wide variety of purposes. The most common was "going over core teaching material", and the remainder were, in order, "teaching new material", "going over tutor-marked assignments", "academic problem-solving", "debating", "guidance and assessment", "examination preparation", "feedback on projects", "counselling", and "discussing summer schools". Tutors accepted that it was important to find a substitute for face-to-face for students who were scattered geographically, and, in general, they preferred Cyclops to the telephone.

The corresponding analysis of students' responses was more extensive. All 260 students who had taken part in Cyclops tutorials in the first year were sent a questionnaire at the end, and 65% of them responded. There were three principal findings, the first concerned with attendance, the second how acceptable the students found the medium, and the third their attitude towards it. Attendance, it emerged, was comparable to face-to-face — as high as 100% on some occasions, but typically rather lower — and, of students who attended no tutorials at all, over 75% cited personal circumstances. There was no evidence that Cyclops had been a deterrent.

As to the acceptability of the medium, the main analysis was based on the students' comparisons between a variety of possible arrangements: Cyclops in the study centre, with other students present; Cyclops at home, using an individual desk-top unit; face-to-face on a week-day evening; Cyclops in a study centre, without other students; sound-only conference call from home; and half-day face-to-face Saturday school. Ratings for each alternative were requested on five-point scales, and what emerged was the rank-order I have given (Table 5.4), from group Cyclops tutorials at the top to a half-day Saturday school at the bottom. The most interesting points, perhaps, were that the respondents preferred not to be alone with a Cyclops machine in a study centre — though they would have been happy to use an individual desk-top model at home — and that they disliked half-day schools, which, at the time, were the only alternative the Open University normally offered. Home Cyclops machines, it should be added, were not yet available, but the Open University will be considering them for the future.

TABLE 5.4. *McConnel and Sharples (1983): Students' preferences for type of tutorial*

	Very acceptable/ acceptable	Unsure	Unacceptable/ very unacceptable
1. Cyclops tutorials with other students present in study centre	76	11	13
2. Cyclops tutorial from student's home (with desk-top unit)	72	14	14
3. Face-to-face tutorial on weekday evening (50 miles round trip)	63	7	30
4. Cyclops tutorial alone in study centre	58	11	31
5. Telephone tutorial (voice only) from student's home	53	21	26
6. Half-day Saturday school with tutor (100 miles round trip)	49	22	20

Note: Figures represent percentage of students who made each response. $N = 169$.

TABLE 5.5. *McConnell and Sharples (1983): Student's responses to the Cyclops screen screen.*

	Strongly agree/ agree	Unsure	Disagree/ strongly disagree
The Cyclops screen:			
– provides a visual focus of attention	80	11	8
– is of little importance to the success of the tutorial	31	16	53
– makes it easier to assimilate information	70	15	15
– is not large enough for displaying handwriting	64	19	17

Note: Figures represent percentage of students who made each response. $N = 169$.

The remaining analysis examined students' attitudes towards the special technical and ergonomic features of the medium. Eighty per cent agreed that the screen provides a focus for the meeting — though 31% said it was of little importance to the success of the tutorial — and 70% said that it helped them to assimilate information. Over 60%, however, complained that the screen was too small for displaying handwriting (Table 5.5). As to the light-pen, although most of the information on the screen is normally produced by the tutor, over 70% of the students reported that they had used it at some point. More than 50%, however, complained that it was difficult to handle, and more than 60% found difficulty writing on the smooth glass surface of the screen. Since the light-pen is crucial, the authors found these particular results a little disappointing, but other comments by the students suggested that the pen had a number of virtues: it helped to clarify difficult material; it increased the students' involvement with the tutor and with the students in the other centres; and it made them think about the academic issues they were discussing, as they tried to express their thoughts on the screen.

At the end of their report, McConnell and Sharples were able to conclude that Cyclops is a viable and acceptable alternative to face-to-face — more so than the telephone, perhaps — though their analysis had not, it should be remembered, examined the *educational* merits of the system to any extent. Cyclops is expensive, they concluded, because it is not mass-produced, but it has a promising future. To those designing and managing similar systems, however, they offered these words of advice: the system must be simple and easy to use; there must be an efficient bridge and a competent operator; a trained administrator should be appointed to run the entire network; and there must be good relations with whoever provides the telephone lines. The success of the system ultimately, how-ever, will rest with the tutors and students themselves. There must be briefing sessions at the start of the course; tutorials must be carefully planned and organised; tutors must be willing to experiment with teaching styles; and tutors and students alike must always remember that any system has limitations as well as strengths.

CONCLUSIONS AND THEORETICAL IMPLICATIONS

Our research on teaching by telephone was designed with two main aims, the first of which was to explore whether the literature on visual communication might be of practical value. As in the other areas of application — interviewing and counselling, for example — evaluative research has concentrated on economics and cost-effectiveness, but the theoretical literature *has* played a significant part. At UWEX, there is now a variety of instructional packages for telephone tutors, which makes explicit use of research in nonverbal communication; and in Britain, our own findings have been an important factor in the development of training at the Open University (Robinson, 1979, 1981).

The second of our aims was to test how far our laboratory findings on seeing and cuelessness would generalise outside the laboratory. Content, style, and outcome, we had found, were all affected by the number of usable social cues available, and now we were able to show that there was once again a clear pattern: the fewer the social cues, the greater the retreat into the "traditional" roles required by the task. Both face-to-face and over the telephone, we found, the discussion was consistently "academic", but it was the telephone which produced the more striking way of *handling* that discussion: tutors asked questions and imposed structure; students answered.

Effects of cuelessness on the perception and execution of roles are familiar from previous research (Stephenson, Ayling and Rutter, 1976; Morley and Stephenson, 1977), but, as a final conclusion to our discussion, there are two points of caution to make. First, in many encounters, participants do not have "prescribed" roles — everyday conversations between friends, for example — and there we would not expect a pattern to emerge, for role differentiation will develop only when the roles are reasonably defined at the outset. Second, as we have seen already, sometimes one's role over the telephone is explicitly to behave in an *intimate*, *personal* way — Samaritans and hotline counsellors, for example. Here, our "normal" finding of reduced personal content will disappear or even reverse (for example, Rutter *et al.*, 1984; Kemp and Rutter, 1986), for the "traditional" distinction between "task" and "person" will break down because to be personal *is* the task. Nevertheless, the key remains psychological distance, for the *anonymity* of the system this time encourages psychological *proximity,* and it is cuelessness which makes that anonymity possible. Of all the variables to pursue in future, role and task are among the most important.

REFERENCES

HAMMOND, S., YOUNG, I. and COOK, A. (1978) *Teaching by Telephone*. Final Report to Social Science Research Council of Great Britain.

HOLLOWAY, S. and HAMMOND, S. (1975) Tutoring by telephone: a case study in the Open University. *Communications Studies Group* paper No. P/75025/HL.

KEMP, N.J. and RUTTER, D.R. (1986) Social interaction in blind people: an experimental analysis. *Human Relations*, **39**, 195–210.

L'HENRY-EVANS, O. (1982) Anatomy of a tutorial (or when is a tutorial not a tutorial?). *Teaching at a Distance*, **21**, 71–5.

McCONNELL, D. (1982) CYCLOPS telewriting tutorials. *Teaching at a Distance*, **22**, 20–5.

McCONNELL, D. and SHARPLES, N. (1983) Distance teaching by CYCLOPS: an educational evaluation of the Open University's telewriting system. *British Journal of Educational Technology*, **14**, 109–26.

MORLEY, I.E. and STEPHENSON, G.M. (1977) *The Social Psychology of Bargaining*. London: Allen & Unwin.

MURGATROYD, S. (1980) What actually happens in tutorials? *Teaching at a Distance*, **18**, 44–53.

PARKER, L.A. and MONSON, M.K. (1980) *More than meets the eye: the effectiveness of broadcast audio and two-way instruction for distant learning*. Madison: University of Wisconsin-Extension.

PARKER, L.A. and ZORNOSA, A. (1979) *Unit Assessment and Future Implications*. Madison: University of Wisconsin-Extension.

PARKER, L.A. and ZORNOSA, A. (1980) *Five Year Plan*. Madison: University of Wisconsin-Extension.

READ, G.A. (1978) *CYCLOPS — an audio-visual system*. Milton Keynes: Open University Press.

REID, F.J.M. and CHAMPNESS, B.G. (1983) Wisconsin Educational Telephone Network: how to run educational teleconferencing successfully. *British Journal of Educational Technology*, **14**, 85–101.

ROBINSON, B. (1979) *Briefing and Training for Telephone-Teaching: Some Guidelines*. Milton Keynes: Open University Press.

ROBINSON, B. (1981) Telephone tutoring in the Open University: a review. *Teaching at a Distance*, **20**, 57–65.

RUTTER, D.R. (1984) *Looking and Seeing: the role of visual communication in social interaction*. Chichester: Wiley.

RUTTER, D.R., DEWEY, M.E., HARDING, A. and STEPHENSON, G.M. (1984) Medium of communication and group size: effects of cuelessness on the content, style, and outcomes of discussions. Unpublished. University of Kent, Canterbury.

RUTTER, D.R. and ROBINSON, B. (1981) An experimental analysis of teaching by telephone: theoretical and practical implications for social psychology. *In* G.M. Stephenson and J.H. Davis (eds.), *Progress in Applied Social Psychology*, Vol. 1, 345–74. Chichester: Wiley.

STEPHENSON, G.M., AYLING, K. and RUTTER, D.R. (1976) The role of visual communication in social exchange. *British Journal of Social and Clinical Psychology*, **15**, 113–20.

Index